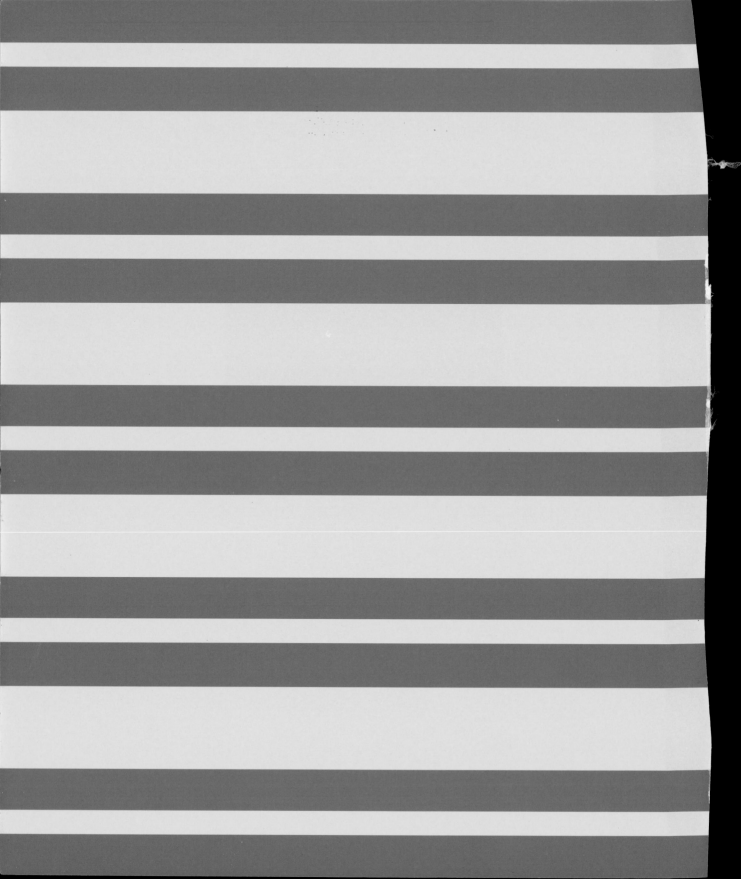

PERFECT
CAKES

■ HarperCollinsPublishers

PERFECT
CAKES

NICK
MALGIERI

Photographs by Tom Eckerle

Designed by Joel Avirom and Jason Snyder
Design assistant: Meghan Day Healey
Illustrations by Laura Hartman Maestro
Food Styling by Barbara Bria Pugliese with Faith Drobbin,
Rebecca Millican, Cara Tannenbaum, and Andrea Tutunjian
Prop Styling by Ceci Gallini

HarperCollins books may be purchased for educational, business, or sales promotional use. For information, please write: Special Markets Department, HarperCollins Publishers Inc., 10 East 53rd Street, New York, NY 10022.

FIRST EDITION

Printed on acid-free paper

Library of Congress Cataloging-in-Publication Data

Malgieri, Nick.
    Perfect cakes / Nick Malgieri.
        p. cm.
    Includes bibliographical references and index.
    ISBN 0-06-019879-6
    1. Cake. I. Title.

TX771 .M3148 2002   2002017338
641.8'653—dc21

02 03 04 05 06   ❖/TOP   10 9 8 7 6 5 4 3 2 1

For Maida Heatter, the Queen of Cakes

CONTENTS

INTRODUCTION

CAKES PLAY AN IMPORTANT PART IN OUR LIVES. The dramas of christenings, birthdays, bar mitzvahs, graduations, and, of course, weddings, always include a cake as part of the festivities. Cakes have only been with us for a few hundred years.

In most countries, a cake is a pound cake or fruitcake. Layer cakes and molded cakes with mousse or other soft fillings are more often referred to as desserts, but we use the term *cake* for all these sweet treats. In this book, I use the term to describe round, rectangular, or loaf-shaped baked desserts that may be filled or not, and that may have only one or several layers—in short, what we Americans generally think of as cakes. Although there are some recipes that straddle the line between cake and pastry, I have used the general rule that if there is a dough that has to be rolled out, then it is a pastry dough, resulting in a pie, not a cake. A pie or pastry is made from a dough, a cake is made from a batter. The one exception is yeast-risen coffee cakes; the mixtures for those are almost always doughs and sometimes need to be rolled.

This introduction will take you through all you need to know about cake ingredients and equipment. Begin with the principle professional bakers use: Get organized. If you are making a simple cake (mix-bake-cool-eat), you need only make sure you have all the ingredients before you start. If the cake is more elaborate, with multiple components (cake layer, moistening syrup, filling, frosting, garnish) consider preparing them over a several-day period before you assemble the cake: you will have a much easier time of it, and the whole process will be a pleasure instead of a chore.

A quick explanation about the recipes: One of my greatest pleasures is sharing recipes with family, friends, students, and acquaintances. Many of the recipes in my books, in turn, are ones people have given me. When I use someone else's recipe, I always test it thoroughly and often make adjustments in the ingredients and/or instructions to ensure good results. When a recipe comes from a book or periodical, it has been subjected to the same process—that is why such a recipe is described as "based on" another. If I have researched a particular recipe in many books and the result is a synthesis of all I've learned, then the names of those books appear in the bibliography, as it would not be practical to name all of the sources in the introduction to the recipe.

These cake recipes are the product of a lifetime of collecting and baking. I hope you enjoy them.

New York City
September 2001

INGREDIENTS

Using the best—and the correct—ingredients makes all the difference between success and failure in cake baking. It will take you only a few minutes to go over the descriptions of the ingredients below, but doing so will ensure that you use the right ones when you try the recipes.

FLOUR

Flour used for cake baking is milled from wheat of the botanical genus of *Triticum*. Wheat may be "hard" or "soft," terms that refer to the actual hardness or softness of the wheat berries, or kernels, themselves. Hard wheat produces flour rich in gluten-forming proteins—substances that make doughs elastic and springy, desirable in a bread dough or some pastry doughs, but not in a cake batter. This is why cake recipes call for all-purpose flour or cake flour, both of which are made from soft wheat and are weaker than the strong hard wheat flours.

ALL-PURPOSE FLOUR All-purpose flour is used for some cakes, especially ones that don't rise to great heights. All-purpose flour may be bleached or unbleached. Although unbleached all-purpose flour has a slightly higher protein content than bleached, the two can be used interchangeably in the recipes here that call for all-purpose flour.

CAKE FLOUR Finely milled and always bleached, making it suitable for very delicate cakes, such as sponge and angel cakes. It is used in many other types of cakes too. If you have to substitute all-purpose flour for cake flour, use 14 tablespoons (1 cup minus 2 tablespoons) all-purpose flour for every cup of cake flour called for.

SELF-RISING CAKE FLOUR This is cake flour with salt and baking powder added. Use it only in recipes that specify it—it can not be substituted for regular cake flour.

CORNSTARCH A pure starch extracted from corn and very finely milled. It is used in combination with wheat flour to produce cakes with an especially fine and delicate texture.

POTATO STARCH Very similar in both appearance and results to cornstarch, it is sometimes used in Passover cakes, for which no grain may be used.

CRUMBS Bread or cake crumbs are sometimes called for in recipes. Make sure they are fresh. Making bread crumbs yourself—a simple matter in the food processor—from either hard or soft bread is always superior to using commercial bread crumbs.

Sugar

Sugar contributes more than sweetness to cakes. In butter cakes, it helps the batter absorb air through friction between the butter and sugar during mixing. In any cake, it contributes tenderness and crust color and enhances the cake's ability to retain moisture.

GRANULATED SUGAR Regular granulated sugar is called for in all the recipes. I never use superfine sugar, which is very finely ground granulated sugar.

BROWN SUGAR Refined sugar that has molasses added to it for flavor and color, brown sugar may be light or dark, depending on the amount of molasses added. Granulated light brown sugar is also available; it works the same in recipes as the moist kind.

CONFECTIONERS' SUGAR Very finely ground granulated sugar, this always has about 3 percent cornstarch added by weight to prevent clumping. The cornstarch would add a chalky taste if the confectioners' sugar were added to whipped cream so it is best to use granulated for this purpose. It is dusted over some cakes as a garnish and is also a standard ingredient in simple icings made by just adding liquid to confectioners' sugar and heating before applying to a cake.

CORN SYRUP Corn syrup is a liquid sweetener made from corn. Light (colorless) corn syrup may be added to cooked sugar syrups or to other sugar-rich recipes such as boiled icing or seven-minute frosting to make them pliable and easy to spread. Light corn syrup is the moistening added to marzipan. Dark corn syrup functions in the same way, but it is used only when its molasses-y or slightly caramelized flavor is desired.

HONEY Though there are many specialty honeys, I usually buy a fairly dark natural honey, but I have used the plain old supermarket variety too. Dark honey has a deeper flavor and seems to impart more taste and less sweetness than lighter honeys.

MOLASSES Used often in old-fashioned cake recipes, molasses is a by-product of the sugar refining process. Molasses labeled "unsulphured" is milder in flavor than molasses that has been treated with sulphur to purify it. The latter type is not identified as sulphured molasses—the label usually states that it is "robust flavored." I usually buy unsulphured molasses because even a mild molasses flavor is fairly strong. However, most of the recipes in this book that use molasses call for such small amounts that I can't imagine substituting the stronger-flavored one would make any difference.

Leaveners

The additives that make cakes rise are called leaveners. Yeast, a natural leavener, is a living plant organism that releases carbon dioxide as part of its life cycle and helps some cake batters to rise. Chemical leaveners such as baking powder and baking soda cause carbon dioxide gas to be formed before and/or during baking so that batters rise. Many older recipes call for both baking powder and baking soda—I tend to use one or the other, because an abundance of chemical leaveners can give a cake a strange soapy taste. Many cakes, of course, rise simply through the expansion of air cells in the eggs or egg whites that are part of the batter.

Baking Powder Originally considered a substitute for yeast, baking powder enables mixtures that would otherwise remain dull and leaden to rise into delicate cakes. It was already popular by the last quarter of the nineteenth century, when it was made from a combination of cream of tartar (acid) and baking soda (alkali). This primitive baking powder formed carbon dioxide gas in the batter when the acid-and-alkali combination encountered liquid. Nowadays, double-acting baking powder is a more sophisticated combination of chemicals that cause the batter to leaven first from the presence of liquid and then in the heat of the oven.

Baking Soda Baking soda or bicarbonate of soda, predated baking powder as the first chemical leavener. Highly alkaline, it reacts with an acid ingredient in a batter. The most common ones of these are: cocoa, chocolate, honey, molasses, brown sugar, sour cream, yogurt, and buttermilk.

Yeast Before baking powder or baking soda, yeast was much used in cake making. Coffee cakes such as the brioche-based ones in Chapter 1 owe their light texture to yeast. Though these cakes have one foot firmly planted in the world of breads, they have been sweetened and enriched to the point that they really are cakes.

Flavorings

Whether it's a spoonful of vanilla extract or a little grated lemon zest, flavoring can transform an ordinary cake into a perfumed delicacy.

Vanilla Extract I use Nielsen-Massey Bourbon vanilla extract. Available in specialty food stores and by mail (see Sources), it imparts the vanilla flavor that I most enjoy. A few of these recipes call for vanilla beans, the cured seed pods of the vanilla orchid, from which the extract is made.

To use a vanilla bean, split it along the length, then use the point of a paring knife to scrape out the black paste of tiny seeds and add this to the preparation that calls for it. The rest of the bean need not go to waste—if you embed the scraped-out vanilla bean in a sack or canister of sugar, the sugar will absorb the vanilla flavor left in the bean. Some recipes, notably those in which the vanilla is added to liquid that will be heated, just call for the vanilla bean to be split. Heating and whisking the preparation will release the seeds and flavor inside the bean.

OTHER EXTRACTS I regularly use lemon, orange, almond, and anise extracts. Make sure the ones you purchase are pure, natural extracts. Sometimes the tiny print on the label will reveal that the little bottle is filled with artificial extracts.

FLAVORING OILS There are excellent citrus oils available. Use them just as you would extracts, but in smaller quantities (see Sources).

LIQUORS AND LIQUEURS I sometimes use spirits (distilled alcohol) and liqueurs (alcohol mixed with flavoring and sugar) to enhance cakes and/or fillings. Follow these simple rules to use liquor in a recipe: Use more if the liquor is to be baked in the batter, because the alcohol will evaporate substantially and so will some of the flavor. If the liquor is to be added to a cooled cake, make sure it is diluted with sugar syrup, or the cake may take on a strong, even bitter, alcohol flavor. When flavoring icings and buttercreams, add liquors and liqueurs slowly and sparingly. Too much liquid, or liquid added too quickly, can make glazes too thin and cause delicate buttercreams to separate. By the way, cheap brands of liquors and liqueurs tend to have a pretty cheap taste. Just as with most foods, the best quality is often more expensive, but worth it for its superior flavor.

COFFEE

It's easy to use instant coffee or instant espresso for flavoring a cake, mousse, or buttercream, but nothing beats the flavor of fresh-brewed coffee. When I can, I steep 3 Illy coffee pods—premeasured doses of coffee wrapped in paper, a little like a tea bag—in ¾ cup boiling water until the coffee has cooled completely. Then I squeeze out the pods and keep the resulting triple-strength espresso in the refrigerator in a covered jar. It adds such an excellent coffee flavor that you don't need to use very much. You can do the same thing with ground Illy coffee: Steep 3 heaping tablespoons of the coffee in ¾ cup boiling water. When it has cooled, strain first through a fine strainer to remove most of the grounds, then again through a coffee filter or paper towel set inside a strainer to remove all the grounds. Store as above.

FRUIT

Ripe fresh fruit may be difficult to find in this era of plastic-wrapped trays and sticky-labeled fruit. Below is a list of good staple fruits to use in the recipes here. Locally grown height-of-the-season produce can always be substituted with excellent results.

APPLES Golden Delicious is a good all-purpose apple, but if you like a tarter flavor, Granny Smith works well. McIntosh is the best for applesauce, and tiny lady apples make a pretty platter decoration when they are in season in the fall.

PEARS The all-around best pear for use in fillings, poaching, and cakes is a Bartlett. When a Bartlett pear is ripe, its buttery, melting flesh is exquisitely perfumed and although it is sweet, a good Bartlett always retains a slight undertone of acidity in its flavor. If you can find only underripe pears, place them in a closed paper bag at room temperature, and they will ripen perfectly in a day or two.

CITRUS FRUIT

LEMONS I usually buy supermarket lemons, mainly the Eureka variety that is available all over the United States. When I can find them, I like to use sweeter Meyer lemons for frostings and fillings. Meyer lemons are not necessarily a one-for-one substitute for more acidic lemons—you'll probably need about half again as many for a good lemon flavor. Meyer lemons make fine lemon curd, but I find them weak for flavoring buttercream.

ORANGES California Valencia oranges, which are most easily available where I live, are a perfect all-purpose orange for juice, zest, and for segmenting or slicing. I also use Florida juice oranges for their juice; their zest is a little bitter. Florida Honeybells are good for everything during their short midwinter season.

TANGERINES A good tangerine is usually fairly loose skinned. Aside from the American-grown ones available in fall and winter, I use the tiny, sweet clementines imported from Israel, Morocco, and Spain.

LIMES Persian limes, available in supermarkets, are fine for lime-flavored cakes. I tend not to use the zest, which is bitter. Key limes from Florida, in season in the late fall, have a more tart flavor than Persian limes and can be a good substitute, but you have to be careful that they do not make the cake or filling too tart. Never use the zest of Key limes—it is extremely bitter.

STONE FRUIT

PEACHES They must be ripe to have any flavor at all. Although there is a snobbish preference for white-fleshed peaches in some circles, they aren't any good if they aren't perfectly ripe. Locally grown peaches will always be best for any purpose; if the season is short, use them as often as possible, then wait until next year for good ones again.

APRICOTS One of the most elusively flavored of all fruits, apricots are seldom found ripe. Even my local farmers' market has taken to selling underripe apricots that are more sour than any lemon you can imagine. Although they will soften if left at room temperature, they really won't develop more sugar. So always taste if possible before purchasing apricots. A little acidity is fine to balance the sweetness, but too much will annihilate all flavor.

PLUMS The plums I use the most for baking are the prune plums, sometimes called Italian plums, that come at summer's end. I always think of them as "back to school" plums, because they were always a component of my school lunch in early September when I was a child. Although there are several varieties of this type of plum, they are fairly similar in flavor and texture. They work best in a crumb cake or other coffee cake–type presentation with enough sweet ingredients to offset their tartness.

CHERRIES Sweet or Bing cherries are an excellent dessert in themselves, but they are a little bland and too sweet for making cakes. For baking, I prefer a Montmorency or any one of several other varieties of sour cherries. Sour cherries have a fairly short season compared to their sweet counterparts, but they are well worth waiting for. Where I live in New York City, sour cherries from southern New Jersey and upstate New York are available for a couple of weeks only between mid-June and mid-July. The exact season changes every year and may be longer or shorter depending on weather conditions during both the blossoming and fruiting of the trees. If I can't get sour cherries for a pie or crumb cake, I'll make a blueberry pie or cake, rather than substituting sweet cherries–they just don't have the right taste.

Berries

This category encompasses strawberries, raspberries, blueberries, blackberries, currants (red, black, and white), and gooseberries.

Strawberries Most of the United States gets good California-grown berries throughout the year. But if you live in an area where you can get locally grown strawberries, these are the ones to use for shortcakes (or just serve with a bowl of whipped cream and a shaker of sugar). A ripe local strawberry is hard to beat—it has the color, flavor, and perfume that hothouse berries lack.

Raspberries Although raspberries are now available throughout most of the year, local berries have only a short season where I live; occasionally there are sweet and virtually seedless black raspberries and beautiful golden ones in the fall. As a result, raspberries are one fruit I often use in frozen form. I prefer IQF (individually quick frozen) raspberries when I can get them. These are bags of individual berries that have nothing added to them. When I use the frozen berries for a puree, I add sugar and a drop of water and cook them down, then puree and strain them. Cooking them down concentrates the flavor, and the puree can be used to make a great Bavarian cream, sauce, or glaze.

Blueberries I'm actually lucky that fresh blueberries are available only for part of the year, because I would make cakes and pies with them weekly if I could. I love the way they melt to that jam-like consistency after baking—they are my favorite berry. Most of the blueberries I buy in New York come from southern New Jersey. At the end of August and beginning of September, we sometimes get tiny, very spicy-flavored wild blueberries from Maine. If you can get some, by all means use them. Unfortunately, most of the wild Maine blueberries are bought up by industrial bakers for muffin mixes and canned pie fillings.

Blackberries Aside from wild ones that I pick on walks in the country, I don't often use blackberries. They are available during a short season in my local farmers' market, and they are also to be found in IQF form. They are a berry that I more often associate with pies and cobblers, or serving with sugar and cream, than I do with cakes.

Currants Usually used to make jelly or jam, fresh currants are a rarity. The beautiful clusters of fruit, like diminutive bunches of grapes, make a great decoration for a simple cake, though they are a bit tart to eat uncooked and unsweetened. Black currants are called *cassis* in French.

GOOSEBERRIES The tart green globes of gooseberries can be great in a crumb cake, though I have to admit I seldom use them.

CHOCOLATE

Good chocolate tastes good before you add it to other ingredients. With the exception of unsweetened chocolate, which is found in the baking aisle of most grocery stores, I usually tell people to buy their chocolate for baking in the candy aisle—bars of imported or domestic bittersweet, semisweet, milk, and white chocolate sold to eat out of hand usually have a better flavor and perform better than "baking chocolate." Nowadays there are more than a dozen brands to choose from, including the brands available at specialty food stores. For recipes that center on chocolate (such as Ganache, page 281, or Chocolate Glaze, page 287), it is especially important to choose a chocolate that tastes good on its own. If the recipe mixes chocolate with butter, eggs, sugar, flour, and flavoring, the taste of the chocolate isn't quite as clear as it is in simpler recipes. Of course you should use the best chocolate possible for this type of recipe too, but the flavor of the most delicate chocolates may be somewhat overwhelmed by the other ingredients.

COCOA I always use alkalized (Dutch-process) cocoa for cakes. It has a superior flavor and performs better than nonalkalized cocoa. The alkalizing process (treating the cocoa with a chemical like baking soda) reduces bitterness and improves the color of the cocoa.

NUTS AND NUT PRODUCTS

Besides being an essential ingredient in many cake batters, nuts and nut products are also often used to garnish and decorate.

ALMONDS Most of these come from California, with some arriving from Spain and a very few from Sicily. I usually use blanched almonds, whole or sliced, for cake baking. Store almonds, like all nuts, in a tightly sealed plastic bag in the freezer. If you can't find blanched whole almonds, place unblanched almonds in a saucepan, cover them with water, and bring to a boil. Drain the almonds in a strainer and pop them out of their skins while they are still warm. (If the skin is still on the sliced almonds you buy, you can't remove it.) If you need to grind the almonds, or plan to keep them before using them, place them on a jelly-roll pan and dry them in a 300-degree oven for about 10 minutes. Cool before using or storing in the freezer.

To enable you to grind almonds, or any nutmeats successfully, they must be at room temperature. Bring nuts stored in the freezer to room temperature for an hour or so before grinding them, or warm them on a jelly-roll pan at 300 degrees for 10 minutes, then cool them before you grind. Grind the almonds in the food processor fitted with the metal blade, pulsing the machine on and off at 1-second intervals and occasionally scraping the inside bottom edges of the bowl with a table knife or metal spatula between pulses. Use the same technique for grinding all nuts.

Bitter almonds are not eaten in the United States, but they are used with sweet almonds to make almond extract. That essential bitter almond perfume is their contribution.

ALMOND PASTE This is made from equal quantities of blanched almonds and sugar and is used as an ingredient in cake batters and in marzipan. The best almond paste comes in a can, not in a sausage shape in a cellophane wrapping. There are several good national brands of almond paste available in supermarkets or specialty stores (see Sources).

HAZELNUTS These are grown in Oregon, but many come from the Piemonte in northwestern Italy and from Turkey. Hazelnuts are usually used chopped or ground. I find chopping them with a knife difficult, so I usually wrap them in a towel and crush them with the bottom of a heavy saucepan. Nuts first broken that way won't roll all over your cutting board, and you can then chop them finer with a knife. To grind hazelnuts, see Almonds, above.

To blanch hazelnuts, place them in a jelly-roll pan and toast them in a 350-degree oven for about 10 to 15 minutes. To test whether or not they are ready, remove a hazelnut from the pan, let it cool for a few seconds, and then rub it to see if the skin flakes off easily. If it doesn't, toast a few seconds longer. Pour the toasted hazelnuts onto a damp towel and gather the towel around them. Rub the hazelnuts in the towel to loosen the skins, then go over them one by one to separate them from the skin; it doesn't matter if every speck of skin doesn't come off.

PRALINE PASTE A delicious flavoring made from hazelnuts and sugar, praline paste is available in specialty stores (also see Sources). One of my favorite buttercreams is made with praline paste, and it is a natural and luxuriously smooth and rich partner with chocolate of all kinds.

WALNUTS For decorating, I use walnut halves, or walnut pieces if the recipe calls for them to be chopped or ground. Walnuts can become very pasty when they are ground. To avoid this, add a few tablespoons of the sugar from the recipe to the walnuts in the food processor. Otherwise, follow exactly the same rules as for almonds, above, but scrape the bottom of the bowl every few pulses to prevent caking.

PECANS A close cousin to that all-American nut, the hickory nut, pecans come from the Southern states. They are also very popular in Mexico and more recently, in Australia. I always have to restrain myself from eating more pecans than I'm putting into the recipe. Their sweet and buttery flavor is difficult to resist. When grinding pecans, follow the directions above for walnuts; they are less likely to get pasty than walnuts.

PISTACHIOS These delicious green gems come from California and the Middle East. A small quantity of Sicilian pistachios are imported, and they are worth seeking out for their exotic bitter almond flavor and incredibly bright green color. In general, California pistachios are not as green as the Middle Eastern and Sicilian varieties. To blanch pistachios, start the same way as for almonds, above, but after you drain the pistachios, rub them in a towel and go over them one by one to separate them from the skins. Dry them in the oven afterwards as with almonds, but be careful that they don't start to toast, or they will lose their color.

PINE NUTS Nineteenth-century French baking author Pierre Lacam recommended substituting pine nuts for almonds because they were so much cheaper. Today the opposite is true, but pine nuts can still contribute a very delicate flavor to cakes. I like them especially in light fruit cakes or combined with a crumb topping on a delicately flavored cake with fresh fruit.

EGGS

Eggs are the most essential ingredient in cake baking, responsible for the structure, lightness, and richness of cakes, fillings, and frostings. I always use large eggs (24 ounces per dozen). Remember that the weight is by the dozen and the weight of individual eggs may vary. This doesn't much affect recipes that use whole eggs or yolks, but sometimes if I'm preparing meringues, I like to measure the egg whites by volume, using a liquid-measure cup. In this book, recipes calling for egg whites include a measure such as ½ cup. If I have leftover egg whites, I store them in a covered glass jar in the refrigerator for a few days or freeze them for up to a month. Plastic snack bags and half-pint plastic containers are ideal for a few egg whites—just be sure to mark the bag or container with indelible pen to indicate the number of egg whites in it. To use the whites, thaw them in the refrigerator overnight, or at room temperature. If you have thawed them at room temperature, use them right away.

Leftover yolks will keep well for up to a day or two if stored like this: Place the unbroken yolks in a small bowl, sprinkle with a teaspoon of water, and press plastic wrap directly against the yolks, without breaking them. Keep refrigerated for no more than 48 hours, and use right from the refrigerator. Egg yolks can be frozen by stirring a teaspoon of light corn syrup into every 3 or 4 yolks and pressing plastic wrap directly against the surface, before sealing the container.

DAIRY PRODUCTS

BUTTER My personal favorite baking ingredient, butter has to be of good quality to make an out-standing cake or buttercream. Always use unsalted butter, and make sure it is fresh by using this simple test: Unwrap a stick of butter and scrape the surface with a dull knife, removing a strip about ¼ inch wide. If the butter below the surface is lighter in color, the butter has oxidized—it has been exposed to air and the outside has begun to turn rancid. Never accept oxidized butter from a store; if you have taken it home, return it immediately. Sometimes butter that has begun to oxi-dize is put on sale so the store can get rid of it. Unfortunately, it is no bargain at any price.

Recipe testing has proven it dozens of times—a cake batter made with butter that has been allowed to soften is lighter and has a better texture than one made with cold butter beaten until it is soft. When a recipe calls for softened butter, make sure you leave the butter, still in its wrap-per or covered with plastic wrap, outside the refrigerator for at least an hour. Don't place the butter in the sun or put it on a hot stove to hasten the process—that will melt the butter, not soften it. If you're very careful, you can place the butter in a microwave-safe bowl and mi-crowave it for a few seconds at a time to soften it.

MILK The recipes in this book use whole milk. Honestly, though, if you are making a yeast-risen cake that requires only a small amount of milk, it doesn't really matter if you use a low-fat milk. However, I always use whole milk when making anything custardy. I don't think lower-fat milks make a good pastry cream or crème anglaise.

CREAM I use heavy whipping cream that is 36 percent butterfat. Although richer cream is available to chefs (40 percent butterfat), we tested all the recipes in this book with the ultrapas-teurized cream that you can buy in the supermarket. Remember, for whipped cream, have the bowl, beater, and cream cold.

SOUR CREAM I never use reduced-fat sour creams in recipes, though I suppose they are okay on a baked potato.

Among the richest ingredients for baking, cheese is made by slightly curdling milk, cream, or a combination and draining off the resulting liquid.

CREAM CHEESE I used to think it was important to use cream cheese without vegetable gum additives, but I discovered that cheesecakes, notably, are less smooth when made with the drier and rougher-textured cheeses. Now I use regular full-fat cream cheese from the supermarket for baking.

MASCARPONE A luscious Italian cream cheese, mascarpone has a softer texture than our cream cheese. It is an essential ingredient in Tiramisù (page 252) and in some of the cheese-cake recipes.

RICOTTA Another Italian cheese, ricotta is a deliciously milky curd cheese. Though it has a somewhat rough texture, when eggs and other ingredients are added, ricotta smooths out very well. If I use it uncooked for a mousse recipe, I usually process the ricotta in the food processor to make it smoother. The best-tasting and firmest ricotta is the freshly made kind you can find in an Italian deli. If you don't have one near you, try to find a local commercially made brand.

In the course of my travels to teach at cooking schools around the United States, I have encountered supermarket ricotta that has been frozen and defrosted before it was sold: the resulting ricotta has a dry, chalky texture and has completely lost its milky flavor and rich texture.

EQUIPMENT

HAVING THE RIGHT EQUIPMENT makes baking even more of a pleasure. The good news is that you don't have to buy it all at once. I've been collecting baking equipment for thirty-five years and I still can't visit a kitchenware store, no matter what state or country I'm in, without emerging with a few cookie cutters or an implement (and recipe) necessary to the preparation of a local specialty. Although the best things are not always the most expensive, buying high-quality pans, tools, and small appliances means that they will last a lifetime. I still have my first KitchenAid mixer, which I bought when I was in high school—close to forty years later, it whips up egg whites and everything else to perfect peaks.

ELECTRICAL APPLIANCES

HEAVY-DUTY STAND MIXER This makes quick work of mixing, beating, and whipping. Use the flat paddle for all general mixing purposes such as preparing butter and pound cake batters, cheesecake batters, and any firm mixture, such as marzipan. Use the whisk attachment only for incorporating air, as in whipping egg whites or cream. It's nice to have an extra mixer bowl and whisk for those batters that require whipping whites and yolks separately.

HAND MIXER If you're just starting out baking and have a limited budget, a hand mixer will do all but the most heavy-duty jobs, such as beating marzipan or mixing bread doughs. Having an extra set of beaters is handy for batters that require separately beaten egg whites.

FOOD PROCESSOR Back in the dark ages, before there were food processors, we used hand grinders, graters, and knives to—slowly and laboriously—do everything the food processor now does in seconds. A food processor can be used to mix some simple batters, though I usually rely on my stand mixer for that. The processor mixes ingredients very efficiently, but it doesn't incorporate air in the process, which is why I always prefer the mixer for batters. A processor, though, can't be beat for grinding nuts.

BLENDER I think a blender makes better purees—and does so more quickly—than a food processor.

Hand Tools

A good assortment of whisks, rubber spatulas, and wooden spoons is essential for all cooking and baking. If you have not done a lot of baking, you may need to purchase the following few specialty items before you begin using this book.

Spatulas I like small and large offset (the smooth blade steps down from the handle) spatulas for finishing cakes. A wide griddle spatula—whether or not it has a perforated blade—can be useful for transferring cake layers to cooling racks and onto platters.

Thermometers A thermometer can be a great help in getting consistent results with recipes. Excellent battery-operated digital thermometers are available as close as your local hardware store. These are perfect for tempering chocolate or monitoring the heat of delicate mixtures such as crème anglaise.

Knives This is definitely an area where you want to get the very best you can afford. The three essential knives for cake baking are a paring knife, a chef's chopping knife, and a serrated bread knife, for slicing through cake layers. The latter should have as long a blade as you can find. For the paring and chef's knives, buy whatever size feels comfortable in your hand. I also like a long thin narrow-bladed slicing knife for cutting cakes into portions.

Chocolate Chopper A four-pronged ice pick does a great job of breaking chocolate into ½- to ¼-inch pieces. Be careful: the ends of the picks are sharp and can ruin a countertop or wooden cutting board. I use a less expensive nylon board for chopping chocolate; then the board makes a quick trip through the dishwasher to remove the chocolate stains—difficult to do by hand.

Baking Pans Most of the baking pans I own are aluminum. I have nested sets of 2-inch-deep round cake pans in 8-, 9-, 10-, and 12-inch diameters—all of these are used in the recipes here. Both 9 × 5 × 3-inch and 8½ × 4½ × 2¾-inch loaf pans are called for, as are both 10 × 15-inch and 12 × 18-inch jelly-roll pans. To round out the assortment, you'll need a 12-cup Bundt pan and a 10-inch tube pan with a removable bottom for angel cakes. Add a couple of springform pans—9- and 10-inch—for molded cakes and cheesecakes, and you've got all the pans you'll need to make the recipes in this book.

A *Bundt pan* is a fluted tube pan with a rounded bottom, so that when the cake is unmolded, it has a curved, gently rounded, ridged top. The most common size is 10 inches in diameter and holds 12 cups, and that's the one you'll need for all the recipes that call for Bundt pans.

Angel food cake pans come in two pieces: the bottom and tube are one part and the pan sides another. I keep a separate one just for angel food and sponge cakes that need to be baked in ungreased pans, as any trace of fat in the pan would prevent such cakes from rising properly.

DESSERT RINGS Known as *entremet* rings in French, these are sturdy round metal rings. For molded cakes, they are placed on a cardboard round, set on a sheet pan or cookie sheet, and filled with layers of cake and filling. The dessert ring is removed after the cake has chilled, leaving it on the cardboard base. They are available in many diameters.

SILPAT This is a silicone mat used to line a baking sheet and provide a perfect nonstick surface. A Silpat is very useful when you are making ladyfingers. They are also excellent for cookies such as tuiles and tulipes that spread and need to be lifted while still hot from the pan and shaped.

FLEXIPAN These flexible silicone baking pans come in a variety of shapes and sizes and provide a nonstick medium for baking cakes and smaller items such as madeleines and financiers. If you use them, always remember to place them on a jelly-roll pan before you fill them, or they could buckle on the way to the oven and spill their contents.

DECORATING EQUIPMENT

PASTRY BAGS These used to be made from canvas, and were a real pain to clean. Nowadays I often use disposable bags (see Sources). If you want reusable pastry bags, the nylon or plastic-coated canvas ones are thin, flexible, waterproof (important when you are piping whipped cream), and easy to clean: soak them in soapy water with a little bleach added, then rinse thoroughly under running water. (Sometimes I just rinse these bags and add them to kitchen laundry to be run through the washing machine; I don't think they would survive a trip through the dryer.)

TUBES These tips, which are inserted into the end of the pastry bag, come in many shapes and sizes. Recipes here that require piping always state the Ateco tube number as these are easy to find. Tubes are widely available in kitchenware stores and through mail-order (see Sources).

PAPER GOODS

PARCHMENT PAPER Invaluable for lining pans, making cones (instant disposable pastry bags), and transferring dry ingredients to the mixer, parchment paper comes in rolls or in large sheets. The large sheets, designed to be used on commercial sheet pans, are approximately 18 by 24 inches. These are useful because the standard roll of parchment paper isn't wide enough to line both the bottom and sides of some rectangular pans. Lacking parchment paper, I use wax paper or aluminum foil for lining pans.

CARDBOARD ROUNDS I like putting a cardboard round under a layer cake when I'm finishing it. The convenience of having a cake on a base that you can pick up and move around is a real advantage. See Sources.

MEASURING

Accurate measuring can make the difference between a successful cake and a failure.

LIQUID MEASURES I always use Pyrex measuring cups for liquids. Place the glass (or clear plastic) measuring cup on a level surface and fill it so that the liquid reaches the top of the line for the measurement you need. If you have low countertops, it may be necessary to do a deep knee bend to read the level. Or stand the cup on a shelf at eye level to get a good reading. Measuring cups that hold 2 or more cups are excellent for measuring large amounts, but I never use a large cup measure for measuring less than a cup, because these can be less accurate for smaller amounts.

DRY MEASURES Nested dry-measure cups that come in ¼-, ⅓-, ½-, and 1-cup gradations are used to measure dry ingredients. If you buy a set of dry-measure cups that also has ⅔- and ¾-cup measures, send those immediately to the potting bench or the sandbox—it is too easy to mistake one of those cups for another size and ruin a recipe. To use the cups for powdery dry ingredients such as flour, confectioners' sugar, and cocoa powder, put the correct-size cup on a piece of wax paper and gently spoon in the ingredient until the cup overflows, then level it with the back of a knife or with a metal spatula. Granulated sugar can be scooped up with a cup measure, but it is the only ingredient I measure that way.

MEASURING SPOONS I usually scoop up ingredients with measuring spoons—the quantities being measured are small enough that I don't think it matters if the ingredient is slightly packed in the spoon. To measure spoonfuls of liquid, pour the liquid into the spoon—just don't do the pouring over your bowl of batter, or any excess will overflow into it.

PERFECT
CAKES

I COFFEE CAKES

THESE ARE THE CAKES for when that familiar feeling comes over you: "I want something really good to eat but I don't know what I want." These are cakes that you don't necessarily bake for a special occasion, but because you want to have something in the house in case someone drops by. They're also great to take on picnics or send to school for lunches and to whip up when you want to bake something quick to take to a friend or neighbor who doesn't have time to bake.

A coffee cake should be easy to prepare: no fussy procedures and no fancy, time-consuming touches. One of the cakes in this chapter has a chocolate glaze—it is a more "sitting down for coffee at the dining room table" type of coffee cake. All the others can be prepared quickly, even mixed by hand, in one step.

The name *coffee cake* distinguishes these recipes from dessert cakes, because they are more simple both in preparation and in flavor. Serve them in slices or wedges, and with a favorite beverage.

A few of these recipes call for yeast; they are the only ones in the book that use it. Here are a few hints about working with yeast.

1 Always store dry yeast in the freezer to prolong its life.

2 If you buy dry yeast in bulk, make sure you keep in mind its expiration date.

3 Always use warm, not hot, water to dissolve yeast. Warm water activates the yeast quickly; hot water would kill it.

4 Always allow yeast dough to rise in an area free of drafts. Cool air can chill the yeast and keep the dough from rising.

5 If you prefer to use compressed (fresh) yeast, a 2-ounce yeast cake equals a strip of three dry yeast envelopes. So, if you only need one envelope for the recipe, use a third of the yeast cake. Crumble the yeast and use it the same way you would dry yeast, whisking it into warm liquid.

6 Don't be afraid to try baking with yeast—it's really easy and well worth it for the great things you can make.

CINNAMON COFFEE CAKE

~⸲9 ⸲~

I REMEMBER TRYING THIS FUN AND EASY RECIPE as one of my first attempts at baking. I found it in a pamphlet put out by a baking powder company that was part of the recipe collection I inherited from my maternal grandmother. The cake is still as good today as it was forty years ago. Thanks also to Andrea Tutunjian, who shared a similar recipe from her grandmother Antoinette Bianco.

Because there's such a small quantity of batter, I've given instructions for preparing it by hand. Of course, you can also use a mixer with the paddle attachment.

1 Set a rack in the middle of the oven and preheat to 350 degrees.

2 Stir together the flour, baking powder, cinnamon, and salt in a bowl.

3 Place the butter in a large mixing bowl and beat in the sugar with a wooden spoon or a rubber spatula. Continue to beat for about a minute, then beat in the eggs one at a time, beating until smooth after each addition.

4 Stir in half the flour mixture, then stir in the milk. Stir in the remaining flour mixture. Beat the batter for about a minute. Pour into the prepared pan.

5 To make the crumb topping, mix the flour, sugar, and cinnamon in a bowl. Stir in the butter until evenly distributed. Using your hands, rub the mixture to coarse crumbs. Scatter the crumbs over the batter.

CAKE BATTER

2 cups all-purpose flour (spoon flour into dry-measure cup and level off)

2 teaspoons baking powder

1 teaspoon ground cinnamon

1/8 teaspoon salt

4 tablespoons (1/2 stick) unsalted butter, softened

3/4 cup sugar

2 large eggs

1/2 cup milk

CRUMB TOPPING

1 1/4 cups all-purpose flour (spoon flour into dry-measure cups and level off)

1/2 cup sugar

1/4 teaspoon ground cinnamon

8 tablespoons (1 stick) unsalted butter, melted

One 2-inch-deep 9-inch round cake pan, buttered and the bottom lined with buttered parchment or wax paper

6 Bake for about 40 minutes, until the cake is well risen and deep gold and a toothpick inserted in the center emerges clean.

7 Cool the cake in the pan for about 15 minutes. Invert the cake onto a plate and lift off the pan. Peel off the paper and the cake onto a rack to cool. If some of the crumbs fall off in the process, replace them on the top of the cake.

STORAGE: Wrap in plastic wrap and keep at room temperature, or wrap well and freeze for longer storage; thaw the cake covered, then refresh briefly on a cookie sheet in a 375-degree oven for about 5 minutes; let cool.

MAKES ONE 9-INCH CAKE, ABOUT 12 SERVINGS

IRISH CURRANT AND RAISIN CAKE

RIGHTFULLY THIS CAKE belongs in the chapter with the other cakes that contain dried fruit, but to me it is the quintessential coffee cake. It is a quick and easy version of a cake that I remember from my childhood, made by the mother of my school friend the late Noel Giles. Noel and I consumed about a ton of this cake per year between the ages of twelve and eighteen—a taste of it still makes me feel like a teenager.

2¼ cups unbleached all-purpose flour (spoon flour into dry-measure cups and level off) plus 1 tablespoon

1 teaspoon baking powder

½ teaspoon baking soda

½ teaspoon salt

8 tablespoons (1 stick) unsalted butter, softened

¾ cup sugar

1 large egg, at room temperature

½ cup currants

½ cup golden raisins

¾ cup buttermilk or milk

One 2-inch-deep 8-inch round cake pan, buttered and bottom lined with parchment or wax paper

1 Set a rack in the middle of the oven and preheat to 350 degrees.

2 Stir together the 2¼ cups flour, the baking powder, baking soda, and salt in a bowl.

3 In the bowl of a heavy-duty mixer, beat the butter and sugar with the paddle on medium speed until soft and light, about 5 minutes. Add the egg, beating until smooth.

4 Decrease the mixer speed to low and beat in half the flour mixture. Stop and scrape down the bowl and beater with a rubber spatula. Beat in the buttermilk, then the remaining flour mixture.

5 Give the batter a final mix with the rubber spatula.

6 Toss the currants and raisins with the remaining 1 tablespoon flour and fold them into the batter. Scrape the batter into the prepared pan and smooth the top.

7 Bake for about 45–55 minutes, or until the cake is well risen and deep gold and a toothpick inserted in the center emerges clean.

8 Cool in the pan on a rack for about 30 minutes, then invert the cake onto a rack and remove the pan and paper. Invert the cake onto another rack and cool completely.

STORAGE: Wrap in plastic and keep at room temperature, or double-wrap and freeze for longer storage.

MAKES ONE 8-INCH CAKE, ABOUT 12 SERVINGS

ORANGE POPPY SEED CAKE

CRUNCHY POPPY SEEDS and mellow orange flavor complement each other perfectly in this lovely Australian cake.

1 Set a rack in the middle of the oven and preheat to 350 degrees.

2 Combine the flour, baking powder, and baking soda in a bowl and stir to mix.

3 In the bowl of a heavy-duty mixer, beat the butter and sugar with the paddle on medium speed until soft and light, about 5 minutes. Beat in the eggs one at a time, beating until smooth after each addition.

4 Decrease the mixer speed to low and add half the flour mixture. Stop the mixer and scrape down the bowl and beater with a rubber spatula. Beat in the sour cream, then the remaining flour mixture.

5 Use a large rubber spatula to give the batter a final mix. Fold in the poppy seeds. Scrape the batter into the prepared pan.

6 Bake for about 1 hour, or until the cake is well risen and deep gold and a toothpick inserted in the center emerges clean.

CAKE BATTER

1¾ cups all-purpose flour (spoon flour into dry-measure cups and level off)

1 teaspoon baking powder

1 teaspoon baking soda

½ pound (2 sticks) unsalted butter, softened

1 cup sugar

3 large eggs

One 8-ounce container sour cream

½ cup poppy seeds

ORANGE SYRUP

2 tablespoons finely grated orange zest

¾ cup strained fresh orange juice

¾ cup sugar

Strips of orange zest for decorating

One 9-inch springform pan, buttered and bottom lined with buttered parchment or wax paper

7   While the cake is baking, prepare the syrup: Combine all the ingredients in a nonreactive saucepan and bring to a simmer, stirring occasionally to dissolve the sugar. Strain through a fine-mesh strainer into a measuring cup.

8   When the cake is baked, place it on a jelly-roll pan. Use a skewer to poke about 20 holes into the cake. Gradually pour the syrup all over the top of the cake until it is all absorbed. If any of the syrup leaks out of the springform pan, spoon it back over the cake. The cake absorbs the syrup rather slowly.

9   Transfer the cake to a rack and cool to room temperature.

10   Remove the pan sides and slide the cake, on the paper, onto a platter. Run a sharp knife between the cake and the paper and pull out the paper.

STORAGE: Keep under a cake dome at room temperature.

MAKES ONE 9-INCH CAKE, ABOUT 12 TO 16 SERVINGS

ONTBIJTKOEK

Dutch Breakfast Cake

୨ ୧

THIS IS PRETTY MUCH A STAPLE on the Dutch breakfast table, available in every bakery, supermarket, and convenience store. This version from my friend cookbook dealer Bonnie Slotnick has an extra fillip of crystallized ginger.

In Holland, this cake is eaten with butter, but I think it's fine on its own.

1 Set a rack in the middle of the oven and preheat to 350 degrees.

2 In a large bowl, stir together the flour, baking powder, and spices.

3 Place the brown sugar in a medium bowl and stir in the milk, adding it slowly so the sugar doesn't lump. Pour the milk mixture all at once into the flour mixture and stir until the batter is smooth. Stir in the crystallized ginger, if using.

4 Pour the batter into the prepared pan.

5 Bake for 1 hour, or until the cake begins to leave the sides of the pan and is nicely browned and a toothpick inserted in the center emerges clean.

6 Cool the cake in the pan on a rack for about 15 minutes, then invert onto the rack and let cool completely.

7 Wrap the cake well in plastic wrap and let age at room temperature or in the refrigerator for at least a day. (Served too

2 cups all-purpose flour (spoon flour into dry-measure cup and level off)

1 teaspoon baking powder

1 teaspoon ground cinnamon

½ teaspoon freshly grated nutmeg

½ teaspoon ground ginger

½ teaspoon ground allspice

1 cup firmly packed dark brown sugar

1 cup milk

½ cup (about 3 ounces) crystallized ginger, cut into ¼-inch pieces, optional

One 8½ × 4½ × 2¾-inch loaf pan, buttered and bottom lined with buttered aluminum foil

soon, it has a rubbery quality that disappears otherwise.)

STORAGE: Wrapped well in plastic, this keeps almost indefinitely at room temperature.

MAKES ONE 8½ × 4½-INCH LOAF CAKE, 16 SLICES

CHOCOLATE CHIP– CREAM CHEESE COFFEE CAKE

～⁹ℓ ℓ～

Just reading the name of this cake makes me want to get up and bake one. Its rich texture, surprise of the chocolate chips inside, and crisp topping make a memorable cake.

1 Set a rack in the middle of the oven and preheat to 350 degrees.

2 In a medium bowl, stir together the flour, baking powder, baking soda, and salt.

3 In the bowl of a heavy-duty mixer, beat the cream cheese, butter, and sugar with the paddle on medium speed until soft and light, about 5 minutes. Add the eggs one at a time, beating until smooth after each addition.

4 Decrease the mixer speed to low and add half the dry ingredients. Stop the mixer and scrape down the bowl and beater. Beat in the milk, then beat in the remaining dry ingredients.

5 Give the batter a final mix with a large rubber spatula. Fold in the chocolate chips, and spread the batter evenly in the prepared pan.

6 To make the crumb topping, stir all the dry ingredients together in a mixing

CAKE BATTER

2 cups cake flour (spoon flour into dry-measure cup and level off)

1 teaspoon baking powder

¼ teaspoon baking soda

¼ teaspoon salt

One 8-ounce package cream cheese, softened

½ pound (2 sticks) unsalted butter, softened

1¼ cups sugar

2 large eggs

¼ cup milk

One 12-ounce bag semisweet chocolate chips

CRUMB TOPPING

½ cup all-purpose flour (spoon flour into dry-measure cup and level off)

½ cup rolled oats

¼ cup firmly packed light brown sugar

1 teaspoon ground cinnamon

4 tablespoons (½ stick) unsalted butter, melted

One 12-cup straight-sided tube pan, buttered and floured

bowl, mixing well. Stir in the butter and continue stirring until the mixture forms large crumbs. Sprinkle the crumb topping evenly over the batter.

7   Bake for about 50 to 55 minutes, or until the cake is well risen, the crumbs are golden, and a toothpick inserted into the center emerges clean.

8   Cool the cake in the pan on a rack for about 15 minutes. Invert the cake to a plate, remove side and bottom of pan, then invert again onto the rack to cool completely.

9   Slide the cake onto a platter.

STORAGE: Wrap in plastic and keep at room temperature for up to several days, or double-wrap and freeze for longer storage.

MAKES ONE 9-INCH CAKE, ABOUT 12 SERVINGS

SOUR CREAM COFFEE CAKE

~·~

I REMEMBER MAKING THIS coffee cake as a teenager, probably from the same recipe. It comes from my Aunt Virginia. She has always liked to bake, and this is a recipe she makes frequently. Thanks also to Alan Cohen, who shared a similar recipe.

1 Set a rack in the middle of the oven and preheat to 350 degrees.

2 Stir together the flour, baking powder, and baking soda in a bowl, mixing well.

3 In the bowl of a heavy-duty mixer, beat the butter and sugar with the paddle on medium speed until soft and light, about 5 minutes. Beat in the eggs one at a time, beating until smooth after each addition.

4 Decrease the mixer speed to low and beat in one-third of the flour mixture, followed by half the sour cream. Stop the mixer and scrape down the bowl and beater. Beat in another third of the flour mixture, then the remaining sour cream. Stop and scrape again. Beat in the remaining flour mixture.

5 Give the batter a final mix with a large rubber spatula.

6 To make the topping, stir the ingredients together until evenly mixed.

CAKE BATTER

2 cups all-purpose flour (spoon flour into dry-measure cup and level off)

1 teaspoon baking powder

½ teaspoon baking soda

½ pound (2 sticks) unsalted butter, softened

1½ cups sugar

2 large eggs

One 8-ounce container sour cream

WALNUT TOPPING

1 cup (about 4 ounces) walnuts, coarsely chopped

¼ cup sugar

2 teaspoons ground cinnamon

One 12-cup tube pan, buttered and floured

7 Scrape half the batter into the prepared pan and sprinkle with half the topping. Cover with the remaining batter and smooth the top. Sprinkle with the remaining topping.

8 Bake for 50 to 55 minutes, or until the cake is well risen and deep gold and a toothpick inserted midway between the side of the pan and the central tube emerges clean.

9 Cool in the pan on a rack for 30 minutes, then invert onto a plate and lift off the pan. Invert the cake onto a rack to cool completely.

STORAGE: Keep wrapped in plastic or under a cake dome at room temperature, or double-wrap and freeze for longer storage.

MAKES ONE 10-INCH TUBE CAKE, ABOUT 16 SERVINGS

(see photograph, pages 2-3)

VARIATIONS

Add ½ cup dark raisins or currants to the topping. Bake in two buttered and parchment- or wax paper–lined 9 × 5 × 3-inch loaf pans (especially good if you intend to freeze one or both of the cakes). They will probably be done in around 45 minutes, but check at 35 to 40 minutes.

NOTE: Sometimes the top of the cake is not perfectly flat after baking because of the topping–don't worry, the cake is okay.

CHOCOLATE COFFEE CAKE

❧ ❧

WHAT GOES BETTER WITH COFFEE than chocolate? This fancy coffee cake comes from David Grice of Dallas.

1 Set a rack in the middle of the oven and preheat to 325 degrees.

2 Stir together the flour, baking soda, and salt in a bowl.

3 In the bowl of a heavy-duty mixer, beat the butter and sugar with the paddle on medium speed until soft and light, about 5 minutes.

4 Stop the mixer, scrape in the chocolate, and beat it in on medium speed. Beat in the eggs one at a time, beating until smooth after each addition. Stop the mixer and use a rubber spatula to scrape down the bowl and beater.

5 Decrease the mixer speed to low and beat in one-third of the flour, followed by half the sour cream. Stop and scrape again. Repeat with another one-third of the flour and the remaining sour cream, then stop and scrape. Beat in the remaining flour mixture.

6 Give a final mix to the batter with a large rubber spatula. Scrape the batter into the prepared pan and smooth the top.

CAKE BATTER

2 cups all-purpose flour (spoon flour into dry-measure cup and level off)

2 teaspoons baking soda

¼ teaspoon salt

½ pound (2 sticks) unsalted butter, softened

1½ cups sugar

8 ounces semisweet or bittersweet chocolate, melted and cooled

4 large eggs

One 8-ounce container sour cream

GANACHE GLAZE

1 cup heavy whipping cream

8 ounces semisweet chocolate, cut into ¼-inch pieces

2 tablespoons triple-strength brewed espresso (see page xiv)

One 12-cup tube or Bundt pan, buttered and floured

7 Bake for about 55–60 minutes, or until the cake is well risen and a toothpick inserted halfway between the side of the pan and the central tube emerges clean.

8   Cool the cake in the pan on a rack for 10 minutes, then invert onto the rack, remove the pan, and let cool completely.

9   When the cake is completely cooled, make the glaze. Bring the cream to a simmer in a saucepan. Remove from the heat, add the chocolate, and allow to stand for 3 minutes to melt the chocolate. Add the espresso to the glaze and whisk until smooth. Let cool to room temperature.

10   Place the cake, on the rack, on a jelly-roll pan to catch drips. Pour the glaze over the cake in a spiral, starting from the center and working outward. Leave the cake on the rack until glaze is set.

11   Use a wide metal spatula to slide the cake onto a platter. (Chill the pan the glaze dripped onto, then scrape the glaze off and save it—you can freeze it, then melt and cool it and use it to flavor a chocolate buttercream.)

STORAGE: Keep the cake under a dome at cool room temperature—refrigeration will dull the glaze.

MAKES ONE 10-INCH TUBE OR BUNDT CAKE, ABOUT 16 SERVINGS

EASY BRIOCHE LOAF

TO ME, BRIOCHE IS THE ULTIMATE coffee cake and this fast, easy version will have you making it often.

1 In a small saucepan, heat the milk over low heat until it is just warm, about 110 degrees. Pour into a small bowl and whisk in the yeast, then stir in 1 cup of the flour. Cover the bowl with plastic wrap and set aside at room temperature while you prepare the other ingredients. (The mixture may begin to rise slightly.)

2 In the work bowl of a food processor fitted with the metal blade, combine the butter, sugar, and salt. Pulse for 1-second intervals until the mixture is soft and smooth, scraping the inside of the bowl several times to ensure even mixing. Add the eggs one at a time, processing until smooth after each addition. If the mixture appears curdled, process for about 1 more minute, until it looks smooth. (It may remain somewhat curdled in appearance—that's okay.)

3 Add the remaining 1¼ cups flour and then the milk-yeast-flour mixture, scraping

½ cup milk

1 envelope (2½ teaspoons) active dry yeast

2¼ cups unbleached all-purpose flour (spoon flour into dry-measure cup and level off)

6 tablespoons (¾ stick) unsalted butter, cut into 6 or 8 pieces

3 tablespoons sugar

½ teaspoon salt

2 large eggs

One 9 × 5 × 3-inch loaf pan, buttered and bottom lined with buttered parchment or wax paper

it from the bowl with a rubber spatula. Pulse for 1-second intervals until a soft, smooth dough forms, then process continuously for 15 seconds.

4 Remove the bowl from the base, remove the blade, and scrape the dough onto a generously floured work surface. Fold it

18

over on itself several times to make it more elastic.

5   Press the dough into a rough rectangle about 9 × 5 inches. Fold about 1 inch of each short side in toward the center and press firmly to seal. Then fold the dough as you would a business letter: fold the top third of the rectangle over, then fold the bottom third of the dough up over it and pinch to seal the seam.

6   Place the dough seam side down in the prepared pan. Press down on the dough firmly with the palm of your hand so it flattens and fills the pan evenly. Cover with a piece of buttered plastic wrap or a towel and allow to rise until it is about 1 inch above the rim of the pan.

7   Position a rack in the middle of the oven and preheat to 350 degrees.

8   Use the corner of a razor blade or the tip of a sharp knife held at a 30-degree angle to the top of the loaf to cut a slash down the middle, beginning and ending about 1 inch from the ends. Bake for about 40 minutes, until the loaf is well risen and deep gold. Place the pan on a rack to cool for 5 minutes, then turn the loaf out onto the rack, lay it on its side, and let cool completely.

STORAGE: Wrap in plastic and keep at room temperature, or double-wrap and freeze for longer storage.

MAKES ONE 9 × 5-INCH LOAF CAKE (OR ENOUGH FOR ANY OF THE OTHER RECIPES IN THIS CHAPTER THAT USE THIS DOUGH)

BRIOCHE BEE STING CAKE

~⚬ ⚬~

CALLED "BEE'S STING" or "Bee's Nest," this popular European coffee cake is an excellent choice when you want something out of the ordinary. The topping is nutty, crunchy, and caramelized, a great textural contrast to the rich, smooth filling.

1 To shape the dough, fold it into a sphere, making sure the outside of the dough is smooth and seamless. Cover the dough with a towel and allow to rest for 5 minutes.

2 Press the dough evenly into the prepared pan and pierce it with a fork all over the top at 1-inch intervals. Cover the pan with a towel and allow the dough to rise until it is half again larger in bulk, about 30 minutes.

3 Uncover the dough and refrigerate it for 20 minutes.

4 Once you have refrigerated the dough, position a rack in the middle of the oven and preheat to 350 degrees.

5 To make the topping, butter a 2-quart, heatproof bowl and set aside. Combine the butter, honey, and sugar in a small saucepan, place over low heat, and bring to a boil, stirring constantly. Stir in the almonds and immediately remove the pan from the heat. Pour the topping into the prepared bowl and cool to room temperature.

Dough for Easy Brioche Loaf, page 18, prepared through Step 4.

ALMOND BRITTLE TOPPING

6 tablespoons (¾ stick) unsalted butter

¼ cup honey

¼ cup sugar

1 cup (about 4 ounces) sliced blanched almonds

PASTRY CREAM FILLING

1 cup milk

¼ cup sugar

2 tablespoons cornstarch

4 large egg yolks

2 teaspoons vanilla extract

1 tablespoon kirsch, optional

8 tablespoons (1 stick) unsalted butter, cut into 8 pieces and softened

One 2-inch-deep 10-inch round cake pan or 9- or 10-inch springform pan, buttered and bottom lined with buttered parchment or wax paper (If you use a springform, wrap the bottom in foil because the topping may leak)

6 Remove the chilled dough from the refrigerator and, using the back of a spoon or a small offset metal spatula, spread the almond topping evenly over the top.

7 Bake for about 30 minutes, until the topping is well caramelized and the dough is firm and baked through and a toothpick comes clean. Remove the pan to a rack to cool for 10 minutes, then loosen the topping from the sides of the pan by running the point of a small sharp knife between the topping and the sides of the pan. Unmold the cake, remove the paper, and set it right side up on a rack to cool.

8 While the cake is baking, prepare the pastry cream filling. Combine ¾ cup of the milk and the sugar in a nonreactive saucepan, set over low heat, and whisk once to mix in the sugar. Bring to a boil.

9 Meanwhile, combine the remaining ¼ cup milk and the cornstarch thoroughly in a small mixing bowl and whisk in the yolks.

10 In a steady stream, whisk the hot milk mixture into the yolks. Replace the pan over low heat and whisk constantly until the cream thickens and comes to a boil, about 2 minutes. Allow the cream to boil, whisking constantly, for about 30 seconds. Remove from heat and whisk in the vanilla and the kirsch, if you are using it. One piece at a time, beat the butter into the cream. Pour the cream into a bowl, scrape the sides of the bowl with a rubber spatula, and press plastic wrap against the surface of the cream to prevent a skin from forming. Refrigerate until cold, about 2 hours.

11 Remove the pastry cream from the refrigerator and whisk until smooth, about 10 seconds.

12 With a sharp serrated knife, slice the cake horizontally in half. Place the bottom layer on a platter. With a small offset metal spatula, spread the layer evenly with the pastry cream. Cut the top of the cake into 10 or 12 wedges and reassemble them in the cream, fitting them together. (Precutting the top makes it easier to serve the cake, and it also reduces pressure on the filling so it won't ooze out.)

SERVING: Serve the cake soon after filling it.

STORAGE: Keep in a cool place for several hours before serving; refrigerate leftovers.

MAKES ONE 10-INCH CAKE, ABOUT 10 TO 12 SERVINGS

VARIATION

TARTE TROPEZIENNE: Replace the almond topping with the crumb topping from the Cinnamon Coffee Cake, page 5. Before adding it, paint the dough with beaten egg to make the topping adhere. Bake, fill, and cut as above.

APRICOT BRIOCHE COFFEE CAKE

I SUPPOSE THAT YOU COULD ARGUE that this is a tart because it is a layer of dough covered with fruit. But really it's a cake—brioche is cakier than standard pastry dough and this has a lovely cakey texture.

1   Press the dough into the prepared pan. Cover and allow to rise for about 45 minutes, until doubled.

2   Set a rack in the middle of the oven and preheat to 375 degrees.

3   When the dough has doubled, arrange the apricot halves, cut side up, over it. Sprinkle with the sugar and almonds.

4   Bake for about 45 minutes, or until the fresh apricots are baked through and tender and a toothpick inserted into the center of the dough emerges clean.

5   Cool in the pan on a rack for about 20 minutes, then lift out of the pan using the paper or foil and place on the rack to finish cooling.

6   To remove the paper, slide the cake onto a cutting board. If necessary, run a thin-bladed knife between the cake and the paper to loosen it, and pull away the paper while supporting the side of the cake from which you are pulling.

Dough for Easy Brioche Loaf, page 18, prepared through Step 4.

TOPPING

18 apricots, halved and pitted, or 36 canned apricot halves, well-drained if canned

½ cup sugar

½ cup (about 2 ounces) sliced blanched almonds

One 9 × 13 × 2-inch baking pan, lined with buttered parchment or foil

SERVING: Cut the cake into squares and serve with whipped cream or crème fraîche.

STORAGE: This is best the day it is baked; cover leftovers with plastic wrap and keep at cool room temperature.

MAKES ONE 9 × 13-INCH CAKE, ABOUT 12 GENEROUS SERVINGS

PEGGY'S COFFEE CAKE

～⚬ ⚬～

THIS UNIQUE RECIPE comes from my friend Peggy Tagliarino. She says her mother, Blanche Levine, still makes it for her when she visits her in Florida.

You will need to plan ahead for this recipe: The dough has to chill for at least 8 hours, or overnight, before filling and rolling it. Then, the chilled dough takes quite a while to rise, about 2 hours or so.

1 To make the dough, warm the milk slightly in a small saucepan over low heat. Pour the milk into a bowl and whisk in the yeast. Set aside while you prepare the other ingredients.

2 In the bowl of a heavy-duty mixer, beat the butter and sugar with the paddle on medium speed until soft and light, about 3 minutes. Beat in the egg yolks one at a time, through the vanilla.

3 Decrease the mixer speed to low and beat in one-third of the flour. Beat in the yeast mixture, then stop and scrape down the bowl and beater with a rubber spatula. Beat in another third of the flour, then the sour cream. Stop and scrape again. Beat in the remaining flour and continue beating for 2 to 3 minutes longer, or until the dough is fairly smooth.

4 Scrape the dough into a large bowl, cover it tightly with plastic wrap, and refrigerate it for at least 8 hours, or overnight.

DOUGH

½ cup milk

2 envelopes (5 teaspoons) active dry yeast

½ pound (2 sticks) unsalted butter, softened

¼ cup sugar

3 large egg yolks

½ teaspoon vanilla extract

4 cups all-purpose flour (spoon flour into dry-measure cup and level off)

½ cup sour cream

FILLING

3 large egg whites

1 cup sugar

2 tablespoons ground cinnamon

½ cup dark raisins

½ cup (about 2 ounces) chopped walnuts

One 10-inch tube pan, buttered

5 Scrape the dough out onto a floured surface and flour it lightly. Press the dough into an even rectangle with your hands, then roll it out to a rectangle about 12 × 18 inches.

6 To make the filling, in the clean, dry mixer bowl, whip the egg whites with the whisk attachment on medium speed until very white and opaque. Increase the speed to medium-high, and add the sugar in a slow stream (if you go too fast, the egg whites will deflate). Continue to whip the egg whites until they hold a firm peak.

7 Spread the meringue over the dough within one inch of the ledge. Sprinkle evenly with the cinnamon, raisins, and nuts. Roll the dough up from a long side, like a jelly roll. Carefully ease the rolled cake into the prepared pan seam-side up (this will eventually be the bottom of the cake), making sure the two ends join.

8 Cover the pan with plastic wrap or a towel and leave to rise for about 2 hours, or until the pan is about three-quarters full.

9 Meanwhile, set a rack in the middle level of the oven and preheat to 350 degrees.

10 Bake for about 1 hour, or until the cake is firm, well risen, and deep gold (the toothpick test doesn't work here because of the soft filling).

11 Cool the cake in the pan on a rack for about 15 minutes, then invert onto the rack to cool completely.

STORAGE: Keep under a cake dome, or wrap well and freeze; defrost, reheat, to refresh in 350° oven for 10 minutes, and cool before serving.

MAKES ONE 10-INCH TUBE CAKE, ABOUT 16 SERVINGS

2 POUND CAKES AND BUTTER CAKES

POUND CAKE BECAME POPULAR in both the British Isles and in America in the eighteenth century, when it was called, simply, "a cake." The "pound cake" name originated from the proportions of the ingredients (one pound each of butter, sugar, eggs, and flour). Rich yet delicate, a good pound cake may be perfumed with vanilla, citrus, or spice. Preparation has only one trick, and it is an easy one to master: make sure the butter is soft before you begin to mix. Many pound cakes are baked as loaves, but I find that pound cakes have an excellent texture and superior lightness when they are baked in a tube pan. A tube pan also bakes the cake more quickly because of the heat conducted into the center of the pan through the tube, and this makes for a moister cake. Any of the recipes in this chapter can be baked in a tube pan—use the basic test for doneness and insert a toothpick in the cake midway between the side of the pan and the central tube: when the toothpick emerges clean, the cake is done.

HINTS FOR PERFECT POUND AND BUTTER CAKES

1 Always start with very soft butter.

2 Don't rush the mixing—many of these batters are leavened only by the air beaten into them during mixing.

3 Always have eggs and any liquids as close to room temperature as possible, and add them to the batter gradually. Adding liquid too quickly, or adding too much at a time can make a cake batter separate, resulting in a heavy, greasy texture instead of a light one.

4 For a loaf cake, line the pan or at least the bottom with parchment paper.

5 If the top of a cake baked for a long time seems to be coloring too deeply, cover the cake loosely with aluminum foil. Placing the cake pan on a heavy cookie sheet or jelly-roll pan will protect the bottom of the cake from coloring too deeply.

6 Cool pound cakes in the pan for a few minutes, then invert onto a rack or board. Invert again so that the cake cools completely right side up.

7　To store pound cakes, keep tightly wrapped in plastic and foil at room temperature for up to a couple of days, or freeze for longer.

8　Although finer than coffee cakes, pound cakes are served in the same way—with a favorite beverage. If the last few slices of a pound cake seem dry, lightly toast them and serve with butter or jam.

ALTERNATING LIQUID AND DRY INGREDIENTS

Many of the recipes that follow call for alternating liquid and dry ingredients when you add them to the batter. For pound cakes or any butter cake, always begin and end with the flour. Here's why: The buttery base of these batters does not absorb a lot of liquid easily. If the butter is forced to absorb too much liquid (usually eggs), the butter will reach its saturation point, and the result will be a separated batter with unabsorbed liquid in it. If this happens, the cake will be heavy. So it's far better to start by adding just some of the liquid to the butter and sugar mixture, then add the rest alternating it with the flour. The flour brings the batter together and prevents separation. For most recipes, these ingredients are incorporated in five additions: flour, liquid, flour, liquid, flour.

CLASSIC POUND CAKE

～୨ ୧～

THIS ALMOST DOESN'T NEED A RECIPE because it is based on the classic proportions of a pound of each of the four main ingredients: butter, sugar, eggs, and flour. I have played with the quantities a little bit so that the recipe doesn't make such a large cake. I like to flavor this type of pound cake with just a little vanilla–it keeps the flavor delicate and doesn't mask the lovely flavor of the butter. If you want more vividly flavored pound cake, try any of the milk-based ones or the high-ratio pound cakes later in the chapter.

1   Set a rack in the middle of the oven and preheat to 325 degrees.

2   Place the butter and sugar in the bowl of a heavy-duty mixer and beat on medium speed with the paddle attachment until very light, about 5 minutes. Beat in the vanilla. One at a time, beat in 3 of the eggs, beating until smooth after each addition.

3   Reduce the mixer speed to low and beat in one-third of the flour, then another egg, beating until smooth after each addition. Stop the mixer occasionally to scrape the bottom and sides of the bowl with a rubber spatula. Beat in another third of the flour, then, after the flour has been absorbed, beat in the final egg. Scrape again and beat in the last of the flour.

4   Use the rubber spatula to give a final mix to the batter, then scrape it into the prepared pan and smooth the top.

½ pound (2 sticks) unsalted butter, softened

1 cup sugar

2 teaspoons vanilla extract

5 large eggs, at room temperature

2 cups cake flour (spoon flour into dry-measure cup and level off), sifted after measuring

One 9 × 5 × 3-inch loaf pan, buttered and bottom lined with parchment or foil

5   Bake for about 1¼ to 1½ hours, or until the cake is well risen, cracked on top, and well-colored and a toothpick inserted into the center emerges dry.

6   Cool the cake in the pan for a few minutes, then unmold it onto a rack and turn right side up to finish cooling.

STORAGE: Wrap the cake in plastic wrap and then foil so it doesn't dry out, and serve within a few days. For longer storage, wrap and freeze; defrost, loosely covered, at room temperature.

MAKES ONE 9 × 5-INCH LOAF CAKE, ABOUT 12 SERVINGS

(see photograph, pages 26–27)

VARIATIONS

VANILLA BEAN POUND CAKE: Omit the vanilla extract. Split a vanilla bean lengthwise and scrape out the seeds with the point of a paring knife. Add the vanilla seeds to the butter and sugar mixture. The vanilla flavor will be stronger than a cake made with extract, and the visible vanilla seeds make a strong "vanilla statement."

MACE POUND CAKE: Add ¼ teaspoon ground mace to the flour.

HINT OF LEMON POUND CAKE: Add the finely grated zest of a large lemon to Classic Pound Cake or Vanilla Bean Pound Cake.

MRS. LINCOLN'S POUND CAKE

~ ୨ ୧ ~

THIS RECIPE WAS GIVEN TO ME by my friend and associate Andrea Tutunjian. It comes from a typewritten collection of recipes amassed by her maternal grandmother, Antoinette Bianco. The famous mid-century food writer Clementine Paddleford wrote about receiving a recipe for this cake from Mrs. Weibert Scott of Bridgeton, New Jersey, who said it came from President Lincoln's family via her cousins the Yorks and the Huckebys.

Regardless of its real or imaginary presidential pedigree, this is an excellent old-fashioned pound cake.

1 Set a rack in the middle of the oven and preheat to 325 degrees.

2 Stir together the flour and mace in a bowl, mixing well.

3 Place the butter and sugar in the bowl of a heavy-duty mixer fitted with the paddle attachment and beat on medium speed until the mixture is very light, about 5 minutes. Beat in the vanilla. One at a time, beat in 3 of the eggs, beating until smooth after each addition.

4 Reduce the mixer speed to low and beat in one-third of the flour, then another egg, beating until smooth after each addition and stopping the mixer occasionally to scrape the bottom and sides of the bowl

2 cups bleached all-purpose flour
  (spoon flour into dry-measure cup
  and level off)
½ teaspoon ground mace
½ pound (2 sticks) unsalted butter,
  softened
1⅔ cups sugar
1 teaspoon vanilla extract
5 large eggs, at room temperature

Two 8½ × 4½ × 2¾-inch loaf pans,
buttered and bottoms lined with
parchment

with a rubber spatula. Beat in another third of the flour, then, after the flour has been absorbed, the remaining egg. Scrape again and beat in the last of the flour.

5 Use the rubber spatula to give a final mix to the batter, then scrape it into the prepared pan and smooth the top.

6 Bake for about 1 hour, or until the cake is well risen, cracked on top, and well colored and a toothpick inserted into the center emerges dry.

7 Cool the cake in the pan for a few minutes, then unmold it onto a rack and turn right side up to finish cooling.

STORAGE: Wrap the cake in plastic wrap and then foil to ensure that it doesn't dry out, and serve within a few days. Or wrap and freeze for longer storage; defrost loosely covered at room temperature.

MAKES TWO 8½ × 4½-INCH LOAF CAKES, ABOUT 12 TO 16 SERVINGS

CREAM CHEESE POUND CAKE

─◦୨ ୧◦─

CREAM CHEESE GIVES this pound cake its richness and density. Many thanks to my dear friend Sheri Portwood of Dallas for the recipe.

1   Set a rack in the lower third of the oven and preheat to 325 degrees.

2   Stir the flour and baking powder together in a bowl, mixing well.

3   Place the butter, cream cheese, and sugar in the bowl of a heavy-duty mixer and beat on medium speed with the paddle attachment until very light, about 5 minutes. Beat in the vanilla. One at a time, beat in 4 of the eggs, beating until smooth after each addition.

4   Reduce the mixer speed to low and beat in one-third of the flour, then another egg, beating until smooth after each addition. Stop the mixer occasionally to scrape the bottom and sides of the bowl with a rubber spatula. Beat in another third of the flour, then, after the flour has been absorbed, the last egg. Scrape again and beat in the last of the flour.

5   Use the rubber spatula to give a final mix to the batter, then scrape it into the prepared pan and smooth the top.

CAKE BATTER

2 cups bleached all-purpose flour
    (spoon flour into dry-measure cup
    and level off)
1 teaspoon baking powder
½ pound (2 sticks) unsalted butter,
    softened
One 8-ounce package cream cheese
    (I use Philadelphia), softened
2 cups sugar
2 teaspoons vanilla extract
6 large eggs, at room temperature

RUM GLAZE

3 cups confectioners' sugar
2 tablespoons white rum
2 tablespoons water

One 12-cup tube or Bundt pan,
buttered and floured

6   Bake for about 65 to 75 minutes, or until cake is well risen, cracked on top, and well-colored and a toothpick inserted into the center emerges dry.

7 Cool the cake in the pan for a few minutes, then unmold it onto a rack and turn right side up to finish cooling.

8 To make the glaze, combine the sugar, rum, and water in a medium saucepan and stir until smooth, then heat over very low heat just until lukewarm. Drizzle over the cake with a spoon, or use a parchment paper cone, or pour the glaze over to cover the entire cake.

STORAGE: Wrap cake in plastic wrap and then foil to ensure it doesn't dry out, and serve within a few days. For longer storage, wrap and freeze; defrost, loosely covered, at room temperature. If you intend to freeze or otherwise keep the cake for more than a day, don't glaze it until the day you intend to serve it.

MAKES ONE 10-INCH TUBE OR BUNDT CAKE, ABOUT 16 SERVINGS

SOUR CREAM POUND CAKE

❧

THERE ARE DOZENS OF RECIPES for sour cream pound cakes and coffee cakes. Some use sour cream for almost all the fat in the batter, while richer ones, such as this cake, use butter as well. This recipe come from the collection of my late aunt, Kitty Rocco. She loved to bake and always had fresh-out-of-the-oven treats in her house.

1   Position a rack in the lower third of the oven and preheat to 350 degrees.

2   Stir together the flour, baking soda, and salt in a bowl, mixing well.

3   Place the butter and sugar in the bowl of a heavy-duty mixer and beat on medium speed with the paddle attachment until very light, about 5 minutes. Beat in the extracts. Beat in the eggs one at a time, beating until smooth after each addition.

4   Reduce the mixer speed to low and beat in one-third of the flour mixture, then half the sour cream, beating until smooth after each addition. Stop the mixer occasionally to scrape the bottom and sides of the bowl with a rubber spatula. Beat in another third of the flour, then, after the flour has been absorbed, the remaining sour cream. Scrape again and beat in the last of the flour.

5   Use the rubber spatula to give a final mix to the batter, then scrape it into the prepared pan and smooth the top.

3 cups bleached all-purpose flour
    (spoon flour into dry-measure
    cup and level off)
½ teaspoon baking soda
½ teaspoon salt
½ pound (2 sticks) unsalted butter,
    softened
2¾ cups sugar
½ teaspoon lemon extract
½ teaspoon orange extract
½ teaspoon vanilla extract
6 large eggs
One 8-ounce container sour cream

One 12-cup tube or Bundt pan,
buttered and floured

6   Bake for about 1¼ to 1½ hours, or until the cake is well risen, cracked on top, and well colored and a toothpick inserted into the cake halfway between the side of the pan and the central tube emerges dry.

7 Cool the cake in the pan for a few minutes, then unmold it onto a rack and turn right side up to finish cooling.

STORAGE: Wrap the cake in plastic wrap and then foil to ensure it doesn't dry out.

For longer storage, wrap and freeze. Defrost loosely covered at room temperature.

MAKES ONE 10-INCH TUBE CAKE, ABOUT 16 SERVINGS

NEWARK CAKE

~ ✑ ✑ ~

I WAS BORN IN NEWARK, NEW JERSEY, and I am completely crazy for anything from, by, or about Newark. So when I found this recipe in Marian Harland's *Breakfast, Luncheon, and Tea* (Scribner, Armstrong, and Company, 1875) I had to try it. Harland was one of the nineteenth-century's most prolific cookbook authors and novelists. Her husband, William Terhune, was a Dutch Reform clergyman and pastor of various churches in the New Jersey–Pennsylvania area, including one in Newark; hence the name of the cake.

1 Position a rack in the lower third of the oven and preheat to 325 degrees.

2 Place the flour, sugar, baking powder, and salt in the bowl of a heavy-duty mixer fitted with the paddle attachment. Add the butter and beat on the lowest speed for about 2 minutes, or until the ingredients are well combined.

3 Meanwhile, whisk together the remaining batter ingredients in a mixing bowl.

4 cups all-purpose flour (spoon flour into dry-measure cup and level off)

2 cups sugar

1 tablespoon baking powder

1 teaspoon salt

½ pound (2 sticks) unsalted butter, softened

6 large eggs

1 cup milk

1 teaspoon freshly grated nutmeg

1 teaspoon almond extract

Confectioners' sugar for finishing

One 12-cup tube or Bundt pan, buttered and floured

4 Increase the mixer speed to medium and add one-third of the liquid ingredients. Beat for 2 minutes, then stop the mixer and scrape down the bowl and beater. Add another third of the liquid, beat for 2 minutes, and scrape. Finally, add the remaining liquid and beat and scrape as before.

5 Use a large rubber spatula to give the batter a final vigorous stir, then scrape it into the prepared pan and smooth the top.

6 Bake for about 1¼ to 1½ hours, or until a toothpick inserted into the cake halfway between the side of the pan and the central tube emerges clean.

7 Cool the cake in the pan on a rack for 10 minutes, then invert onto the rack to finish cooling.

8 Just before serving, dust the cake generously with confectioners' sugar.

STORAGE: Wrap the cake in plastic wrap and then foil to ensure it doesn't dry out, and serve within a few days. For longer storage, wrap and freeze. Defrost loosely covered at room temperature.

MAKES ONE 10-INCH TUBE OR BUNDT CAKE, ABOUT 16 SERVINGS

MORRIS CAKE

~⁙~

THIS IS ANOTHER NINETEENTH-CENTURY CAKE from Marian Harland's *Breakfast, Luncheon, and Tea* (see page 37). I updated the recipe so as to mix the batter in the high-ratio manner (see page 44), but aside from that, it is the same wonderful cake it was about 125 years ago.

1 Position a rack in the lower third of the oven and preheat to 325 degrees.

2 Place the flour, sugar, baking soda, and nutmeg in the bowl of a heavy-duty mixer fitted with the paddle attachment. Add the butter and beat on the lowest speed for about 2 minutes, or until the ingredients are well combined.

3 Meanwhile, whisk all the remaining batter ingredients in a mixing bowl until well combined.

4 Increase the mixer speed to medium and add one-third of the liquid ingredients. Mix for 2 minutes, then stop the mixer and scrape down the bowl and beater. Add another third of the liquid, beat for 2 minutes, and scrape again. Finally, add the remaining liquid and beat and scrape as before.

5 Use a large rubber spatula to give the batter a final vigorous stir, then scrape the batter into the prepared pan and smooth the top.

4 cups all-purpose flour (spoon flour into dry-measure cup and level off)

2 cups sugar

1 teaspoon baking soda

½ teaspoon freshly grated nutmeg

½ pound (2 sticks) unsalted butter, softened

5 large eggs

One 8-ounce container sour cream

1 teaspoon vanilla extract

Confectioners' sugar for finishing

One 12-cup tube or Bundt pan, buttered and floured

6 Bake for about 1¼ to 1½ hours, or until a toothpick inserted into the cake halfway between the side of the pan and the central tube emerges clean.

7 Cool the cake in the pan on a rack for 10 minutes, then invert onto the rack to finish cooling.

8 Just before serving, dust the cake generously with confectioners' sugar.

STORAGE: Wrap the cake in plastic wrap and then foil to ensure it doesn't dry out, and serve within a few days. For longer storage, wrap and freeze; defrost loosely covered at room temperature.

MAKES ONE 10-INCH TUBE OR BUNDT CAKE, ABOUT 16 SERVINGS

CHOCOLATE POUND CAKE

THIS RECIPE COMES FROM A DEAR FRIEND, Zona Spray. When I was just starting to collect recipes for this book, I was staying with Zona and her husband, Grant Starks, in Hudson, Ohio. Zona let me look through a notebook of many recipes given to her by a very talented home cook named Katy Buell.

1 Set a rack in the lower third of the oven and preheat to 325 degrees.

2 Stir together the flour, salt, and soda in a bowl, mixing well.

3 Place the butter and sugar in the bowl of a heavy-duty mixer fitted with the paddle attachment and beat on medium speed until very light, about 5 minutes. Beat in the vanilla. Scrape the chocolate into the mixer bowl and beat until incorporated. Scrape down the bowl and beaters.

4 Add the eggs one at a time, beating well after each addition.

5 Reduce the mixer speed to low and beat in one-third of the flour, then half the

3 cups bleached all-purpose flour (spoon flour into dry-measure cup and level off)

1 teaspoon salt

½ teaspoon baking soda

½ pound (2 sticks) unsalted butter, softened

2 cups sugar

2 teaspoons vanilla extract

4 ounces semisweet chocolate, melted and cooled

4 large eggs, at room temperature

1 cup buttermilk

Confectioners' sugar for finishing

One 12-cup tube or Bundt pan, buttered and floured

buttermilk, beating until smooth after each addition. Stop the mixer occasionally to scrape down the bottom and sides of the bowl. Beat in another third of the flour, then, after the flour has been absorbed, the remaining buttermilk. Scrape again and beat in the last of the flour.

6   Use a large rubber spatula to give a final mix to the batter, then scrape it into the prepared pan and smooth the top.

7   Bake for 1½ to 1¾ hours, or until the cake is well risen and a toothpick inserted into the center emerges dry.

8   Cool the cake in the pan for a few minutes, then unmold it onto a rack to finish cooling.

9   Just before serving, dust the cake with confectioners' sugar.

STORAGE: Wrap the cake in plastic and then foil to ensure it doesn't dry out, and serve within a few days. For longer storage, wrap and freeze; defrost loosely covered at room temperature.

MAKES ONE 10-INCH TUBE OR BUNDT CAKE, ABOUT 16 SERVINGS

VARIATION

Drizzle the cooled cake with Chocolate Glaze, page 287.

GREEN TEA POUND CAKE

〜♀ ♀〜

ON A RECENT TRIP TO PARIS, some friends and I stopped at the beautiful Mariage Frères tea shop in the Marais district to buy some tea. The store also has a tearoom, so we decided to try their special tea-flavored delicacies. The winner was this green tea pound cake. It is flavored with matcha, the powdered green tea used for the Japanese tea ceremony, which gives the cake a unique bittersweet perfume. Many thanks to a dear friend, author and baker Dorie Greenspan, for sharing the recipe with me.

1 Set a rack in the middle of the oven and preheat to 325 degrees.

2 Stir together the flour, tea, and baking powder in a bowl, mixing well.

3 Beat the butter and confectioners' sugar in the bowl of a heavy-duty mixer fitted with the paddle attachment for about 3 minutes, or until light. Beat in the egg yolks one at a time, beating well after each addition and occasionally scraping down the bowl and beater with a rubber spatula. Fold in the flour mixture with the rubber spatula.

4 In a clean, dry mixer bowl, whip the egg whites with the salt on medium speed until they are white and opaque and just beginning to hold their shape. Increase the speed slightly and continue whipping the whites until they hold a soft peak.

2 cups bleached all-purpose flour
   (spoon flour into dry-measure cup
   and level off)
2 tablespoons matcha green tea (see
   Sources)
2 teaspoons baking powder
16 tablespoons (2 sticks) unsalted
   butter, softened
2 cups confectioners' sugar
5 large eggs, separated
Pinch of salt

Two 9 × 5 × 3-inch loaf pans, buttered and lined with buttered parchment or wax paper

5 Quickly scrape the egg whites onto the batter and use a large rubber spatula to fold the whites into the batter, folding just until no streaks of white remain. Scrape the batter into the prepared pan and smooth the top.

6 Bake for about 60 to 70 minutes, or until the cake is well risen and a toothpick inserted in the center emerges dry.

7 Cool the cake in the pan on a rack for 10 minutes, then unmold onto the rack, turn right side up, and cool completely.

STORAGE: Within several days, wrap the cake in plastic wrap and then foil to ensure it doesn't dry out, and serve within a few days. For longer storage, wrap and freeze; defrost loosely covered at room temperature.

MAKES TWO 9 × 5 × 3-INCH LOAF CAKES, ABOUT 16 SERVINGS

A high-ratio cake is one in which the weight of the sugar equals or exceeds the weight of the flour. (This applies to many pound and butter cakes, but not all.) The high proportion of sugar can make the batter separate, resulting in a coarse texture in the baked cake. The "high ratio" mixing method, developed in the 1940s by Procter and Gamble, prevents the batter from separating and yields a particularly fine textured cake.

Basically, you first mix all the dry ingredients with the softened butter. Then the liquids, including the eggs, are combined and added in three parts. The resulting baked cake has a great texture and moist crumb. To convert a recipe to the high-ratio method of mixing, first check to see if the sugar equals or exceeds the flour: calculate 8 ounces for a cup of sugar and 4 ounces for a cup of all-purpose flour. If and only if the recipe passes this test, you can combine all the dry ingredients in the mixer bowl, add the softened butter, and beat for 2 minutes on low speed. Then add the liquids, mixed together, one-third at a time, beating for 2 minutes on medium speed between each addition.

HANNAH GLASSE'S POUND CAKE
An Eighteenth-Century Recipe Modernized

〜⟨⟩〜

ONE OF THE MOST WIDELY INFLUENTIAL cookbooks in the English language, Hannah Glasse's *The Art of Cookery Made Plain and Simple* was first published in London in 1747. It was widely reprinted; I have two editions, one published in London in 1778 and another published in Virginia in 1812. I checked the recipe for pound cake in those two editions against a facsimile of the 1747 edition and found the recipe to be identical in all of them. Here are the original instructions:

> Take a pound of butter, beat it in an earthen pan, with your hand one way, till it is like a fine thick cream; then have ready twelve eggs, but half the whites, beat them well, and beat them up with the butter, a pound of flour beat in it, and a pound of sugar, and a few carraways; beat it all together for an hour with your hand or a great wooden spoon. Butter a pan, and put it in and bake it an hour in a quick oven. For a change, you may put in a pound of currants clean wash'd and pick'd.

We can cook from this today if we halve the ingredients and mix the ingredients as for a high-ratio formula. But beat the batter for considerably less than an hour!

1 Set a rack in the lower third of the oven and preheat to 325 degrees.

2 Place the flour and sugar in the bowl of a heavy-duty mixer fitted with the paddle attachment, add the butter, and beat on the lowest speed for about 2 minutes, or until the ingredients are well combined.

3 Meanwhile, whisk the eggs and yolks together until well combined.

2 cups bleached all-purpose flour (spoon flour into dry-measure cup and level off)

1 cup sugar

½ pound (2 sticks) unsalted butter, softened

3 large eggs, at room temperature

3 large egg yolks

1 teaspoon caraway seeds, optional

1½ cups Zante currants, tossed with 1 tablespoon flour

One 12-cup tube or Bundt pan, buttered and floured

4 Increase the mixer speed to medium and add one-third of the egg mixture. Beat for 2 minutes, then stop the mixer and scrape down the bowl and beater. Add another third of the eggs, for 2 minutes, beat and scrape again. Finally, add the remaining egg and beat and scrape as before.

5 Use a large rubber spatula to give the batter a final vigorous stir. Fold in the optional caraway seeds and floured currants, then scrape the batter into the prepared pan and smooth the top.

6 Bake for about 55 to 65 minutes, or until a toothpick inserted into the cake halfway between the side of the pan and the central tube emerges clean.

7 Cool the cake in the pan on a rack for 10 minutes, then invert onto the rack to finish cooling.

STORAGE: Wrap the cake in plastic wrap and then foil to ensure it doesn't dry out, and serve within a few days. For longer storage, wrap and freeze; defrost loosely covered at room temperature.

MAKES ONE 10-INCH TUBE OR BUNDT CAKE (NOT EXTREMELY TALL), ABOUT 12 SERVINGS

VARIATIONS

Omit the caraway seeds and/or the currants for a plainer cake that's very good sliced and toasted.

ANACHRONISTIC POUND CAKE: For a slightly higher cake, add a teaspoon of baking powder to the flour and sugar (baking powder wasn't available until more than a hundred years after the original recipe was first published).

HIGH-RATIO POUND CAKE

~⚬ ⚬~

THIS RECIPE WAS LITERALLY A FIND. When I sat down to write this chapter, it was in the folder of pound cake recipes I had been collecting. It was handwritten on a recipe card stapled to a typed version of the recipe.

1 Set a rack in the lower third of the oven and preheat to 350 degrees.

2 Place the flour, sugar, baking powder, and salt in the bowl of a heavy-duty mixer fitted with the paddle attachment, add the butter, and beat on the lowest speed for about 2 minutes, or until the ingredients are well combined.

3 Meanwhile, whisk all the remaining ingredients together in a mixing bowl until well combined.

4 Increase the mixer speed to medium, add one-third of the liquid ingredients, and mix for 2 minutes. Stop the mixer and scrape down the bowl and beater. Add another third of the liquid, beat for 2 minutes, and scrape again. Finally, add the remaining liquid and beat and scrape as before.

5 Use a large rubber spatula to give the batter a final vigorous stir, then scrape it into the prepared pan and smooth the top.

2½ cups bleached all-purpose flour (spoon flour into dry-measure cup and level off)

1¾ cups sugar

2 teaspoons baking powder

1 teaspoon salt

½ pound (2 sticks) unsalted butter, softened

¾ cup milk

3 large eggs, at room temperature

1 large egg yolk

2 teaspoons vanilla extract

One 12-cup tube or Bundt pan, buttered and floured

6 Bake for about 1 hour and 15 minutes, or until a toothpick inserted into the cake halfway between the side of the pan and the central tube emerges clean.

7 Cool the cake in the pan on a rack for 10 minutes, then invert onto the rack to finish cooling.

47

STORAGE: Wrap the cake in plastic wrap and then foil to ensure it doesn't dry out, and serve within a few days. For longer storage, wrap and freeze; defrost loosely covered at room temperature.

MAKES ONE 10-INCH TUBE OR BUNDT CAKE, ABOUT 16 SERVINGS

VARIATIONS

LEMON POUND CAKE: Substitute lemon extract for the vanilla.

PECAN, WALNUT, OR HAZELNUT POUND CAKE: Fold 1 cup coarsely chopped pecans, walnuts, or hazelnuts, tossed with 1 tablespoon flour, into the batter when you are giving it the last mix with the spatula.

HIGH-RATIO LEMON-BUTTERMILK POUND CAKE

~⟲ ⟳~

AFTER YOU BAKE THIS CAKE, you soak it with a lemon and vanilla syrup that adds just the right note of tartness and moisture. See the variations at the end of the recipe for a sprightly orange or lemon-lime version. Many thanks to my friend Gary Peese of Austin, Texas, for this recipe.

1 Position a rack in the lower third of the oven and preheat to 325 degrees.

2 Place the flour, sugar, baking powder, and salt in the bowl of a heavy-duty mixer fitted with the paddle attachment, add the butter, and beat on the lowest speed for about 2 minutes, or until the ingredients are well combined.

3 Meanwhile, whisk all the remaining batter ingredients together in a mixing bowl until well combined.

4 Increase the mixer speed to medium and add one-third of the liquid, and mix for 2 minutes. Stop the mixer and scrape down the bowl and beater. Add another third of the liquid, beat for 2 minutes, and scrape again. Finally, add the remaining liquid and beat and scrape as before.

5 Use a large rubber spatula to give the batter a final vigorous stir, then scrape it into the prepared pan and smooth the top.

CAKE BATTER

2½ cups bleached all-purpose flour (spoon flour into dry-measure cup and level off)

2 cups sugar

2 teaspoons baking powder

½ teaspoon salt

½ pound (2 sticks) unsalted butter, softened

4 large eggs, at room temperature

3 large egg yolks

½ cup buttermilk

1 tablespoon grated lemon zest

1 tablespoon strained fresh lemon juice

1 teaspoon vanilla extract

LEMON SYRUP

½ cup water

½ cup sugar

⅓ cup fresh lemon juice, strained

2 teaspoons vanilla extract

One 12-cup Bundt pan, buttered and floured

6   Bake for about 1 hour, or until a toothpick inserted into the cake halfway between the side of the pan and the central tube emerges clean.

7   Cool the cake in the pan on a rack for 10 minutes, then invert onto the rack to finish cooling.

8   To make the syrup, bring the water and sugar to a boil in a small saucepan. Remove from the heat and stir in the lemon juice and vanilla. Brush the hot syrup evenly all over the cake. Gradually brush until it is all absorbed.

STORAGE: Wrap the cake in plastic wrap and then foil to ensure it doesn't dry out, and serve within a few days. For longer storage, wrap and freeze; defrost loosely covered at room temperature.

MAKES ONE 10-INCH BUNDT CAKE, ABOUT 16 SERVINGS

VARIATIONS

LEMON SOUR CREAM OR YOGURT POUND CAKE: Substitute sour cream or plain yogurt for the buttermilk.

ORANGE BUTTERMILK POUND CAKE: Substitute orange zest and juice for the lemon and orange extract for the vanilla extract in the batter. Make the syrup with $\frac{1}{3}$ cup strained fresh orange juice and 2 tablespoons lemon juice. This cake can also be made with sour cream or yogurt as above.

LEMON-LIME BUTTERMILK POUND CAKE: Substitute lime juice for the lemon juice in the batter. Use half lemon and half lime juice for the syrup. This cake can be made with sour cream or yogurt as above.

HIGH-RATIO FRESH GINGER POUND CAKE WITH LEMON GLAZE

⚬ᵔ⚬

IF YOU LOVE THE PUNGENT FLAVOR of fresh ginger, this is the cake to go with your cup of tea. The bit of lemon zest in the batter complements the ginger flavor. I like the cake very gingery, but if you just want a hint of ginger, you can use less. This moist, spicy cake is perfect for a brunch or picnic.

1 Set a rack in the lower third of the oven and preheat to 325 degrees.

2 Place the flour, sugar, baking powder, and salt in the bowl of a heavy-duty mixer fitted with the paddle attachment and add the butter. Beat on the lowest speed for about 2 minutes, or until the ingredients are well combined.

3 Meanwhile, combine all the remaining batter ingredients in a mixing bowl.

4 Increase the mixer speed to medium and add one-third of the liquid ingredients. Mix for 2 minutes, then stop the mixer and scrape down the bowl and beater. Add another third of the liquid, beat for 2 minutes, and scrape again. Finally, add the remaining liquid and beat and scrape as before.

5 Use a large rubber spatula to give the batter a final vigorous stir, then scrape it into the prepared pan and smooth the top.

CAKE BATTER

2½ cups bleached all-purpose flour (spoon flour into dry-measure cup and level off)

2 cups sugar

2 teaspoons baking powder

½ teaspoon salt

½ pound (2 sticks) unsalted butter, softened

4 large eggs

3 large egg yolks

½ cup milk

⅓ cup grated fresh ginger (see Note)

1 tablespoon finely grated lemon zest

1 teaspoon vanilla extract

LEMON GLAZE

3 cups confectioners' sugar

2 tablespoons strained fresh lemon juice

2 tablespoons white rum or water

One 12-cup Bundt or tube pan, buttered and floured

6 Bake for about 1 hour, or until a toothpick inserted into the cake halfway between the side of the pan and the central tube emerges clean.

7 Cool the cake in the pan on a rack for 10 minutes, then invert onto the rack to finish cooling.

8 To make the glaze, stir the sugar, lemon juice, and rum together in a medium saucepan until smooth, adding a teaspoon or two of water, if necessary, to make a smooth glaze. Then heat over very low heat just until lukewarm. Drizzle over the cake with a spoon or use a parchment paper cone.

STORAGE: Wrap the cake in plastic wrap and then foil to ensure it doesn't dry out, and serve within a few days. For longer storage, wrap and freeze; defrost loosely covered at room temperature. If you intend to freeze or otherwise keep the cake for more than a day before serving, don't glaze it until the day you will serve it.

MAKES ONE 10-INCH BUNDT CAKE, ABOUT 16 SERVINGS

NOTE: To get ⅓ cup of grated ginger, you'll need to start with about 3 ounces fresh ginger. Peel the ginger and grate it on a grater with ¼-inch oval holes—if you try to grate it on a finer grater, you'll only get juice. You can also chop the ginger very fine with an extremely sharp stainless steel knife, or coarsely chop it and then whir it in the food processor to mince it.

TORTA DI POLENTA

~9 9 ~

THOUGH THERE ARE MANY fine Italian recipes for similar cornmeal cakes, I developed this one from a high-ratio pound cake recipe, and I like it very much. Cornmeal adds a slight crunch and a subtle sweetness.

1 Position a rack in the lower third of the oven and preheat to 325 degrees.

2 Place the flour, cornmeal, sugar, baking powder, and salt in the bowl of a heavy-duty mixer fitted with the paddle attachment and add the butter. Beat on the lowest speed for about 2 minutes, or until the ingredients are well combined.

3 Meanwhile, combine the remaining batter ingredients except the optional raisins or currants in a mixing bowl.

4 Increase the mixer speed to medium and add one-third of the liquid ingredients. Mix for 2 minutes, then stop the mixer and scrape down the bowl and beater. Add another third of the liquid, beat for 2 minutes, and scrape again. Finally, add the remaining liquid and beat and scrape as before.

5 Use a large rubber spatula to give the batter a final vigorous stir. Fold in the optional floured raisins or currants, if using, then scrape the batter into the prepared pan and smooth the top.

2½ cups all-purpose flour (spoon flour into dry-measure cup and level off)

1 cup stone-ground yellow cornmeal

2 cups sugar

2 teaspoons baking powder

½ teaspoon salt

½ pound (2 sticks) unsalted butter, softened

7 large eggs

1 tablespoon grated lemon zest

1 tablespoon strained fresh lemon juice

2 teaspoons vanilla extract

1 cup golden raisins or Zante currants, tossed with 1 tablespoon flour, optional

Confectioners' sugar for finishing

One 12-cup tube or Bundt pan, buttered and floured

6   Bake for about 65 to 75 minutes, or until a toothpick inserted into the cake halfway between the side of the pan and the central tube emerges clean.

7   Cool the cake in the pan on a rack for 10 minutes, then invert onto the rack to finish cooling.

8   Just before serving, dust the cake generously with confectioners' sugar.

STORAGE: Wrap the cake in plastic wrap and then foil to ensure it doesn't dry out, and serve within a few days. For longer storage, wrap and freeze; defrost loosely covered at room temperature.

MAKES ONE 10-INCH TUBE OR BUNDT CAKE, ABOUT 16 SERVINGS

BOURBON PECAN POUND CAKE

⌒ꝯ ꜿ⌒

BOURBON AND PECANS, both products of the South, are a natural combination. Because of the bourbon, the cake keeps well and stays moist.

1 Position a rack in the lower third of the oven and preheat to 325 degrees.

2 Place the flour, sugar, baking powder, and salt in the bowl of a heavy-duty mixer fitted with the paddle attachment and add the butter. Beat on the lowest speed for about 2 minutes, or until the ingredients are well combined.

3 Meanwhile, combine the remaining batter ingredients except the pecans in a mixing bowl, mixing well.

4 Increase the mixer speed to medium and add one-third of the liquid ingredients. Mix for 2 minutes, then stop the mixer and scrape down the bowl and beater. Add another third of the liquid, beat for 2 minutes, and scrape again. Finally, add the remaining liquid and beat and scrape as before.

5 Use a large rubber spatula to give the batter a final vigorous stir. Fold in the floured pecans, then scrape the batter into the prepared pan and smooth the top.

2½ cups bleached all-purpose flour (spoon flour into dry-measure cup and level off) plus 1 tablespoon

1 cup packed light brown sugar

1 cup granulated sugar

2 teaspoons baking powder

½ teaspoon salt

½ pound (2 sticks) unsalted butter, softened

4 large eggs

3 large egg yolks

½ cup best Kentucky bourbon

2 teaspoons vanilla extract

1½ cups finely chopped (not ground) pecans, tossed with 1 tablespoon flour

Confectioners' sugar for finishing

One 12-cup tube or Bundt pan, buttered and floured

6 Bake for about 65 to 75 minutes, or until a toothpick inserted into the cake halfway between the side of the pan and the central tube emerges clean.

7   Cool the cake in the pan on a rack for 10 minutes, then invert onto the rack to finish cooling.

8   Just before serving, dust the cake generously with confectioners' sugar.

STORAGE: Wrap the cake in plastic wrap and then foil to ensure it doesn't dry out, and serve within a few days. For longer storage, wrap and freeze; defrost loosely covered at room temperature.

MAKES ONE 10-INCH TUBE OR BUNDT CAKE, ABOUT 16 SERVINGS

VARIATIONS

ALMOND RUM POUND CAKE: Substitute chopped blanched whole almonds for the pecans and white rum for the bourbon. Add 1 teaspoon almond extract along with the vanilla extract.

HAZELNUT DARK RUM POUND CAKE: Substitute coarsely ground unblanched hazelnuts for the pecans and dark rum for the bourbon.

3 CAKES MADE WITH FRESH OR DRIED FRUIT

SIMPLE CAKES TAKE BEAUTIFULLY TO FRESH FRUIT. I could possibly live on blueberry crumb cake, pausing only occasionally to vary it with a plum or apricot version. Apple cakes almost received their own chapter—I had literally dozens of them in my folder for this chapter. I combined the best recipes into new versions.

Also included in this chapter are those poor fruitcakes that everyone loves to hate. I'm so tired of the lame attempts at insipid humor at the expense of the fruitcake. People who don't like fruitcake dislike it for one of the following reasons:

1 The fruitcake was probably large and baked at too high a temperature, making it very dark on the outside, with a bitter flavor.

2 The candied fruit used was of dubious quality. Good candied fruit is expensive, there's no way around it. To make it properly, each piece of citrus rind must be treated many times. First it has to be blanched: the rinds repeatedly brought to a boil and drained to remove bitterness. Then the fruit or rind is cooked in small batches in sugar syrup repeatedly over the course of several weeks. The candied fruit in the little plastic containers in the supermarket is not made this way. But you can order excellent candied fruit—see Sources at the end of the book.

A last word about candied fruit—if you do buy the mixed kind sold in the supermarket, read the label: if the first ingredient is grapefruit rind, don't buy it—that's a guarantee it will be very bitter. If you buy candied fruit sold in bulk, taste a piece before purchasing. You'll be able to tell if it's the right kind very easily.

This chapter also contains recipes for cakes made with vegetables. Don't get scared—there are none that contain beets, sauerkraut, or rutabagas, though I like all of those things perfectly well as vegetables. But I've included a few really good carrot, pumpkin, and zucchini recipes. Their purpose in a cake batter is to contribute moisture, and in the case of carrots, there is an extra bonus of sweetness.

FRESH APPLE CAKE FROM MRS. APPENZELLER (5D)

~ ❧ ~

ANA RAMBALDI, A GREAT BAKER of Ukranian-Argentine descent, is also the superintendent of a Greenwich Village apartment building. The recipe came from a tenant with whom Ana traded recipes.

1 Position a rack in the middle of the oven and preheat to 350 degrees.

2 Stir together the flour, baking soda, and spices in a bowl, mixing well.

3 In a large bowl, whisk the eggs just to break them up. Whisk in the sugar in a stream. Continue to whisk for a minute or so to lighten the mixture, then whisk in the oil in a slow stream and vanilla.

4 Use a rubber spatula to fold in the flour mixture. Fold in the apples, raisins, and nuts. Scrape the batter into the prepared pan and smooth the top.

5 Bake for about an hour, or until the cake is well risen and well colored and a toothpick inserted into the center emerges clean.

6 Cool the cake in the pan on a rack for 5 minutes, then turn it out onto another rack, turn it right side up again onto a rack to cool completely.

SERVING: Serve this cake plain or with vanilla or cinnamon ice cream.

2 cups all-purpose flour (spoon flour into dry-measure cup and level off)

1 teaspoon baking soda

1 teaspoon freshly grated nutmeg

½ teaspoon ground cinnamon

3 large eggs

1 cup sugar

1 cup vegetable oil, such as corn or canola

2 teaspoons vanilla extract

3 cups peeled, cored, and chopped Golden Delicious apples (2 to 3 large apples)

½ cup dark raisins, coarsely chopped

½ cup (about 2 ounces) walnuts, coarsely chopped

One 12-cup tube pan, buttered and floured

STORAGE: Wrap the cooled cake in plastic and keep at room temperature for up to several days, or double-wrap and freeze for longer storage.

MAKES ONE 10-INCH CAKE, ABOUT 12 SERVINGS

APPLE RUM CAKE

~⚬ ⚬~

THIS IS A DELICIOUS AUSTRALIAN RECIPE given to me by my friend Maureen McKeon, one of Australia's top food stylists.

1 Set a rack in the middle of the oven and preheat to 350 degrees.

2 Combine all the filling ingredients in a glass or stainless steel bowl and let stand while you prepare the batter.

3 Stir together the flour, baking powder, and salt in a bowl, mixing well.

4 In the bowl of a heavy-duty mixer fitted with the paddle attachment, beat the butter and sugar on medium speed for about 5 minutes, or until light and fluffy. Beat in the eggs one at a time, beating until smooth after each addition. Beat in the vanilla. With a rubber spatula, fold in half the flour mixture.

5 Drain the apples in a colander set over a bowl. Add the milk to any rum that drains into the bowl and stir the liquids into the batter, then fold in the remaining flour mixture.

6 Spread half the cake batter evenly in the prepared pan. Scatter with the sliced apple mixture. Scrape the

APPLE FILLING

2 tart apples, such as Granny Smith, peeled, halved, cored, and sliced, about ⅛ inch thick
½ cup golden raisins
2 tablespoons dark rum

CAKE BATTER

2¼ cups bleached all-purpose flour (spoon flour into dry-measure cups and level off)
2 teaspoons baking powder
½ teaspoon salt
12 tablespoons (1½ sticks) unsalted butter, softened
¾ cup sugar
3 large eggs
½ teaspoon vanilla extract
2 tablespoons milk

RUM GLAZE

1 cup confectioners' sugar
2 tablespoons dark rum

One 9-inch springform pan, buttered and bottom lined with buttered parchment or wax paper

remaining batter onto the filling and smooth it with an offset metal spatula.

7 Slide a foil-lined cookie sheet onto the rack below the middle one to catch any drips. Bake for about 55 to 65 minutes, or until the cake is risen, firm, and deep golden and the apples are cooked through and tender.

8 Cool the cake in the pan for 15 minutes, then loosen the cake by running a sharp paring knife around the inside of the pan, scraping the knife against the pan, not the cake. Remove the sides and slide the cake off the base to a rack to finish cooling.

9 When the cake has cooled completely, invert the cake onto a plate, remove the paper, and invert the cake onto the rack again so it is right side up.

10 To make the glaze, stir together the confectioners' sugar and rum in a small saucepan, mixing well. Place over medium heat and stir until warm and fluid.

11 Drizzle half the glaze over the top of the cake in a series of parallel lines. Rewarm the glaze if necessary and drizzle another series of lines on a diagonal to the first ones. Wait until the glaze dries, then slide the cake onto a platter.

SERVING: Serve with ice cream or whipped cream.

STORAGE: This cake is best on the day it is baked. Keep it under a cake dome at room temperature.

MAKES ONE 9-INCH CAKE, ABOUT 8 SERVINGS

WALNUT APPLESAUCE CAKE WITH HONEY–CREAM CHEESE FROSTING

~⊙ ⊙~

THIS CAKE IS BASED ON A RECIPE I FOUND inside a cookbook I bought at a used book store. It was on a fine fold-over note, written in a cultivated hand and dated July 21, 1952; the note is addressed to Louise and is signed Mary. This is a perfect cake for the early fall, when the first McIntosh apples come into season.

CAKE BATTER

3 cups all-purpose flour (spoon flour into dry-measure cup and level off)

1½ teaspoons baking soda

½ teaspoon salt

1 teaspoon ground cinnamon

½ teaspoon ground cloves

½ teaspoon freshly grated nutmeg

1½ cups dark raisins or currants

1½ cups (about 6 ounces) walnut pieces

½ pound (2 sticks) unsalted butter, softened

1 cup granulated sugar

1 cup firmly packed dark brown sugar

4 large eggs

1½ cups unsweetened applesauce (see Note)

CREAM CHEESE FROSTING

8 tablespoons (1 stick) unsalted butter, softened

One 8-ounce package cream cheese, softened

⅓ cup mild honey

1 teaspoon vanilla extract

½ cup (about 2 ounces) chopped toasted walnuts

One 9 × 13 × 2-inch baking pan, buttered and lined with buttered parchment or foil

1   Position a rack in the middle of the oven and preheat to 350 degrees.

2   Stir together the flour, soda, salt, and spices in a bowl, mixing well. In a small bowl, combine the raisins and walnuts. Add 2 tablespoons of the flour mixture, tossing to coat; set aside.

3   In the bowl of a heavy-duty mixer fitted with the paddle attachment, beat together the butter and sugars on medium speed until soft and light. Beat in the eggs one at a time, beating until smooth after each addition.

4   Beat in one-third of the flour mixture, then beat in half the applesauce. Scrape down the bowl and beater. Beat in another third of the flour mixture, then the remaining applesauce, and scrape again. Beat in the remaining flour mixture. Fold in the raisins and walnuts.

5   Scrape the batter into the prepared pan and smooth the top.

6   Bake for about 45 minutes, or until a toothpick inserted in the center of the cake emerges clean. Cool in the pan on a rack.

7   To make the frosting, combine the butter, cream cheese, honey, and vanilla in the bowl of a heavy-duty mixer fitted with the paddle and beat on medium speed until soft and light, about 3 minutes.

8   Invert the cake onto a cardboard rectangle or a platter and remove the paper. Run knife around the sides to release the cake. Spread the frosting on the top of the cake, then sprinkle with the chopped walnuts.

STORAGE: Store under a cake dome. Unfrosted, this cake keeps well for a few days at room temperature if well wrapped in plastic, or double-wrap and freeze for longer storage; defrost before frosting.

MAKES ONE 9 × 13-INCH CAKE, ABOUT 24 SERVINGS

NOTE: To make applesauce, peel, core, and slice 4 medium McIntosh apples. Combine them with ¼ cup water in a nonreactive pan and cook until the apples are very soft and falling apart. Puree in a food processor or blender if desired (for a very smooth puree), then measure out 1½ cups for the recipe.

AUNTIE RAE'S APPLE CAKE

~ ⊙ ⊙ ~

THE AUNTIE IN QUESTION IS NOT MINE, but that of a friend, cookbook dealer Bonnie Slotnick. This recipe has been in Bonnie's family for a long time. I like it not only because it is delicious, but also because it is one of those unusual recipes in which cake and pastry meet. The same mixture is used for both the cake base under the apple filling and for the crumb topping that covers it—my idea of efficient.

1 Set a rack in the middle level of the oven and preheat to 350 degrees.

2 To make the cake mixture, combine the flour, baking powder, and salt in a bowl, mixing well.

3 In a large bowl, whisk the eggs to break them up, then whisk in the sugar, oil, and vanilla. Using a rubber spatula, stir in the flour mixture.

4 Place half the mixture in the prepared pan. With the floured palm of one hand, press it into an even layer. Cover the remaining mixture and chill until firm.

5 Meanwhile, combine the sugar and cinnamon, mixing well. Sprinkle the apples with half the cinnamon sugar and spread them evenly over the cake layer in the pan.

6 When the remaining cake mixture is cold, grate it through the coarse holes of a box grater over the apples, moving the grater all over the filling; avoid pressing

CAKE MIXTURE

4 cups all-purpose flour (spoon flour into dry-measure cup and level off)

1½ teaspoons baking powder

½ teaspoon salt

2 large eggs

¾ cup sugar

½ cup vegetable oil, such as corn or canola

1½ teaspoons vanilla extract

CINNAMON SUGAR

½ cup sugar

1 tablespoon ground cinnamon

APPLE FILLING

6 large apples (about 3 pounds) such as Golden Delicious, peeled, halved, cored, coarsely grated, and sprinkled with 1 tablespoon fresh lemon juice

Confectioners' sugar for finishing

One 13 × 9 × 2-inch baking pan, lined with buttered foil that extends an inch or so above the rim of the pan

down or moving the mixture around too much to avoid compressing it. Sprinkle the top with the remaining cinnamon sugar.

7 Bake for about an hour, or until the top of the cake is crisp and deep golden and the apples are bubbling. Cool in the pan on a rack.

8 To unmold, lift up the cooled cake by the foil onto a cutting board, then slide the foil out from under the cake. Use a long serrated knife to trim the edges and cut the cake into 2-inch squares.

9 Just before serving, dust the cake lightly with confectioners' sugar.

STORAGE: Keep the cake covered at room temperature, or double-wrap and freeze for longer storage. Leftovers are best reheated and cooled before serving.

MAKES ONE 13 × 9-INCH CAKE, ABOUT 24 SERVINGS

Cakes Made with Fresh or Dried Fruit

PHYLLIS VACARELLI'S PUMPKIN PECAN LOAF CAKE

～૭ ౬～

THIS IS A SPECIALTY of Los Angeles cooking school owner and teacher Phyllis Vacarelli. It is an easy cake to prepare—all the ingredients are just stirred together.

1 Position a rack in the middle of the oven and preheat to 350 degrees.

2 Combine 3 cups of the flour and all the remaining ingredients except the pecans and raisins in the bowl of a heavy-duty mixer fitted with the paddle attachment. Beat for 2 minutes on low speed.

3 Toss the pecans and raisins with the remaining 2 tablespoons flour and fold them into the batter. Scrape the batter into the prepared pans and smooth the tops.

4 Bake for about 1 hour, or until a toothpick inserted in the center emerges clean.

5 Cool for 10 minutes, then invert onto a rack and turn right side up to cool completely.

SERVING: This is a perfect breakfast or brunch cake.

STORAGE: Wrap and keep at room temperature, or freeze for longer storage.

MAKES TWO 9 × 5-INCH LOAF CAKES, ABOUT 16 TO 18 SERVINGS

3 cups all-purpose flour (spoon flour into dry-measure cup and level off) plus 2 tablespoons

1 cup firmly packed dark brown sugar

1 cup granulated sugar

1 teaspoon freshly grated nutmeg

1 teaspoon ground cinnamon

1 teaspoon baking soda

1 teaspoon baking powder

½ teaspoon salt

One 16-ounce can unsweetened pumpkin

⅓ cup water

1 cup vegetable oil, such as corn or canola

2 teaspoons vanilla extract

6 large eggs

2 cups (about 8 ounces) pecans, coarsely chopped

½ cup (about 3 ounces) dark or golden raisins

Two 9 × 5 × 3-inch loaf pans, buttered and floured

MARTHA TURNER'S CARROT CAKE

〜◞◝〜

THE QUINTESSENTIAL CARROT CAKE. This is one of the few cakes in which I ever use canned fruit. The pineapple makes it moist and tart. Thanks to Martha Turner of Greensboro, North Carolina, for the recipe.

CAKE BATTER

2 cups all-purpose flour (spoon flour into dry-measure cup and level off)

2 teaspoons baking powder

1½ teaspoons baking soda

2 teaspoons ground cinnamon

4 large eggs

2 cups sugar

1½ cups vegetable oil, such as corn or canola

2 cups peeled and finely grated carrots (about 4 large carrots)

One 8-ounce can crushed pineapple in juice

¾ cup (about 3 ounces) pecans, coarsely chopped

CREAM CHEESE ICING

12 ounces cream cheese, softened

12 tablespoons (1½ sticks) unsalted butter, softened

1 tablespoon vanilla extract

1 cup (about 4 ounces) pecans, coarsely chopped and lightly toasted

6 cups confectioners' sugar, sifted after measuring

Three 2-inch deep 9-inch round cake pans, buttered and bottoms lined with buttered parchment or wax paper

1 Set the racks in the upper and lower thirds of the oven and preheat to 325 degrees.

2 Stir together the flour, baking powder, baking soda, and cinnamon in a bowl, mixing well.

3 Whisk the eggs in a large mixing bowl. Whisk in the sugar and continue whisking briefly until light, about 1 minute. Whisk in the oil in a slow stream.

73

4   Stir in the carrots, the pineapple with its juice, and the pecans, then fold in the dry ingredients. Scrape the batter into the prepared pans and smooth the tops.

5   Bake for about 45 minutes, switching the position of the pans top and bottom and back to front, once during baking, until the cake layers are firm and golden and a toothpick inserted in the center emerges clean.

6   Cool the cake in the pans for 10 minutes, then invert onto racks to finish cooling. Remove the paper before icing.

7   To make the icing, in the bowl of a heavy-duty mixer fitted with the paddle, beat the cream cheese, butter, and vanilla on medium speed until very soft and light, about 5 minutes. Decrease the mixer speed to low and gradually beat in the confectioners' sugar. Once all the sugar is incorporated, increase the speed to medium and beat for 5 minutes longer.

8   To assemble the cake, place one layer on a platter or cardboard round and spread with one-third of the icing. Top with another layer and spread with another third of the icing. Place the last layer on top, bottom side up, and, using a large offset spatula, frost the top and sides of the cake with the remaining icing. Sprinkle the toasted pecan pieces on top of the cake, and press into sides.

STORAGE: Keep under a cake dome at room temperature.

MAKES ONE 9-INCH THREE-LAYER CAKE, ABOUT 16 SERVINGS

CHOCOLATE CHUNK ZUCCHINI CAKE

〜◦❧ ❦◦〜

THE ZUCCHINI IN THIS rich chocolate and spice cake provides moisture. Thanks to Chris Hubbuch of KitchenAid for the recipe.

1 Set a rack in the middle level of the oven and preheat to 325 degrees.

2 Stir together the flour, cocoa, baking soda, salt, and spices in a bowl, mixing well.

3 Beat the butter and oil in the bowl of a heavy-duty mixer fitted with the paddle on medium speed until well mixed. Add the sugar and continue beating for about 5 minutes, or until light. Beat in the eggs one at a time, beating until smooth after each addition. Beat in the vanilla.

4 Decrease the mixer speed to low and beat in half the flour mixture, then beat in the buttermilk. Scrape the bowl and beater with a rubber spatula. Beat in the remaining flour mixture, then scrape the bowl and beater again. Fold in the zucchini and chocolate chunks.

5 Scrape the batter into the prepared pan and smooth the top. Sprinkle with the chocolate chips.

2¼ cups all-purpose flour (spoon flour into dry-measure cups and level off)

¼ cup alkalized (Dutch-process) cocoa powder, sifted after measuring

1 teaspoon baking soda

1 teaspoon salt

1 teaspoon ground cinnamon

¼ teaspoon ground cloves

8 tablespoons (1 stick) unsalted butter, softened

½ cup vegetable oil, such as corn or canola

1¾ cups sugar

2 large eggs

1 teaspoon vanilla extract

½ cup buttermilk or milk

2 cups grated unpeeled zucchini (about 3 medium zucchini)

4 ounces semisweet chocolate, cut into ½-inch chunks

One 6-ounce bag semisweet chocolate chips

One 9 × 13 × 2-inch baking pan, buttered and lined with buttered parchment or foil that extends at least an inch above the top of the pan

6 Bake for about 50 minutes, or until the cake is well risen and a toothpick inserted in the center emerges clean. Cool the cake in the pan on a rack.

7 Lift the cake out of the pan, using the paper or foil, and place on a cutting board. Run a knife or spatula between the paper and the cake and pull away the paper. Cut the cake into squares or rectangles.

SERVING: Serve with whipped cream or ice cream.

STORAGE: Wrap well and keep at room temperature.

MAKES ONE 13 × 9-INCH CAKE, ABOUT 12 GENEROUS SERVINGS

FRUITCAKES

THE CAKES IN THE FOLLOWING RECIPES contain preserved fruits. The simplest are merely enriched with raisins or candied peel, the more complex are the all-out, whole-bottle-of-rum type of fruitcake that's aged for a few months before serving. If you have been wary of fruitcake in the past, try a simple one first, then work your way up to the extravaganzas.

AGING FRUITCAKE

Some fruitcakes benefit from a long rest before they are served. The cake becomes tender and less likely to crumble when sliced, and the flavor mellows. To age a cake, sprinkle it liberally with dark rum or other strong spirits of your choice. Not only does the rum flavor the cake, it also acts as a preservative. Cut off about a foot of new cheesecloth (more for larger cakes) and soak it with the same spirits. Wrap the fruitcake in the soaked cheesecloth, then wrap in several layers of plastic wrap and finish with a double layer of aluminum foil. As a further precaution, place the cake in a plastic container or tin with a tightly fitting cover. Store the cake in the coolest place you can find, but not the refrigerator or kitchen. Check the cake occasionally and sprinkle with a little more rum if it seems to be drying out.

STORING FRUITCAKE

To store fruitcake for any length of time, follow the directions for aging above. Or, if you don't want to use alcohol, wrap it well and store in the freezer.

TEXAS FRUITCAKE

THIS RECIPE COMES FROM Texas food writer Sidney Carlisle. In 1980, she wrote about a Fort Worth man who made annual holiday fruitcakes. I find the recipe fascinating because it doesn't contain butter, as most traditional fruitcakes do.

1 Position a rack in the middle of the oven and preheat to 250 degrees.

2 Stir together the nuts and fruits in a large bowl, mixing well. In a medium bowl, mix together the dry ingredients, and stir them into the bowl of fruit.

3 In another medium bowl, whisk together the eggs and vanilla. Use a large rubber spatula to mix the eggs into the rest of the ingredients, folding them in until completely incorporated.

4 Scrape the batter into the prepared pan(s). Bake for about 2 hours for a tube cake, about 1 hour and a half for loaf cakes, or until a toothpick inserted into the center emerges clean.

5 Cool completely on a rack.

6 Unmold the cake(s) onto a rack and peel off the paper. Turn loaf cakes right side up.

SERVING: Serve cut into very thin slices.

STORAGE: Keep well wrapped in plastic and foil at room temperature for up to a week.

1 pound pecans, coarsely chopped

1 pound pitted dates, quartered

8 ounces candied cherries, halved

8 ounces candied pineapple, cut into ½-inch pieces

1 cup sugar

1 cup all-purpose flour (spoon flour into dry-measure cup and level off)

2 teaspoons baking powder

½ teaspoon salt

1 teaspoon freshly grated nutmeg

4 large eggs

1 teaspoon vanilla extract

One 12-cup tube pan or four 6 × 3 × 2-inch mini-loaf pans, sprayed with vegetable cooking spray and lined with parchment paper

Or, for longer storage, see Aging Fruitcakes and Storing Fruitcakes, page 78.

MAKES ONE 10-INCH TUBE CAKE, ABOUT 20 SERVINGS, OR FOUR 6 × 3-INCH LOAF CAKES, ABOUT 20 SERVINGS

MACAO CHRISTMAS CAKE

～♪ ♪～

THIS RECIPE COMES FROM A DEAR FRIEND, chef and cookbook author Rosa Ross. Rosa's mother, Edris de Carvalho, made this cake every holiday season at their family home in Macao, the former Portuguese colony near Hong Kong. The food of Macao is mainly Chinese and Portuguese, but there is also a broad vein of English influence (from the British presence in Hong Kong), evident in food like this fruitcake. Don't be put off by the quantity of nutmeg, or be tempted to reduce it or leave it out—the spice gives the cake a delicate and pleasant perfume.

1 Set a rack in the lower third of the oven and preheat to 275 degrees.

2 In a large bowl, stir together the dried and candied fruit and the almonds, mixing well. Toss with ¼ cup of the flour.

3 In a medium bowl, combine the remaining 2¾ cups flour, the nutmeg, and baking powder, mixing well.

4 In the bowl of a heavy-duty mixer fitted with the paddle, beat the butter and sugar on medium speed for about 5 minutes, or until light and fluffy. Beat in the eggs one at a time, beating until smooth after each addition. Beat in one-third of the flour, then the brandy. Scrape down the bowl and beater with a rubber spatula. Beat in another third of the flour, then beat in the crème de cacao. Scrape again. Beat in the remaining flour.

5 Use the rubber spatula to give a final mix to the batter. Fold in the floured fruit.

8 ounces dark raisins

8 ounces golden raisins

8 ounces dried currants

4 ounces candied orange peel, cut into ¼-inch dice

4 ounces candied lemon peel, cut into ¼-inch dice

½ cup (about 2 ounces) slivered blanched almonds

3 cups all-purpose flour (spoon flour into dry-measure cup and level off)

2½ whole nutmegs, finely grated

1½ teaspoons baking powder

½ pound (2 sticks) unsalted butter, softened

1 cup sugar

6 large eggs, at room temperature

½ cup Cognac or other brandy

¼ cup crème de cacao

One 12-cup tube or Bundt pan, buttered and floured

6 Scrape the batter into the prepared pan and smooth the top. Bake for about 2 to 2½ hours, or until a toothpick inserted into the cake halfway between the side of the pan and the central tube emerges clean.

7 Cool the cake in the pan on a rack for about 20 minutes, then invert onto a rack, remove the paper, and cool completely.

SERVING: Serve thin slices of this cake with coffee or tea. Around the holidays, it is always on my table at teatime.

STORAGE: See Aging Fruitcake and Storing Fruitcake, page 78. Wrap in Cognac- or brandy-soaked cheesecloth, but do not moisten the cake itself—it is too delicately flavored and would take on a harsh alcohol taste—or keep at room temperature for up to a week.

MAKES ONE 10-INCH TUBE OR BUNDT CAKE, ABOUT 24 SERVINGS

Cakes Made with Fresh or Dried Fruit

SULEIKA'S TORTE

꧁ ⁓ ꧂

THIS EXOTICALLY NAMED SPECIALTY comes from the Confiserie Heini in Lucerne, Switzerland, which is owned by two brothers, Bruno and Hans Heini. Suleika's Torte, which was developed by their grandfather, is an astonishing fantasy of chocolate walnut cake and dried-fruit–studded butter cake baked with a layer of sweet orange marmalade in between.

CHOCOLATE BATTER

4 tablespoons (½ stick) unsalted butter, cut into 8 pieces

6 ounces best-quality bittersweet chocolate, cut into ¼-inch pieces

1 ounce unsweetened chocolate, cut into ¼-inch pieces

2 large eggs

⅓ cup sugar

Pinch of salt

1 cup (about 4 ounces) walnuts, coarsely chopped

⅔ cup all-purpose flour (spoon flour into dry-measure cup and level off)

⅔ cup sweet orange marmalade

FRUIT BATTER

¼ cup Zante currants

⅓ cup golden raisins

2 tablespoons (about 1 ounce) finely diced candied orange peel

2 tablespoons (about 1 ounce) finely diced candied lemon peel

1 tablespoon dark rum

⅔ cup all-purpose flour (spoon flour into a dry-measure cup and level off)

1 teaspoon baking powder

6 tablespoons (¾ stick) unsalted butter, softened

½ cup sugar

1 teaspoon vanilla extract

3 large eggs, separated

2 large egg yolks

Pinch of salt

Confectioners' sugar for finishing

One 10-inch round cake pan, buttered and bottom lined with buttered parchment or wax paper

1 Set a rack in the middle of the oven and preheat to 350 degrees.

2 To make the chocolate batter, melt the butter in a 1½-quart saucepan over medium heat. Swirl the pan every so often so that the butter melts evenly. Off the heat, add both chocolates and swirl the pan to submerge them in the hot butter. Set aside.

3 Whisk the eggs in a large bowl. Whisk in the sugar in a slow stream, then whisk in the salt. Using the whisk, whisk the chocolate mixture until smooth, then use a rubber spatula to scrape it into the egg mixture. Fold the chocolate mixture into the egg mixture, then fold in the walnuts and flour.

4 Scrape the batter into the prepared pan and spread it evenly. Spread the marmalade over the chocolate batter, leaving about a ½-inch plain border all around.

5 To make the fruit batter, combine the currants, raisins, orange peel, and lemon peel in a small bowl. Stir in the rum and set aside.

6 Stir together the flour and baking powder, mixing well.

7 In the bowl of a heavy-duty mixer fitted with the paddle, beat the butter and ¼ cup of the sugar on medium speed until very light, about 5 minutes. Beat in the egg yolks and vanilla, beating until smooth after each addition. Reduce the speed to low and beat in the flour mixture.

8 In a clean, dry mixer bowl, whip the egg whites and salt with the whisk attachment on medium speed until very white and foamy. Increase the speed and add the remaining ¼ cup sugar in a stream. Continue to whip until the whites hold a soft, glossy peak. Fold half the egg whites into the batter, then fold in the fruit. Fold in the remaining egg whites. Spread the batter over the marmalade and smooth the top.

9 Bake for 50 to 60 minutes, or until the cake is well risen and firm and a toothpick inserted into the fruit batter emerges clean (the marmalade and chocolate batter will remain a little wet).

10 Cool the cake in the pan for at least 20 minutes, then invert it onto a rack. Peel off the paper and invert the cake onto another rack to cool completely.

11 Just before serving, dust the cake with confectioners' sugar.

SERVING: Serve with coffee or tea—this rich cake needs no other accompaniment.

STORAGE: Wrap the cooled cake in plastic and keep at room temperature for 1 week, or double-wrap and freeze for longer storage.

MAKES ONE 10-INCH CAKE, ABOUT 12 GENEROUS SERVINGS

Cakes Made with Fresh or Dried Fruit

PANFORTE DI SIENA

～⌒⚬⌒～

THIS MEDIEVAL FRUITCAKE COMBINES toasted nuts, honey, and fruit in a spicy batter that bakes into an unusual cross between cake and candy. *Panforte* (the name, meaning "strong bread" in Italian, may come from either its spiciness or its texture) is a specialty of Siena, and in its native town is found in many different varieties. The panforte made for export is a very thin, usually an inedible hard disk about five or six inches in diameter and half an inch thick (most of them could actually be used as a weapon). Making panforte yourself is the only way, short of going to Siena, to taste it the way it was meant to be—moist, tender, chewy, and sweet.

Although most of the ingredients for panforte are as close as your local market, the bottom of the cake is usually covered with wheat starch paper—the same material used in Catholic churches for altar breads or hosts. It is available by mail-order (see Sources), but you can use the alternative pan preparation given below. It doesn't change the quality of the panforte at all. The "covering flour" in the recipe is used to prevent the top of the panforte from becoming crusty in the oven—it comes right off as soon as it is baked.

Edible wheat starch paper for preparing the pan OR 1 tablespoon *each* dry bread crumbs and ground almonds

CAKE BATTER

⅔ cup all-purpose flour (spoon flour into dry-measure cup and level off)

1½ teaspoons ground cinnamon

½ teaspoon ground coriander

½ teaspoon ground cloves

½ teaspoon freshly grated nutmeg

⅔ cup honey

⅔ cup sugar

⅔ cup (about 4½ ounces) candied citron or candied melon rind, cut into ¼-inch dice

⅔ cup (about 4½ ounces) candied orange peel, cut into ¼-inch dice

1⅓ cups (about 5½ ounces) blanched almonds, lightly toasted and coarsely chopped

COVERING FLOUR

2 tablespoons all-purpose flour

½ teaspoon ground cinnamon

One 8-inch round cake pan, bottom lined with foil and buttered

1 Set a rack in the middle level of the oven and preheat to 300 degrees. Line the bottom of the buttered pan with slightly overlapping pieces of wheat starch paper, or sprinkle the bread crumbs and almonds evenly over it.

2 Stir together the flour and spices in a bowl, mixing well.

3 In a 2-quart saucepan, combine the honey and sugar and stir well to mix. Place the pan over low heat and stir occasionally until the mixture reaches a full rolling boil. Allow to boil hard for about 15 seconds, then remove from the heat. Stir in the candied fruit and almonds, then fold in the flour-and-spice mixture.

4 Scrape the batter into the prepared pan. Slightly oil the palm of your hand and smooth the top of the cake.

5 Mix together the flour and cinnamon, then sift it over the top of the pan through a small strainer.

6 Bake the panforte for about 20 minutes, checking a few times to make sure that it is not starting to bubble; if it shows signs of simmering, slide the cake pan onto a heavy cookie sheet to finish baking. Cool in the pan on a rack.

7 Invert the cooled cake to remove the covering flour, then peel away the foil.

SERVING: Serve tiny wedges. This is really not a dessert cake as much as it is something to have with coffee after dinner, like a confection or cookie.

STORAGE: Wrap well in plastic wrap and foil and store in a tin or plastic container with a tight-fitting cover.

MAKES ONE 8-INCH CAKE, ABOUT 16 SMALL SERVINGS

VARIATION

CHOCOLATE PANFORTE: Add ½ teaspoon salt to the flour mixture. Add 5 ounces bittersweet chocolate, cut into ¼-inch pieces, to the honey mixture when you remove it from the heat. Allow to stand for a minute to melt the chocolate, then whisk until smooth.

CHOCOLATE-DATE TIPSY CAKE

❧ ❧

A "TIPSY" CAKE USUALLY MEANS it has been flavored with spirits. I like to bake this in a large rectangular pan, then cut it into squares and serve it right from the pan.

CAKE BATTER

1 cup (about 4 to 5 ounces) pitted dates, finely chopped

½ cup (about 3 ounces) mixed candied fruit, cut into ¼-inch dice

1 teaspoon baking soda

2 tablespoons alkalized (Dutch-process) cocoa powder

2 tablespoons Lyle's Golden Syrup available in British or specialty stores or honey

1 teaspoon ground ginger

1 cup boiling water

¼ cup Cognac or other brandy

2 cups all-purpose flour (spoon flour into dry-measure cup and level off)

½ cup (about 2 ounces) pecans, coarsely chopped

2 teaspoons baking powder

½ teaspoon salt

8 tablespoons (1 stick) unsalted butter

1 cup sugar

3 large eggs

SYRUP

1 cup sugar

2 tablespoons unsalted butter

⅓ cup water

⅓ cup sweet sherry

¼ cup Cognac or other brandy

1 teaspoon vanilla extract

One 9 × 13 × 2-inch baking pan, buttered and floured

1 Position a rack in the middle of the oven and preheat to 350 degrees.

2 Stir together the dates, candied fruit, cocoa, baking soda, ginger, golden syrup, and boiling water in a large bowl. Set aside to cool slightly, then stir in the brandy.

3 Combine the flour, pecans, baking powder, and salt in a bowl and stir well to mix.

4 In the bowl of a heavy-duty mixer fitted with the paddle attachment, beat the butter and sugar on medium speed for 3 to 4 minutes, or until lightened. Beat in the eggs one at a time, beating until smooth after each addition.

5 Decrease the mixer speed to low and beat in one-third of the flour mixture, then half the date mixture. Stop the mixer and scrape the bowl and beater. Beat in another third of the flour, followed by the remaining date mixture. Stop and scrape again. Beat in the remaining flour mixture.

6 Use a large rubber spatula to give a final mix to the batter, then scrape it into the prepared pan and smooth the top.

7 Bake for about 30 to 40 minutes, or until the cake is well risen and well colored and a toothpick inserted in the center emerges clean. Cool the cake in the pan on a rack.

8 To make the syrup, combine the sugar, butter, water, sherry, brandy, and vanilla in a 2-quart saucepan and bring to a boil over medium heat. Lower the heat to a simmer and cook for 5 minutes. Poke 20 holes in the cake with a skewer and carefully pour the hot syrup over the entire surface of the cake (in the pan).

Serving: Serve the cake as soon as you've poured the syrup over it or after it has cooled. It's great with whipped cream or ice cream.

Storage: Wrap the cooled cake, in the pan, well, and store at room temperature.

Makes one 13 × 9-inch cake, about 24 servings

Cakes Made with Fresh or Dried Fruit

ALMOST ALL OF THE WORLD'S DESSERT CUISINES have their own version of cheesecake. Creamy, smooth, rich, and with just a tiny sour tinge to temper the sweetness, cheesecake heads the list of the richest and most requested of all cakes.

Though I too love cheesecake, I have always been mystified that it appears on steak-house menus—who could eat a piece of such a rich cake after such a rich main course? With that thinking in mind, I usually serve only the lightest cheesecakes for dessert. The richer ones I reserve for midafternoon tea or coffee—or if I do serve one as a dessert, it is only after a very light lunch or supper. In my childhood, cheesecake always appeared as one of the dozen or so desserts after Thanksgiving dinner. I could never resist it, but even as a child I always regretted indulging in it.

The cheesecakes in this chapter fall into several different categories.

1 Cream-Cheese Cakes: Plain, or with the addition of sour cream, these are the classic New York–style cheesecakes. They probably entered the American baking repertoire with immigrants from Eastern Europe, as this type of cheesecake is eminently a Russian or Polish-style dessert.

2 Curd-Cheese Cakes: These are the ones made from ricotta, cottage cheese, or farmer cheese and hail primarily from Italy, in the case of ricotta, or from Germany and Eastern Europe, in the case of the other curd cheeses.

3 Unbaked Cheesecakes: These are really mousses based on cream cheese, yogurt, or some other cheese, held with dissolved gelatin and usually lightened with a cooked meringue. Much lighter than the baked variety of cheesecake, these are fancy party desserts and can be served after a rich meal.

CHEESECAKE RULES

Cheesecakes aren't difficult to make, but you have to follow these very simple rules:

1 When a recipe says have the ingredients at room temperature, it means it. Room-temperature cream cheese, sugar, and eggs will combine to make a smooth lump-free batter.

2 Don't overmix the batter. If the ingredients are at room temperature, the batter will smooth out with almost no effort. If the ingredients are cold and firm, no amount of beating will

smooth them—you're just beating unwanted air into the batter, which will make the cheesecake rise too much while it is baking, only to sink dismally in the center as it cools.

3 Bake most cheesecakes in a pan of water. This helps reduce bottom heat so that the cheesecake sets without rising and developing a soufflé-like texture.

4 Don't overbake the cheesecake. If it looks as though it has puffed a little and it has taken on a tiny bit of color, and the baking time stated in the recipe has elapsed, take the cheesecake out of the oven. Yes, it will still look a little wobbly in the center—it's supposed to.

PREVENTING CRACKS

Following the three rules above will also help prevent the top of the cheesecake from cracking. Before baking, loosening the top of the cheesecake from the side of the pan by running the point of a sharp paring knife between the cheesecake and the side of the pan (just about ½ inch down) all around—press the knife against the pan, not the cake—will also help prevent cracks. If despite all your precautions there is a tiny crack or two, then it's time for that strawberry topping—see page 97.

CHEESECAKE CRUSTS

I decided not to have any pastry doughs that need to be rolled out in a book about cakes, but there are quite a few alternatives for the bottom of a cheesecake.

1 Nothing: Butter the bottom of the pan, cut a disk of parchment paper the same size as the bottom of the pan, place it in the pan, and butter it, too.

2 Crumb base: Line the pan with buttered paper as above, then scatter a ⅛-inch layer of graham cracker, cookie, or cake crumbs, evenly over the bottom of the pan and press them down firmly. Some of these recipes call for a mixture of butter and cookie crumbs.

3 Crisp crust: This is like a crumb topping mixture that you press onto the buttered paper; see page 9.

4 Cake: Place a thin slice of a sponge or butter cake on the buttered paper before pouring in the batter. Ideally, a cake layer to be used as a cheesecake base should be baked in a pan

larger than the cheesecake pan and then cut to size. If you bake it in a pan of the same size, the base will be too small because the cake will shrink a little as it cools.

SPRINGFORM OR OTHER PANS

All the recipes here call for springform pans, but you can also use a 3-inch-deep round cake pan of the same diameter. Such pans are actually called cheesecake pans and are available from several equipment suppliers. If you use a pan that doesn't have removable sides, you'll have to invert the cheesecake to unmold it. Don't worry—it's easy.

UNMOLDING CHEESECAKES

To unmold a baked cheesecake successfully, follow the instructions below as though your life depended on it:

1 Wrap the cooled-to-room-temperature cheesecake very well in plastic wrap and chill it overnight. No, two hours in the refrigerator isn't a replacement for twelve; several hours in the freezer can be, though.

2 Remove the cheesecake from the refrigerator and unwrap it. Save the plastic wrap. If there is a little condensation on the chilled cheesecake, leave it there. If not, dribble or spray about 1 teaspoon water evenly over the top of the cheesecake.

3 Loosen the cheesecake from the sides of the pan with a thin sharp knife: insert it between the pan and the cheesecake and run it around the entire inside of the pan, scraping against the pan, not the cake.

4 Turn on a burner on your stove to a moderate flame, or halfway between low and high if electric. Place the cheesecake pan on the burner and rotate it so that the entire bottom of the pan becomes slightly heated—the whole process should take only 5 seconds.

5 Place the plastic wrap over the pan—you don't need to press it against the top of the cheesecake.

6 Cover the plastic wrap with a perfectly flat plate, platter, cutting board, or piece of stiff cardboard—a cake circle is ideal.

7 Invert the pan onto the plate or other surface. The cheesecake should drop right out. If it doesn't, give the bottom of the pan a bit of a swat. If that doesn't work, invert the whole package, remove the plate or cardboard and plastic wrap, and reheat the pan bottom.

8 Once you succeed in getting the cheesecake to drop out of the pan, remove the paper from the bottom of the cheesecake.

9 Place a flat platter or cardboard over the bottom of the cheesecake and invert the whole package again. Remove the top platter or cardboard and the plastic wrap (which will not have stuck to the cheesecake because of the little bit of moisture on the cheesecake top). Gently pat the top of the cake dry with a paper towel, without pressing too hard.

For cheesecakes in springform pans: If you have a wide metal spatula, you may be able simply to loosen the cheesecake base from the pan bottom and slide it onto a platter, without inverting it—it really depends on how firm the cheesecake is when you do it. This works best with a very well chilled baked cheesecake. I have tried this with chilled cheesecakes that have sponge cake bases though, and sometimes they buckle.

You can also invert a cheesecake baked in a springform pan to unmold it, following the instructions above. It's easier to do because you'll only need to remove the pan bottom and paper. I strongly suggest doing this, especially if you like to take cheesecakes to friends—you'll never lose another springform bottom again.

CHEESECAKE BASES

The following recipes for cheesecake bases are all interchangeable, though I like the crumb-type bases best with baked cheesecakes. The more delicate sponge base is better with unbaked cheesecakes.

PLAIN CHEESECAKE BASE

~⌒⊙⌒~

THIS IS AN EASY WAY to make a pastry-like base for a cheesecake without the bother of rolling out dough. The crumbly flour and butter mass is pressed into the bottom of the buttered and paper-lined pan. Not only does having a base under the cheesecake make it easier to cut and serve, but it makes the cake easier to unmold after it is baked and chilled.

1 Position a rack in the middle of the oven and preheat to 350 degrees.

2 Using a heavy-duty mixer fitted with the paddle, or a wooden spoon, beat together the butter and sugar until light and fluffy. Beat in the yolk until smooth. Combine the flour, baking powder, and salt and gently fold into the butter mixture with a rubber spatula. The mixture will be crumbly.

3 Place the mixture in the pan and use your hands to pat it down evenly and firmly over the bottom. Pierce the surface at 1-inch intervals with a fork.

4 Bake for 15 to 20 minutes, or until the crust is golden and firm. Transfer to a rack to cool slightly before covering with the cheesecake batter.

MAKES A BASE FOR ONE 9- OR 10-INCH CHEESECAKE

3 tablespoons unsalted butter, softened

3 tablespoons sugar

1 large egg yolk

1 cup all-purpose flour (spoon flour into dry-measure cup and level off)

½ teaspoon baking powder

⅛ teaspoon salt

One 9-inch springform pan, bottom buttered and lined with buttered parchment paper

VARIATION

COCOA CHEESECAKE BASE: Reduce the 1 cup flour to ¾ cup and add 3 tablespoons alkalized (Dutch-process) cocoa powder, sifted after measuring, to the dry ingredients.

SPONGE BASE

ॐ

THIS IS A SPONGE CAKE BATTER that is piped or spread on a pan and baked. (For a detailed explanation of this type of layer, see the sponge cake chapter, page 111.) Made this way you get a single thin layer of cake that doesn't need to be cut from a larger cake. A little trimming will be required, though, to make the layer fit the cheesecake pan.

1 Position a rack in the middle of the oven and preheat to 350 degrees.

2 Using a 9-inch round cake pan as a pattern, with a very dark pencil, trace a 9-inch circle on the parchment paper on the jelly-roll pan. Turn the paper over so that the pencil marking is underneath.

3 In the bowl of a heavy-duty mixer, whisk together the yolks, vanilla, and 3 tablespoons of the sugar. With the whisk attachment, whip the mixture on medium speed for about 5 minutes, until well aerated.

4 In a clean, dry mixer bowl, combine the whites and salt. With the clean, dry whisk attachment, whip on medium speed until very white and opaque. Increase the speed and whip in the remaining 3 tablespoons sugar in a stream. Whip until the whites hold a very firm peak.

5 Use a rubber spatula to fold in the yolks, then sift the cake flour over the mixture and fold it in gently.

2 large eggs, separated
½ teaspoon vanilla extract
¼ cup sugar
Pinch of salt
6 tablespoons cake flour

One 10 × 15-inch jelly-roll pan or baking sheet, lined with parchment

6 Using a pastry bag fitted with a ½-inch plain tip (Ateco 806), pipe the batter in a continuous spiral from the center of the traced circle outward, forming a 9-inch disk.

7 Bake for about 15 minutes, or until golden and firm. Transfer the layer, still on the paper, to a rack to cool.

MAKES ONE 9- OR 10-INCH LAYER, ABOUT ½ INCH THICK

SOUR CREAM CHEESECAKE

❧

WHEN PEOPLE TALK ABOUT REAL NEW YORK cheesecake, this is the recipe they mean. Rich and creamy, this cheesecake has just a hint of acidity from the sour cream.

1 Position a rack in the middle of the oven and preheat to 350 degrees.

2 To make the base, beat together the butter and sugar by hand until light and fluffy. Beat in the yolk until smooth. Combine the flour, baking powder, and salt and, with a rubber spatula, gently fold into the butter mixture. The mixture will be crumbly.

3 Place the dough in the pan and use your hands to pat it down evenly and firmly over the bottom.

4 Bake for about 25 minutes, until the crust is golden and baked through. Transfer to a rack and reduce the oven temperature to 325 degrees.

5 To make the batter, in the bowl of a heavy-duty mixer fitted with the paddle attachment, beat the cream cheese on the lowest speed just until smooth, no more than 30 seconds. Stop the mixer and scrape down the bowl and beater. Add the sugar in a stream, mixing for no more than 30 seconds. Stop and scrape again. Add 1 cup of the sour cream and mix only until it is

CHEESECAKE BASE

3 tablespoons unsalted butter, softened

3 tablespoons sugar

1 large egg yolk

1 cup bleached all-purpose flour (spoon flour into dry-measure cup and level off)

¼ teaspoon baking powder

⅛ teaspoon salt

CHEESECAKE BATTER

1 pound cream cheese

1 cup sugar

One 16-ounce container sour cream

3 large eggs

2 teaspoons vanilla extract

One 3-inch-deep 9-inch springform pan, bottom buttered and lined with parchment or wax paper; one 10 × 15-inch jelly-roll pan or roasting pan

absorbed, no more than 30 seconds. Repeat with the remaining sour cream. Add the eggs one at a time, mixing only until each is absorbed; stop and scrape after each addition. Beat in the vanilla extract.

6 Wrap heavy-duty aluminum foil around the bottom of the springform pan so it comes at least 1 inch up the sides. Pour the batter into the pan. Place the pan in a jelly-roll pan or roasting pan and pour warm water into the pan to a depth of ½ inch.

7 Bake the cheesecake for about 55 minutes, or until it is lightly colored and firm except for the very center. Remove from the oven and lift the cheesecake out of the hot water. Remove the foil and let cool completely on a rack. Wrap the cheesecake and chill overnight.

8 To unmold the cheesecake, run a knife or thin spatula around the inside of the pan, pressing the knife against the pan, not the cake. Unbuckle the pan side and lift off. Leave the cake on the base, or run a spatula under the cake base and slide the cake onto a platter.

MAKES ONE 9-INCH CHEESECAKE, ABOUT 12 SERVINGS

(see photograph, pages 88–89)

VARIATION

STRAWBERRY CHEESECAKE: Rinse, hull, and slice 2 pints strawberries. Starting at the outer edge of the baked and chilled cheesecake, arrange the strawberry slices in concentric circles, points outward, like the petals of a flower. Heat ½ cup currant jelly and reduce until slightly thickened, then glaze the berries, using a pastry brush.

PAUL'S CHEESECAKE

~⌒⌒~

THIS EXCELLENT CHEESECAKE comes from my friend Paul Kinberg of Dallas.

1 Position a rack in the middle of the oven and preheat the oven to midway between 300 and 325 degrees.

2 In the bowl of a heavy-duty mixer fitted with the paddle, beat the cream cheese on low speed until smooth. Beat in the sugar in a stream. Beat in the eggs one at a time, stopping to scrape the bowl and beater with a rubber spatula each time and beating until smooth after each addition. Beat in the vanilla, then beat in the sour cream.

3 Pour the batter into the prepared pan.

4 Bake for exactly 1 hour. Turn off the oven, without opening the door, and leave the cheesecake in the oven for exactly 1 hour more.

5 Cool the cheesecake in the pan on a rack, then wrap in plastic and refrigerate until firm. Unmold according to the instructions on page 97.

CHEESECAKE BATTER

1½ pounds cream cheese

1½ cups sugar

6 large eggs

1½ teaspoons vanilla extract

One 16-ounce container sour cream

1 Cheesecake Base, page 96, baked and cooled

One 9- or 10-inch springform pan, buttered

SERVING: Serve thin wedges of this rich cake.

STORAGE: Wrap leftovers in plastic and refrigerate. Bring to room temperature before serving.

MAKES ONE 9- OR 10-INCH CHEESECAKE, ABOUT 12 SERVINGS

COTTAGE CHEESE CAKE

～♡～

THIS RECIPE WAS GIVEN TO ME by my friend and associate, Andrea Tutunjian, who got it from her maternal grandmother, Antoinette Bianco. When I looked at the recipe, I was struck by the similarity to another recipe I had seen and I phoned my friend Ann Nurse to see if we could get to the bottom of the similarity. Sure enough, the recipe was the same as Ann's except that Ann uses ricotta instead of cottage cheese. She said that she had been given the recipe about forty years ago and told that it was a secret recipe, not to be shared with anyone. To her immense surprise, one day she happened to read the side panel on a box of cornstarch, and there was the "secret" recipe! The success of this easy recipe depends on the accuracy of your oven. Bake it for a few minutes too long, or at a temperature higher than called for, and the cheesecake will crack miserably.

1 Position a rack in the middle of the oven and preheat to 325 degrees.

2 In the bowl of a heavy-duty mixer fitted with the paddle, beat the cream cheese on medium speed until smooth, about a minute. Beat in the cottage cheese and beat until smooth again.

3 Mix the sugar with the flour and cornstarch, stirring to remove any lumps. Decrease the mixer speed to low and add the sugar mixture in a stream, stopping to scrape down the bowl and beater twice. Still on low speed, beat in the eggs one at a time, stopping to scrape down the bowl and beater each time and beating until smooth after each addition. Beat in the lemon juice and vanilla extract, and finally the butter.

1 pound cream cheese, softened

One 16-ounce container cottage cheese

1½ cups sugar

3 tablespoons all-purpose flour

3 tablespoons cornstarch

4 large eggs

2 tablespoons strained fresh lemon juice

1 teaspoon vanilla extract

8 tablespoons (1 stick) unsalted butter, melted and cooled

One 16-ounce container sour cream

One 9-inch springform pan, buttered

4   Use a large rubber spatula to fold in the sour cream. Pour the batter into the prepared pan and smooth the top.

5   Bake for exactly 1 hour. Turn off the oven and without opening the door, leave the cake in the oven for exactly 1 hour longer.

6   Transfer the cake to a rack. Run a sharp paring knife around the inside of the pan, scraping against the pan rather than the cake.

7   Cool the cheesecake in the pan on the rack, then wrap in plastic and refrigerate until firm. Unmold according to the instructions on page 97. Bring to room temperature to serve.

SERVING: Serve thin wedges of this rich cake. Sliced sugared strawberries, or a combination of raspberries and strawberries, would make a nice accompaniment.

STORAGE: Wrap leftovers in plastic and refrigerate. Bring to room temperature before serving.

MAKES ONE 9-INCH CHEESECAKE, ABOUT 16 SERVINGS

LESLIE'S LAYERED CHEESECAKE

THIS IS A GREAT CHOCOLATE-AND-VANILLA cheesecake that won first prize for Leslie Sutton, a very talented baker and artist, at a Connecticut cheesecake baking contest.

CHOCOLATE COOKIE CRUST
1¾ cups chocolate wafer crumbs
5 tablespoons unsalted butter, melted

CHEESECAKE BATTER
1½ pounds cream cheese, softened
1 cup sugar
Pinch of salt
3 large eggs
One 8-ounce container sour cream

1 teaspoon vanilla extract
7 ounces semisweet chocolate, melted

TOPPING
One 16-ounce container sour cream
¼ cup sugar

One 3-inch-deep 9-inch springform pan, bottom buttered and lined with parchment or wax paper

1   Position a rack in the middle of the oven and preheat to 350 degrees.

2   To make the crust, put the cookie crumbs in a bowl and stir in the butter with a fork. Press the mixture evenly and firmly over the bottom and most of the way up the sides of the pan.

3   To make the batter, in the bowl of a heavy-duty mixer fitted with the paddle attachment, beat the cream cheese, sugar, and salt on low speed until smooth. Beat in the eggs one at a time, stopping often to scrape down the bowl and beater. Beat in the sour cream and vanilla.

4   Pour half the batter into prepared pan.

5   Stir the melted chocolate into the remaining batter and carefully pour it over the plain batter.

6   Bake the cheesecake for 40 minutes.

7   While the cheesecake is baking, prepare the topping. Stir the sour cream and sugar together until smooth.

8   Pour the topping over cheesecake and smooth it with a spatula. Increase the oven temperature to 450 degrees and bake for 10 minutes.

9   Cool the cheesecake in the pan on a rack, then wrap in plastic and refrigerate until firm. Unmold according to the instructions on page 97.

SERVING: Serve thin wedges of this rich cake.

STORAGE: Wrap leftovers in plastic and refrigerate. Bring to room temperature before serving.

MAKE ONE 9-INCH CHEESECAKE, ABOUT 16 SERVINGS

DARK AND WHITE
CHOCOLATE CHEESECAKE

〜৩ ৩〜

TWO LAYERS OF CHOCOLATE CAKE LAYERS make this cheesecake complex and elegant.

1 Position a rack in the middle of the oven and preheat to 350 degrees.

2 In the bowl of a heavy-duty mixer fitted with the paddle attachment, beat half the cream cheese on the lowest speed until smooth, no more than 30 seconds. Stop the mixer and scrape down the bowl and beater. Add ½ cup of the sugar in a stream, beating for no more than 30 seconds. Stop and scrape again. Add the melted dark chocolate, beating only until it is absorbed, no more than 30 seconds. Beat in 1 teaspoon of the vanilla. Add 3 of the eggs, one at a time, mixing only until each is absorbed. Stop and scrape after each addition and transfer to another bowl if you only have one mixer bowl.

3 Make the white chocolate batter following the same procedure as for the dark chocolate batter, using the remaining ingredients.

CHEESECAKE BATTER

2 pounds cream cheese

1 cup sugar

5 ounces bittersweet or semisweet
    chocolate, melted

2 teaspoons vanilla extract

6 large eggs

5 ounces white chocolate, melted

One 9-inch layer 1942 Devil's Food Cake,
    page 212, sliced into two layers

One 3-inch-deep 9-inch springform pan, bottom buttered and lined with parchment or wax paper; one 10 × 15-inch jelly-roll pan

4 Wrap heavy-duty aluminum foil around the bottom of the springform pan to come at least 1 inch up the sides. Place one of the cake layers in the bottom of the pan. Pour the dark chocolate batter into the pan. Place the other cake layer on the batter and pour in the white chocolate batter.

5 Place the pan in the jelly-roll pan and pour warm water into the pan to a depth of ½ inch. Bake the cheesecake for about 75 minutes, or until it is lightly colored and firm except for the very center. Remove from oven and take the cheesecake pan out of the hot water. Remove the foil and cool completely on a rack.

6 Wrap the cheesecake and chill overnight. Unmold according to the directions on page 97.

MAKES ONE 9-INCH CHEESECAKE, ABOUT 16 SERVINGS

SHARI'S INDIVIDUAL
MASCARPONE CHEESECAKES

❧ ❧

THE RECIPE FOR THIS DELICIOUS CHEESECAKE was given to me by Shari Lepore, an old friend who is also a cooking teacher.

1 Position a rack in the middle of the oven and preheat to 300 degrees.

2 In the bowl of a heavy-duty mixer fitted with the paddle attachment, beat the cream cheese and sugar on medium speed until smooth. Add the mascarpone and beat until smooth. Beat in eggs one at a time, scraping down the bowl and beater often. Beat in the vanilla.

3 Place the prepared molds in the roasting pan and fill the molds to within ½ inch of the top. Pour about an inch of warm water into the pan.

4 Bake for about 30 minutes, or until the cakes are no longer liquid in the center.

5 Turn off the oven and leave door ajar. Cool the cheesecakes in the oven for about 30 minutes, then chill the cheesecakes until firm.

6 To unmold, invert and remove the cups and paper.

2 pounds cream cheese, softened
2¼ cups sugar
One 500-gram (about 18 ounces or 1¾ cups) container imported mascarpone, softened
7 large eggs
1 tablespoon vanilla extract

Eighteen 4-ounce aluminum foil cups, buttered and bottoms lined with buttered parchment or wax paper; a shallow roasting pan large enough to hold the cups

SERVING: Serve with sliced sugared strawberries or raspberries, or a combination.

STORAGE: Wrap leftovers in plastic and refrigerate. Bring to room temperature before serving.

MAKES 21 INDIVIDUAL CHEESECAKES

PIZZA DOLCE DI RICOTTA

~ ᕦ ᕤ ~

THIS MOST TYPICAL ITALIAN DESSERT is often served as an Easter specialty in southern Italy. The flavorings vary slightly according to the region, and toasted slivered almonds, chopped chocolate, and grated lemon and orange zest are sometimes included.

1 Position a rack in the middle of the oven and preheat to 350 degrees.

2 Using a wooden spoon, beat the ricotta in a large bowl until smooth. Stir in the sugar, then stir in the eggs one at a time. Being careful not to overmix, stir in the anisette, vanilla, and ½ teaspoon of the cinnamon.

3 Pour the mixture over the crust and sprinkle the top with the remaining ½ teaspoon cinnamon.

4 Bake for about 45 minutes, or until the cheesecake is well colored, slightly puffed, and firm except in the very center.

5 Cool the cake in the pan on a rack, then wrap in plastic and refrigerate until firm. Unmold according to the instructions on page 97.

SERVING: Serve thin wedges of this rich cake.

RICOTTA BATTER

3 pounds whole-milk ricotta

1 cup sugar

8 large eggs

2 tablespoons anisette

2 teaspoons vanilla extract

1 teaspoon ground cinnamon

1 Cheesecake Base with Ground Nuts, made with almonds, baked and cooled

One 2-inch-deep 12-inch round cake pan, bottom buttered and lined with buttered parchment or wax paper

STORAGE: Wrap leftovers in plastic and refrigerate. Bring to room temperature before serving.

MAKES ONE 12-INCH CHEESECAKE, ABOUT 16 SERVINGS

LEMON AND ALMOND CHEESECAKE

THIS UNBAKED CHEESECAKE is always a big hit, and it is easy to prepare. To avoid last-minute panic, always prepare this type of cheesecake the day before, so you'll be sure it's completely set before you unmold it.

1 To make the filling, combine the rum and lemon juice in a medium heatproof bowl and sprinkle the gelatin over the surface. Allow to soak for 5 minutes, then place the bowl over a small pan of gently simmering water and stir several times to melt the gelatin, about 1 minute. Remove the bowl from the pan and cool the gelatin slightly.

2 In the bowl of a heavy-duty mixer fitted with the paddle attachment, beat the cream cheese at medium speed until soft and light, scraping the bowl and beaters often. Beat in the cream until smooth.

3 Combine the egg whites and sugar in the clean, dry bowl of the electric mixer and heat over simmering water, whisking constantly, until the egg whites are hot and the sugar is dissolved. Attach the bowl to the mixer and whip with the whisk attachment at medium speed until cold and firm.

4 Beat one-quarter of the cream cheese mixture into the dissolved gelatin, then beat the gelatin mixture into the remaining cream cheese. Fold in the meringue in several additions. Pour the filling into the prepared pan and refrigerate until at least 6 hours, or overnight.

5 To prepare the almonds, position a rack in the middle of the oven and preheat to 325 degrees.

6 Put the almonds in a jelly-roll pan, pour the egg white over them, and rub the almonds between the palms of your hands to coat evenly. Stir in the sugar.

7 Bake for about 20 minutes, stirring often, until the almonds are well toasted and sugar has caramelized slightly. Cool, and store in a tin or jar at room temperature until ready to use.

8 To make the glaze, combine the water and lemon juice in a small bowl and sprinkle the gelatin over the surface. Allow to soak for 5 minutes.

9 Bring the jelly to a boil and add the gelatin mixture. Return to a boil, and remove from heat. Add the food coloring and cool the glaze to room temperature.

10 Strain the cooled glaze over the cheesecake and chill again to set the glaze.

11 Unmold the cheesecake according to the directions on page 97. Press the sugared almonds around the sides.

To serve, cut the cake into wedges with a knife warmed in hot water and wiped dry.

STORAGE: Keep refrigerated until time to serve; refrigerate leftovers.

MAKES ONE 9-INCH CHEESECAKE, ABOUT 12 SERVINGS

1 Cheesecake Base with Ground Nuts, made with almonds, baked and cooled

CHEESE FILLING

2 tablespoons white rum

2 tablespoons fresh lemon juice

1 envelope gelatin

1½ pounds cream cheese, softened

½ cup heavy cream

4 large egg whites

⅔ cup sugar

SUGARED ALMONDS

1 cup (4 ounces) sliced blanched almonds

1 tablespoon beaten egg white

½ cup sugar

LEMON GLAZE

⅓ cup water

2 tablespoons fresh lemon juice, strained

1 envelope unflavored gelatin

⅔ cup apple jelly

A drop of yellow food coloring

One 3-inch-deep 9-inch springform pan; one 10 × 15-inch jelly-roll pan

RASPBERRY CHEESECAKE

~◦ ◦~

THIS EXCEPTIONALLY LIGHT CHEESECAKE has fresh raspberries hidden in a light and silky cheese mousse.

1   Trim the sponge base to an even 8½- or 9½-inch diameter, depending on the pan you are using (the base needs to be slightly smaller than the pan so that its sides will be covered when the filling is poured in). Place it in the springform pan.

2   To make the filling, beat the cream cheese until smooth and light. Gradually beat in the yogurt.

3   Combine framboise and water in a small heatproof bowl, sprinkle the gelatin over the surface, and let soak for 5 minutes. Set the bowl over simmering water and stir to melt the gelatin. Remove and cool slightly.

4   Whisk the egg whites and sugar in the mixer bowl over simmering water until the egg whites are hot and the sugar is dissolved. Attach the bowl to the mixer and beat on medium speed until cool.

5   Beat the gelatin mixture into the cheese mixture, then fold in the meringue.

1 Sponge Base, page 95, baked and cooled

CREAM CHEESE FILLING

1 pound cream cheese

One (8-ounce) container yogurt

2 tablespoons framboise (raspberry eau-de-vie)

¼ cup water

1½ envelopes gelatin

4 large egg whites

¾ cup sugar

¼ cup seedless raspberry preserves

One ½-pint basket raspberries

RASPBERRY GLAZE

1 envelope unflavored gelatin

2 tablespoons water

⅓ cup raspberry puree (see Note)

½ cup currant jelly

One 3-inch-deep 9- or 10-inch springform pan

6   To assemble, spread the sponge base with the preserves, then with one-quarter of the cheese mousse. Arrange the raspberries on the mousse, then cover with the remaining mousse. Chill until set, at least 6 hours, or overnight.

7   To make the glaze, sprinkle the gelatin over the water in a small bowl and let soak for 5 minutes. In a small saucepan, combine the puree and jelly and bring to a boil, stirring occasionally. Add the soaked gelatin and return to a boil, then strain into a bowl. Cool to room temperature.

8   Pour the glaze through a strainer over the top of the cheesecake. Return to the refrigerator to set the glaze.

9   To unmold, run a sharp knife around the inside of the pan. Unhook the springform buckle and lift off the ring. Smooth the sides with a metal spatula if necessary.

SERVING: Cut the cake into wedges with a knife warmed in hot water and wiped dry.

STORAGE: Keep refrigerated until time to serve; refrigerate leftovers.

MAKES ONE 9- OR 10-INCH CHEESECAKE, ABOUT 16 SERVINGS

NOTE: To make raspberry puree, cook 1 cup frozen raspberries until thick, then puree and strain.

FROM THE POINT OF VIEW OF BAKING CHEMISTRY, sponge and foam cakes are some of the most interesting. Relatively few of these light cakes contain a leavening such as baking powder or soda. Most rise from the expansion of air cells beaten into the eggs during mixing. Once the batter goes into the oven, the heat makes the air cells expand and cause the cake to rise.

There are four main types of sponge and foam cakes.

1 Angel Food: These are almost always made exclusively with egg whites. I like to serve these extremely light and delicate cakes with sweetened fruit or berries.

2 Génoise: This very delicate French-style sponge cake is made with whole eggs that are combined with sugar and heated over simmering water before being whipped by machine; then the dry ingredients are folded in. Génoise layers form the bases of many layered, rolled, and molded cakes, and they are often moistened with sugar syrup for extra moisture and flavor.

3 Separated-Egg Sponge, called *Biscuit* (bees-kwee) in French: For this type: the yolks are whipped with part of the sugar, the whites are whipped separately, the remaining sugar is incorporated, and then the two foams are combined and the dry ingredients folded in. Many sponge cakes are made in this way, including ladyfingers, sponge bases for mousse and Bavarian cakes, tube cakes, Passover sponge cake, and even the Italian pan di Spagna.

4 Chiffon Cakes: These are barely more than fifty years old—the recipe was supposedly developed by a salesman who then sold it to General Mills. Most chiffon cake recipes descend from the same source, pamphlets and other promotional material circulated by General Mills in the 1940s and '50s. The one I used as the basis for these recipes was published by General Mills in 1948. Chiffon cakes are made by mixing all the ingredients (which include baking powder and vegetable oil) except the egg whites, then whipping the egg whites and folding the rest of the batter into the whites. A cake with a delicate texture and more flavor than an ordinary sponge cake, is the result.

A NOTE ABOUT SIFTING

Though I don't sift flour before measuring it, in these recipes the flour (or a combination of flour and cornstarch and/or cocoa) is sifted over the batter before it is folded in. This makes it easier to incorporate the dry ingredients into the batter and consequently results in less mixing and more air (for leavening) in the batter.

CLASSIC ANGEL FOOD CAKE

❧ ❧ ❧

UNTIL VERY RECENTLY, I had always made angel food cakes with self-rising cake flour—the baking powder in the flour providing a little "insurance" that the cake would rise no matter what. When I started working on an angel food recipe for this book, I was haunted by a comment made by Marion Cunningham, one of the founders of The Baker's Dozen in San Francisco, author of many cookbooks, and an expert baker. Marion had found, in recent tests, that all-purpose flour also worked for angel food and that the resulting baked cakes had more body and character than those made with cake flour. I experimented, and this is the result—the best angel food cake you'll ever bake or eat. Adding lemon juice to the egg whites not only imparts a pleasant delicate flavor, but it also helps to stabilize the egg whites by slightly toughening the walls of the bubbles formed during whipping. Many other recipes use cream of tartar for this purpose.

1 Set a rack in the middle level of the oven and preheat to 325 degrees.

2 Put ¾ cup of the sugar in a small bowl. In another small bowl, mix the remaining ¾ cup sugar evenly with the flour. Sift the mixture three times to aerate it.

3 In the bowl of a heavy-duty mixer fitted with the whisk attachment, whip the egg whites and salt on medium speed until foamy. Add the lemon juice and vanilla and continue whipping until the whites are very white and opaque and beginning to hold a shape. Increase the speed to medium-high and whip in the sugar from the bowl in a slow stream. Continue to whip until the egg whites hold a soft, glossy peak.

1½ cups sugar

1 cup bleached all-purpose flour (spoon flour into dry-measure cup and level off)

1½ cups egg whites (from about 12 large eggs)

¼ teaspoon salt

1 tablespoon strained fresh lemon juice

1 teaspoon vanilla extract

One 10-inch tube pan with removable bottom, ungreased; a narrow-necked bottle (such as a wine bottle) to hang the cake on after it is baked (see Note); a strainer or sifter

4 Quickly sift one-third of the flour and sugar mixture over the egg whites. Gently fold in with a rubber spatula, making sure you scrape across the bottom of the bowl as you fold to prevent the flour mixture from accumulating there and possibly causing lumps. Repeat with another third of the flour and sugar mixture, then finally with the remainder.

5 Scrape the batter into the pan and run the spatula through the batter to eliminate any large air pockets.

6 Bake for about 45 to 55 minutes, or until the cake is well risen, well colored, and firm to the touch. Be careful not to overbake, or the cake will fall. Invert the central tube of the pan onto the neck of the bottle and allow the cake to cool completely upside down.

7 To remove the cooled cake from the pan, run a long thin knife all around the sides of the pan, scraping against the pan rather than the cake. Remove the pan sides and run the knife around the central tube under the cake. Invert the cake onto a platter, easing it off the central tube with your fingers.

SERVING: Serve with whipped cream and/or fruit.

STORAGE: Wrap in plastic or keep under a cake dome at room temperature, or wrap well and freeze for longer storage.

MAKES ONE 10-INCH TUBE CAKE, ABOUT 12 SERVINGS

VARIATIONS

CINNAMON ANGEL FOOD CAKE: Add 2½ teaspoons ground cinnamon to the flour and sugar mixture, stirring it in thoroughly. (You can use the same proportions for any other spice, such as ginger.)

FIVE-SPICE ANGEL FOOD CAKE: Chinese five-spice powder has a stronger flavor than any single spice so add just 2 teaspoons of it to the flour mixture.

COCOA ANGEL FOOD CAKE: Add 3 tablespoons alkalized (Dutch-process) cocoa powder to the flour mixture and sift together once to eliminate any lumps in the cocoa.

NOTE: Make sure the cake pan is completely clean, dry, and free of grease of any kind. If you have never baked an angel food cake before, first invert the pan onto the bottle to make sure the pan's central tube will fit over the neck of the bottle. The cake needs to hang to cool after it is baked; it would compress and fall if cooled right side up.

PLAIN GENOISE

❧ ❧

THIS RICH, DELICATE CAKE forms the basis for many filled, frosted, and glazed cakes. A good plain génoise is hard to beat—it has an elegance that derives from its simplicity, and I even like them unadorned. Many recipes for génoise add butter as an enrichment. Unfortunately, sometimes the extra manipulation the incorporation of the butter necessitates causes these light batters to fall. So I prefer to add a few extra egg yolks instead—they not only help enrich the cake, they also provide greater stability to the foam, ultimately making the batter easier to prepare.

1   Set a rack in the middle level of the oven and preheat to 350 degrees.

2   Half-fill a medium saucepan with water and bring it to a boil over high heat. Lower the heat so the water is simmering.

3   Whisk the eggs, yolks, salt, and sugar together in the bowl of a heavy-duty mixer. Place over the pan of simmering water and whisk gently until the mixture is just lukewarm, about 100 degrees (test with your finger). Attach the bowl to the mixer and, with the whisk attachment, whip on medium-high speed until the egg mixture is cooled (touch the outside of the bowl to tell) and tripled in volume. The egg foam will be thick and will form a slowly dissolving ribbon falling back onto the bowl of whipped eggs when the whisk is lifted.

4   While the eggs are whipping, stir together the flour and cornstarch.

3 large eggs
3 large egg yolks
Pinch of salt
¾ cup sugar
½ cup cake flour (spoon flour into dry-measure cup and level off)
¼ cup cornstarch

One 9-inch round cake pan or 9-inch springform pan, buttered and bottom lined with buttered parchment or wax paper; a strainer or sifter

5   Sift one-third of the flour mixture over the beaten eggs. Use a rubber spatula to fold in the flour mixture, making sure to scrape all the way to the bottom of the bowl on every pass through the batter to prevent the flour mixture from accumulating there and making lumps. Repeat with another third of the flour mixture and finally with the remainder.

6 Scrape the batter into the prepared pan and smooth the top.

7 Bake the génoise for about 25 minutes, or until well risen, deep gold, and firm to the touch.

8 Immediately use a small paring knife to loosen the cake from the sides of the pan. Invert the cake onto a rack, then reinvert onto another rack and let the cake cool right side up on the paper. Remove the paper when the cake is cool.

STORAGE: Wrap in plastic wrap and refrigerate for several days, or double-wrap and freeze for up to a month.

MAKES ONE 9-INCH ROUND LAYER

VARIATIONS

CHOCOLATE GENOISE: Reduce the cake flour to ⅓ cup, increase the cornstarch to ⅓ cup, and add ¼ cup alkalized (Dutch-process) cocoa powder to the flour and cornstarch mixture, sift.

GENOISE SHEET: Bake either the plain or chocolate batter in a 10 × 15-inch jelly-roll pan that has been buttered and lined with buttered parchment at 400 degrees for about 10 to 12 minutes. Make sure the cake doesn't overbake and become too dry, especially if it is to be rolled. (Makes one 10 × 15-inch layer.)

BISCUIT BATTER

~⚬~

THIS IS A CLASSIC FRENCH PREPARATION for making ladyfingers and also for making piped-out thin sponge-cake bases for under mousse-type desserts. If you like, you may also use a thin slice of a piped biscuit disk under a cheesecake, either baked or unbaked. The name, by the way, has nothing to do with baking powder biscuits, and it's pronounced "bee-skwee"—a very old name in French for a cake layer.

    To make this easier to prepare, like any sponge cake with separated eggs, it's good to have two bowls and whisks for your mixer. If you don't, either use a hand mixer for the yolks and your heavy-duty mixer for the whites, or use the bowl and whisk for the yolks, scrape them into another bowl, and wash the bowl and whisk in hot soapy water and dry them before proceeding to whip the whites.

1 Set racks in the upper and lower third of the oven and preheat to 350 degrees.

2 Whisk the yolks, half the sugar, and the vanilla in the bowl of a heavy-duty mixer. Place the bowl on the mixer with the whisk attachment and whip on medium speed until very aerated and pale yellow, about 3 minutes.

3 In a clean, dry mixer bowl combine the egg whites and the salt. Whip on medium speed with the whisk attachment until the whites are very white and opaque. Increase speed to medium-high, and whip in the remaining sugar in a stream, continuing to whip the whites until they hold a firm, dull peak.

4 large eggs, separated
½ cup sugar, divided
1 teaspoon vanilla extract
Pinch of salt
1 cup cake flour or bleached all-
    purpose flour (spoon the flour into
    dry-measure cup and level off)
Confectioners' sugar for dusting the
    tops of the ladyfingers

Two cookie sheets or jelly-roll pans lined with parchment (if you are going to make a disk or disks, trace a 9-inch circle on the paper and turn the paper over)

4 Remove the bowl from the mixer and fold the yolks into the whites with a large rubber spatula.

5 Put the flour in a strainer or sifter and sift it over and fold it into the batter in three additions, making sure to scrape the bottom of the bowl with the spatula to keep the flour from accumulating there.

6 Fit a pastry bag with a ½-inch plain tube (Ateco #806). Spoon about a third of the batter into the bag and twist the top of the bag to seal.

7 To pipe fingers, touch the tube to the paper on the pan and squeeze gently while pulling the bag back toward you, making a 3-inch finger. To stop the flow of the batter, stop squeezing and proceed to the next finger, positioning the tube about 2 inches away from the first finger. You can pipe 3 rows of 6 fingers on a typical jelly-roll pan—see the illustration for positioning the fingers on the pan. Immediately after you have piped a full pan of the fingers, generously sift the confectioners' sugar over them and put them right in the oven. Continue with the remaining batter.

8 To pipe a disk, start with the bag perpendicular to the pan in the center of the traced circle. Squeeze gently, keeping the end of the tube about ½-inch above the surface of the pan and allowing the batter to flow out the same diameter as the end of the tube. Continue gently squeezing until the circle is filled in. Alternatively, take several large spoonfuls of the batter and spread them in the circle with a small offset spatula. It doesn't matter if you don't pipe or spread a perfect circle, you can trim it later. It is important to keep the batter at a fairly even thickness on the pan.

9 The disks don't have to be dusted with confectioners' sugar because they are inside the dessert.

10 Bake the fingers and/or disk(s) for about 15 minutes, until they are well risen, deep golden, and firm when pressed with a fingertip.

11 Slide the papers from the pans to racks to cool. Use the fingers and disks as soon as they are cooled.

STORAGE: The disks may be wrapped and refrigerated or frozen. The fingers don't hold up as well—they tend to bruise on the surface or harden if kept more than a day— they are best used freshly baked.

MAKES ABOUT 3 DOZEN LADYFINGERS OR TWO ROUND DISKS, OR A COMBINATION

TUBE PAN SPONGE CAKE

~⦿~

THIS IS THE TYPE OF SPONGE CAKE that should be eaten as is, rather than frosted, filled, or otherwise elaborated upon. Not only is it as fine and delicate a cake as you'll ever find, it is easy to prepare to boot.

1 Set a rack in the middle of the oven and preheat to 325 degrees.

2 Whisk together the yolks, ½ cup of the sugar, and the lemon zest in the bowl of a heavy-duty mixer, then whip with the whisk attachment on medium speed until very aerated and pale yellow, about 3 minutes.

3 In a clean, dry mixer bowl, whip the 8 egg whites and the salt with the clean, dry whisk attachment on medium speed. Add the lemon juice and continue whipping until the whites are very white and opaque and beginning to hold a shape. Increase the speed to medium-high, and whip in the remaining ½ cup sugar in a stream, continuing to whip until the whites hold a firm, dull peak.

4 Use a large rubber spatula to fold the yolk mixture into the whites.

6 large eggs, separated
1 cup sugar
1 teaspoon finely grated lemon zest
2 large egg whites
¼ teaspoon salt
¼ cup strained fresh lemon juice
1 cup bleached all-purpose flour
 (spoon flour into dry-measure cup
 and level off)

One 10-inch tube pan with removable bottom, ungreased; a narrow-necked bottle (such as a wine bottle) to hang the cake on after it is baked

5 In 3 additions, sift the flour through a strainer or sifter over the batter and fold it in. Make sure to scrape the bottom of the bowl with the spatula as you fold to keep the flour from accumulating there and making lumps.

6   Scrape the batter into the pan and run the spatula through the batter to eliminate any large air pockets.

7   Bake for 45 to 55 minutes, or until the cake is well risen, well colored, and firm to the touch. Be careful not to overbake, or the cake will fall. Invert the central tube of the pan onto the neck of the bottle and allow the cake to cool completely upside down.

8   To remove the cooled cake from the pan, run a long thin knife around the sides of the pan, scraping against the pan rather than the cake. Remove the pan sides and run the knife around the central tube and under the cake. Invert the cake onto a platter, easing it off the central tube with your fingers.

SERVING: Serve with whipped cream and/or fruit.

STORAGE: Wrap in plastic or keep under a cake dome at room temperature, or wrap well and freeze for longer storage.

MAKES ONE 10-INCH TUBE CAKE, ABOUT 16 SERVINGS

PASSOVER SPONGE CAKE

꩜

Of course my recipe for Passover sponge cake comes from Kyra Effren, the ultimate *bala-busta*. Kyra is the first one up in North Dallas every morning, and by 6 o'clock, the most entic-ing smells issue from her kitchen. Is it a wonder I look forward to my stays in Dallas?

During Passover, Jews refrain from eating anything made with grain and anything fer-mented or leavened in any way. The only exceptions are matzoh, a cracker made with wheat flour that is prepared under religious supervision, and kosher wine, fermented under supervi-sion. Passover cakes usually contain matzoh meal (ground matzohs) or potato starch, or a com-bination. This cake uses special matzoh cake meal, which is more finely ground than regular matzoh meal. Sponge cake is a popular Passover dessert not only because it is parve (it contains neither meat nor dairy and so can be eaten with any meal), but also because, unlike many other cakes, it works well made with matzoh cake meal and potato starch.

1 Set a rack in the middle of the oven and preheat to 325 degrees.

2 Whisk the yolks and 1 cup of the sugar together in the bowl of a heavy-duty mixer, then whip with the whisk attachment on medium speed until very aerated and pale yellow, about 3 minutes. Whip in the water and lemon juice.

3 In a clean, dry mixer bowl, whip the 8 egg whites and the salt with the clean, dry whisk attachment on medium speed until the whites are very white and opaque. Increase the speed to medium-high, and whip in the remaining ½ cup sugar in a stream. Continue to whip until the whites hold a firm, dull peak.

7 large eggs, separated
1½ cups sugar
2 tablespoons water
1 tablespoon strained fresh lemon juice
1 large egg white
¼ teaspoon salt
½ cup matzoh cake meal (see Note)
½ cup potato starch

One 10-inch tube pan with removable bottom, ungreased; a narrow-necked bottle (such as a wine bottle) to hang the cake on after it is baked

4 With a large rubber spatula, fold the yolks into the whites.

5 Put the matzoh meal and potato starch in a strainer or sifter and, in 3 additions, sift the mixture over the batter and fold it in. Make sure to scrape the bottom of the bowl with the spatula to keep the meal and starch from accumulating there and causing lumps.

6 Scrape the batter into the pan and run the spatula through the batter to eliminate any large air pockets.

7 Bake for 35 to 45 minutes, or until the cake is well risen, well colored, and firm to the touch. Be careful not to overbake, or the cake will fall. Invert the central tube of the pan onto the neck of the bottle and allow the cake to cool completely upside down.

8 To remove the cooled cake from the pan, run a long thin knife around the sides of the pan, scraping against the pan rather than the cake. Remove the pan sides and run the knife around the central tube and under the cake. Invert the cake onto a platter, easing it off the central tube with your fingers.

SERVING: Serve with fruit, if you like.

STORAGE: Wrap in plastic or keep under a cake dome at room temperature, or wrap well and freeze for longer storage.

MAKE ON 10-INCH TUBE CAKE, ABOUT 16 SERVINGS

NOTE: Matzoh cake meal is available in the kosher section of the supermarket around Passover. It is also, of course, available at Passover stores in large Jewish neighborhoods.

PAN DI SPAGNA

~⚬~

THE JURY IS STILL OUT on whether the name of this Italian sponge cake means "Spanish bread," which would be the literal translation, or whether *spagna* is really a corruption of *spugna,* or sponge. Fortunately it doesn't matter–the cake is delicious.

1 Position a rack in the middle of the oven and preheat to 350 degrees.

2 Whisk together the yolks, 6 tablespoons of the sugar, and the vanilla in the bowl of a heavy-duty mixer, then whip with the whisk attachment on medium speed until very aerated and pale yellow, about 3 minutes.

3 In a clean, dry mixer bowl, whip the egg whites and salt with the whisk attachment on medium speed until the whites are very white and opaque. Increase the speed to medium-high, and whip in the remaining 6 tablespoons sugar in a stream. Continue to whip the whites until they hold a firm, dull peak.

4 Use a large rubber spatula to fold the yolks into the whites.

5 Put the flour and cornstarch in a strainer or sifter and, in 3 additions, sift the mixture over the batter and fold it in. Make sure to keep scraping the bottom of the bowl with the spatula to keep the flour from accumulating there and causing lumps.

6 Scrape the batter into the prepared pan and smooth the top.

4 large eggs, separated

¾ cup sugar

1 teaspoon vanilla extract

Pinch of salt

½ cup all-purpose flour (spoon flour into dry-measure cup and level off)

½ cup cornstarch

One 2-inch-deep 9- or 10-inch round cake pan, buttered and bottom lined with parchment or wax paper

7 Bake the cake for 30 to 40 minutes, until it is well risen and feels firm when pressed gently with the palm of your hand. Immediately run a small knife or spatula around the inside of the pan to loosen the cake. Unmold the layer onto a rack. Leave the paper on it and turn the layer right side up onto a rack to cool. Remove the paper when the cake is cool.

STORAGE: Double-wrap the layer in plastic and keep it in the refrigerator up to 5 days, or freeze it for longer storage.

MAKES ONE 9- OR 10-INCH ROUND LAYER

CHOCOLATE SPONGE CAKE

For this recipe, the eggs are separated, yielding a particularly tender and chocolaty result.

1 Set a rack in the middle of the oven and preheat to 350 degrees.

2 Sift together the flour, cornstarch, and cocoa through a fine-mesh strainer onto a piece of wax paper.

3 Whisk together the yolks, 6 tablespoons of the sugar, and the vanilla in the bowl of an electric mixer, then whip on medium speed for about 3 minutes, until the mixture is pale, fluffy, and lemon colored.

4 In a clean, dry mixer bowl, whip the egg whites and salt with the clean, dry whisk attachment on medium speed until white and opaque and beginning to hold a very soft peak. Increase the speed to medium-high and whip in the remaining 6 tablespoons sugar in a stream. Continue to whip until the whites hold a firm, dull peak.

5 Use a rubber spatula to fold the yolk mixture into the whipped whites.

6 In 3 additions, sift the dry ingredients over batter, folding them in with a rubber spatula.

7 Scrape batter into the prepared pan and smooth the top with a spatula.

⅓ cup all-purpose flour (spoon flour into dry-measure cup and level off)

⅓ cup cornstarch

⅓ cup alkalized (Dutch-process) cocoa powder

4 large eggs, separated

¾ cup sugar

1 teaspoon vanilla extract

Pinch of salt

One 2-inch-deep 9-inch round cake pan or 9-inch springform pan, buttered and bottom lined with parchment or wax paper

8 Bake for about 30 minutes, until the layer is well risen and firm to the touch.

9 If necessary, loosen the layer from the sides of the pan with a small knife or spatula. Invert the cake onto a rack. Leave the paper on the cake and invert onto another rack to cool. Remove the paper when the cake is cool.

STORAGE: Double-wrap the layer in plastic wrap and refrigerate for several days, or freeze for several months.

MAKES ONE 9-INCH ROUND LAYER

MARBLE SPONGE CAKE

~⚬⚬~

THIS WINS MORE FRIENDS FOR SPONGE CAKE than any other recipe I know. It's not difficult to make—in fact, the eggs are prepared exactly the same way as for many other sponge
cakes. The only trick is that once you combine the white and yolks and then divide the batter,
you must move quickly so that the white batter doesn't deflate while you are folding the dry ingredients into the chocolate batter.

1 Set a rack in the middle of the oven and
preheat to 350 degrees.

2 In a small bowl stir together ½ cup of the
flour and ¼ cup of the cornstarch, for the
white batter. In another small bowl, stir
together the remaining ¼ cup flour, ¼ cup
cornstarch, and the cocoa, for the chocolate
batter. Set aside.

3 Whisk together the yolks, ½ cup plus 2
tablespoons of the sugar, and the vanilla in
the bowl of a heavy-duty mixer, then whip
with the whisk attachment on medium
speed until very aerated and pale yellow,
about 3 minutes.

4 In a clean, dry mixer bowl, whip the egg
whites and salt with the clean, dry whisk
attachment on medium speed until the
whites are very white and opaque. Increase
the speed to medium-high, and whip in the
remaining ½ cup plus 2 tablespoons sugar in
a stream. Continue to whip until the whites
hold a firm, dull peak. With a large rubber
spatula, fold the yolks into the whites.

¾ cup all-purpose flour (spoon flour
    into dry-measure cups and level off)
½ cup cornstarch
3 tablespoons alkalized (Dutch-process)
    cocoa powder
6 large eggs, separated
1¼ cups sugar
2 teaspoons vanilla extract
Pinch of salt

One 10-inch tube pan with removable
bottom, ungreased, a narrow-necked
bottle (such as a wine bottle) to hang
the cake on after it is baked

5 Pour half the egg mixture into the bowl
in which the yolks were whipped. In 2
additions, sift the dry ingredients for the
white batter over the egg mixture and fold
them in; set the bowl aside. Do the same
with the dry ingredients for the chocolate
batter and the remaining egg mixture.

6 Spoon half the white batter into the tube pan, leaving the top surface somewhat irregular. Spoon half the chocolate batter over the white batter, then repeat with the layering.

7 Bake for about 45 minutes, or until the cake is well risen and feels firm when pressed gently with the palm of the hand. Invert the central tube of the pan onto the neck of the bottle and allow the cake to cool completely upside down.

8 To remove the cooled cake from the pan, run a long thin knife around the sides of the pan, scraping against the pan rather than the cake. Remove the pan sides and run the knife around the central tube and under the cake. Invert the cake onto a platter, easing it off the central tube with your fingers.

SERVING: Serve with whipped cream and/or fruit.

STORAGE: Wrap in plastic or keep under a cake dome at room temperature, or wrap well and freeze for longer storage.

MAKES ONE 10-INCH TUBE CAKE, ABOUT 16 SERVINGS

(see photograph, pages 110–111)

ORANGE SPONGE CAKE

~∽ ၅ ၎ ∿~

THIS RECIPE IS BASED ON ONE from my friends Sheila and Marilynn Brass. It's a lovely change from the more common lemon sponge, and lovers of sponge cake will really appreciate it.

1 Set a rack in the middle of the oven and preheat to 350 degrees.

2 Stir the flour and baking powder together in a bowl, mixing well.

3 In a medium mixing bowl, whisk the yolks to break them up. Whisk in the water, 1½ cups of the sugar, the zest, and orange juice. Continue whisking until the mixture is somewhat lightened, about a minute. Whisk in the flour mixture until smooth, then whisk in the butter.

4 In the clean, dry bowl of a heavy-duty mixer, whip the egg whites and salt with the whisk attachment on medium speed until the whites are very white and opaque and beginning to hold a shape. Increase the speed to medium-high and whip in the remaining ½ cup sugar in a stream. Continue whipping until the egg whites hold a soft, glossy peak.

CAKE BATTER

2 cups all-purpose flour (spoon flour into dry-measure cup and level off)

2 teaspoons baking powder

4 large eggs, separated

1 large egg yolk

⅓ cup water

2 cups sugar

2 teaspoons finely grated orange zest

⅓ cup strained fresh orange juice

4 tablespoons (½ stick) unsalted butter, melted

¼ teaspoon salt

ORANGE GLAZE

1½ cups sifted confectioners' sugar

¼ cup strained fresh orange juice

One 10-inch tube pan, buttered and floured

5 Scrape the whipped egg whites over the batter and gently but thoroughly fold them in. Scrape the batter into the prepared pan and smooth the top.

6 Bake for about 45 minutes, or until the cake is well risen, deep gold, and firm when poked with a fingertip. Immediately unmold onto a rack to cool.

7 When the cake has cooled, prepare the glaze. Stir together the confectioners' sugar and orange juice in a small saucepan and place over low heat. Stir until warm, about 110 degrees.

8 Drizzle on the glaze from a spoon held perpendicular to the cake. After the glaze has set, slide the cake onto a platter.

SERVING: Serve thin slices of this cake with tea or coffee.

STORAGE: Keep under a cake dome at room temperature.

MAKES ONE 10-INCH TUBE CAKE, ABOUT 16 SERVINGS

KYRA'S HOT MILK SPONGE

~~~⌒⌒~~~

THIS IS CERTAINLY THE EASIEST of all sponge cakes to prepare, and it has a moist and delicate texture. It makes great cake layers and is also perfect to use in a trifle.

1 Set the rack in the center of the oven and preheat to 375 degrees.

2 Combine the milk and butter in a 1½-quart saucepan and cook over low heat, stirring occasionally, until the butter is completely melted. Remove from the heat.

3 Meanwhile, stir together the flour and baking powder in a bowl, mixing well.

4 In a medium mixing bowl, whisk the eggs to break them up. Whisk in the salt, then whisk in the sugar in a stream and continue to whisk for about 30 seconds, or until the mixture has lightened somewhat. Whisk in the extracts. Gently whisk in the milk and butter mixture, then use the whisk to gently incorporate the flour mixture in about 4 additions, whisking until smooth after each addition.

5 Divide the batter between the prepared pans. Bake for 15 to 20 minutes, or until the cakes are well risen, smooth, deep gold, and firm when touched in the center with a fingertip.

8 tablespoons (1 stick) unsalted butter, cut into 8 pieces

½ cup milk

1½ cups all-purpose flour (spoon flour into dry-measure cup and level off)

2 teaspoons baking powder

3 large eggs

¼ teaspoon salt

1 cup sugar

¾ teaspoon almond extract

¼ teaspoon vanilla extract

Two 2-inch-deep 9-inch round cake pans buttered and bottoms lined with parchment or wax paper

6 Run a small paring knife around the sides of the pans to loosen the cake. Invert each layer onto a rack, then immediately invert to another rack, leaving the paper on the cake, and let cool. Remove the paper when the layers are cool.

STORAGE: Wrap the layers in plastic wrap and refrigerate for several days, or freeze for up to a month.

MAKES TWO 9-INCH ROUND LAYERS

DELICATE VANILLA CHIFFON CAKE

I ALWAYS THINK OF A CHIFFON CAKE as an angel food cake that has decided to put on the dog. Their appearance–since they are both baked in large tube pans–is similar and so is their characteristic lightness. But chiffon cakes are moister and more tender than angel foods because of the presence of both egg yolks and oil in the batter. A good chiffon cake depends a great deal on getting the egg whites just right, so read Whipping Egg Whites (page 142) before preparing the cake.

1 Set a rack in the middle of the oven and preheat to 350 degrees.

2 Sift the cake flour into the bowl of a heavy-duty mixer. Add 1¼ cups of the sugar and the baking powder and stir well to mix.

3 In a medium bowl, stir together the oil, egg yolks, water, and vanilla. Stir the liquid ingredients into the dry ingredients, then beat with the paddle on medium speed for about a minute, or until smooth.

4 In a clean, dry mixer bowl, whip the egg whites and salt with the whisk attachment on medium speed until very white and opaque and beginning to hold a shape. Increase the speed to medium-high, and whisk in the remaining ¼ cup sugar in a stream. Continue to whip the egg whites until they hold a firm peak.

5 With a large rubber spatula, fold the yolk mixture into the whipped whites, making

2¼ cups cake flour (spoon flour into dry-measure cup and level off)

1½ cups sugar

1 tablespoon baking powder

½ cup vegetable oil, such as corn or canola

4 large egg yolks

¾ cup cold water

2 teaspoons vanilla extract

1 cup egg whites (from 7 or 8 large eggs)

Pinch of salt

One 10-inch tube pan with removable bottom, ungreased; a narrow-necked bottle (such as a wine bottle) to hang the cake on after it is baked

sure you scrape the bottom of the bowl each time the spatula passes through so the batter is thoroughly mixed. Pour the batter into the prepared pan and smooth the top.

6   Bake for about 55 to 60 minutes, or until the cake is deep gold and firm; a toothpick inserted halfway between the side of the pan and the central tube should emerge clean. Invert the central tube onto the neck of the bottle and let the cake cool completely upside down.

7   To remove the cooled cake from the pan, run a long thin knife around the sides of the pan, scraping against the pan rather than the cake. Remove the pan sides and run the knife around the tube and under the cake. Invert the cake onto a platter, easing it off the central tube with your fingers.

SERVING: Use a sharp serrated knife to cut the cake. Serve with whipped cream and/or fruit.

STORAGE: Wrap in plastic or keep under a cake dome at room temperature, or wrap well and freeze for longer storage.

MAKES ONE 10-INCH TUBE CAKE, ABOUT 16 SERVINGS

VARIATIONS

ORANGE CHIFFON CAKE: Substitute strained fresh orange juice for the water and orange extract for the vanilla.

LEMON CHIFFON CAKE: Substitute ⅓ cup strained fresh lemon juice plus enough water to make ¾ cup for the water. Substitute lemon extract for the vanilla.

BROWN SUGAR CHIFFON CAKE: Substitute 1¼ cups firmly packed dark brown sugar for the first sugar added to the batter. Use ¼ cup granulated sugar for the egg whites, as in the recipe above. Brown Sugar Chiffon cake is pictured at right.

CHOCOLATE CHIFFON CAKE

~~ ⟋◞ ◟⟍ ~~

I THINK MOST CHIFFON, angel food, and tube-pan sponge cakes are best left unadorned, but this rather lean chocolate chiffon cake turns into something spectacular with a little chocolate ganache frosting. The ganache is easy to make and complements the lightness of the cake perfectly.

CAKE BATTER

½ cup alkalized (Dutch-process) cocoa powder

¾ cup boiling water

1¾ cups cake flour (spoon flour into dry-measure cup and level off)

1 tablespoon baking powder

1¾ cups sugar

½ cup vegetable oil, such as corn or canola

6 large egg yolks

1 teaspoon vanilla extract

1 cup egg whites (from 7 or 8 large eggs)

½ teaspoon salt

GANACHE

¾ cup heavy whipping cream

1 tablespoon light corn syrup

2 tablespoons butter

10 ounces semisweet or bittersweet chocolate, cut into ¼-inch pieces

One 10-inch tube pan with removable bottom, ungreased; a narrow-necked bottle (such as a wine bottle) to hang the cake on after it is baked

1 Set a rack in the middle of the oven and preheat to 350 degrees.

2 Sift the cocoa into a small mixing bowl. Stir in the boiling water until smooth. Set aside to cool.

3 Sift the cake flour into the bowl of a heavy-duty mixer. Add the baking powder and 1¼ cups of the sugar and stir well to mix.

4 In a medium bowl, stir together the oil, egg yolks, and vanilla. Stir the liquid ingredients and the cooled cocoa mixture into the dry ingredients, then beat with the paddle on medium speed for about a minute, or until smooth.

5 In a clean, dry mixer bowl, whip the egg whites and salt with the whisk attachment

134

on medium speed until very white and opaque and beginning to hold a shape. Increase the speed to medium-high, and whisk in the remaining ½ cup sugar in a stream. Continue to whip the egg whites until they hold a firm peak.

6 With a large rubber spatula, fold the yolk mixture into the whipped egg whites, making sure you scrape the bottom of the bowl each time the spatula passes through so the batter is thoroughly mixed. Pour the batter into the prepared pan and smooth the top.

7 Bake for about 55 to 60 minutes, or until the cake is deep gold and firm; a toothpick inserted halfway between the side of the pan and the central tube should emerge clean.

8 While the cake is baking, prepare the ganache. Bring the cream, corn syrup, and butter to a boil in a medium saucepan. Off the heat, add the chocolate and swirl the pan to make sure all the chocolate is submerged. Allow to stand for 3 minutes, then whisk until smooth. Pour into a bowl and refrigerate until the ganache reaches spreading consistency; check it often to make sure it doesn't harden, or it will be impossible to frost the cake.

9 Remove the cake from the oven, invert the central tube onto the neck of the bottle, and let the cake cool completely.

10 To remove the cooled cake from the pan, run a long thin knife around the sides of the pan, scraping against the pan rather than the cake. Remove the pan sides and run the knife around the central tube and under the cake. Invert the cake onto a cardboard cake round or a platter, easing it off the central tube with your fingers.

11 To finish, spread the top and sides of the cake with the cooled ganache, swirling it on with the tip of an offset metal spatula. Chill the cake briefly to set the ganache.

SERVING: Use a sharp serrated knife to cut the cake.

STORAGE: Keep under a cake dome at room temperature, or wrap loosely and refrigerate; remove from the refrigerator an hour before you serve the cake so that the ganache isn't hard. Or, for longer storage, wrap the unfrosted cake well and freeze; frost the cake after it is defrosted.

MAKES ONE 10-INCH TUBE CAKE, ABOUT 16 SERVINGS

WALNUT CHIFFON CAKE

～❡❡～

THIS DELICATE CHIFFON CAKE is enlivened with chopped walnuts and a bit of walnut oil. Sometimes I also add a bit of some spice to brighten the flavor—see the pecan variation at the end of the recipe.

1 Set a rack in the middle of the oven and preheat to 350 degrees.

2 Sift the cake flour into the bowl of a heavy-duty mixer. Add the brown sugar and the baking powder and stir well to mix.

3 In a medium bowl, stir together the oil, egg yolks, water, and vanilla. Stir the liquid ingredients into the dry ingredients, then beat with the paddle on medium speed for about a minute, or until smooth.

4 In a clean, dry mixer bowl, whip the egg whites and salt with the whisk attachment on medium speed until very white and opaque and beginning to hold a shape. Increase the speed to medium-high, and whisk in the remaining ½ cup sugar in a stream. Continue to whip the egg whites until they hold a firm peak.

5 Use a large rubber spatula to fold the yolk mixture and walnuts into the whipped egg whites. Make sure you scrape the bottom of the bowl each time the spatula passes through to mix the batter thoroughly.

2¼ cups cake flour (spoon flour into dry-measure cup and level off)

1 cup granulated light brown sugar

½ cup granulated sugar

1 tablespoon baking powder

½ cup walnut oil, or a combination of half walnut and half vegetable oil, such as corn or canola

4 large egg yolks

¾ cup cold water

2 teaspoons vanilla extract

1 cup egg whites (from 7 or 8 large eggs)

1 cup walnuts (about 4 ounces), finely chopped by hand (not ground)

One 10-inch tube pan with removable bottom, ungreased; a narrow-necked bottle to hang the cake on after it is baked

Pour the batter into the prepared pan and smooth the top.

6 Bake for about 55 to 60 minutes, until the cake is deep gold and firm; a toothpick inserted halfway between the side of the

pan and the central tube should emerge clean. Invert the central tube of the pan onto the neck of the bottle and allow the cake to cool completely.

7 To remove the cooled cake from the pan, run a long thin knife around the sides of the pan, scraping against the pan rather than the cake. Remove the pan sides and run the knife around the central tube and under the cake. Invert the cake onto a platter, easing it off the central tube with your fingers.

SERVING: Use a sharp serrated knife to cut the cake. Serve with whipped cream and/or fruit.

STORAGE: Wrap in plastic or keep under a cake dome at room temperature, or wrap well and freeze for longer storage.

MAKES ONE 10-INCH TUBE CAKE, ABOUT 16 SERVINGS

VARIATIONS

HAZELNUT CHIFFON CAKE: Substitute chopped blanched hazelnuts (see page xiv for instructions on how to remove the skin) and hazelnut oil for the walnuts and walnut oil.

PECAN CHIFFON CAKE: Substitute chopped pecans for the walnuts. Use vegetable oil instead of walnut oil and add ½ teaspoon ground cinnamon to the dry ingredients.

ALL OF THE CAKES IN THIS CHAPTER have at least one meringue layer. The French Concorde, for instance, is composed exclusively of meringue layers. The Swiss Zuger Kirschtorte combines meringue layers and sponge layers. Whenever I begin to make one of these cakes in a class, someone will invariably say, "I don't like meringue." But later on, when we serve the desserts and the meringue hater tastes the delicate, nutty dacquoise, he or she just as invariably exclaims, "I didn't know meringue tasted like this." The meringue cakes and layers here have nothing to do with Aunt Betty's lemon meringue pie that you were forced to eat as a child. I love the way baked meringue layers provide textural interest in an otherwise soft dessert and the way the crispness of meringue layers shows off a rich, creamy filling such as the buttercream in a dacquoise.

And, not only are meringues fun to make and good to eat, they are also the ultimate bake-ahead cake layer; just keep them in a plastic bag at room temperature. If they absorb some humidity and soften, simply unwrap and bake them on a cookie sheet at your oven's lowest setting for half an hour, and they'll be perfectly crisp again.

MERINGUE TERMINOLOGY

The type of meringue that's piped out and baked into layers is usually referred to as ordinary meringue or French meringue. Raw egg whites are beaten with sugar until stiff, then more sugar (granulated or confectioners') is folded in. The technique of incorporating some of the sugar gently at the end makes meringues that are tender rather than cement-like. Some recipes may call for the addition of an acidic ingredient such as lemon juice, vinegar, or cream of tartar. Acid makes the walls of the bubbles that form in the egg whites firmer so that they don't burst as easily and consequently have better stability during mixing. Sometimes cocoa or ground nuts are added with the second part of the sugar to make a chocolate or nut meringue. Nut meringues have a lot of confusing names: Dacquoise (see page 147), Succès, Progrès, Japonais, Grillage. *Succès* is the most common French term for a nut meringue, and I use it occasionally in a recipe. *Japonais* is the Swiss name for the same thing. But to confuse things further, there is also a Swiss meringue.

Unlike the Japonais, a Swiss meringue is a heated meringue. To make one, you combine the egg white(s) and all the sugar in the mixer bowl and whisk the mixture over a pan of simmering water until it is hot and the sugar is dissolved, then you whip it with the mixer. I like to use this type when the meringue is going to be spread or piped on a cake as an icing or used as a base for a mousse or buttercream. There is another type, called Italian meringue, which is not used in this book. For this, a hot sugar syrup is poured over the egg whites as they are whipping. Italian meringue works very well if made in large quantities, but I don't consider it practical in small ones. Too much of the sugar syrup sticks to the bowl and the whisk, and it's also very difficult to take an accurate temperature reading on a small quantity of syrup.

PIPING MERINGUE DISKS

The most efficient way to make meringue layers is to pipe the meringue. This is really a lot easier than the following directions make it sound. When you pipe the meringue mixture, you want it to fall onto the baking sheet in a cylindrical coil with the same diameter as the tube you're using to pipe it. As long as you use a steady pressure and keep the bag moving, piping these layers is easy and fun.

1 Place the tube in the pastry bag and push it firmly into the narrow opening from the inside. There's no need to try to seal off the tube of the bag, because meringue is too thick to flow out on its own while you are filling the bag. Fold over the top third of the bag to make a cuff. Hold the bag with your non-writing hand, sliding your hand under the cuff and gripping the bag with your open hand, as though you were holding a fat jar.

2 Use a large kitchen spoon or rubber spatula to fill the bag almost to the top fold. Unfold the cuff and twist it to seal the top of the bag.

3 Grip the top of the bag with your writing hand, with the twisted area between your thumb and first finger. This will make it easy to keep the bag closed as you squeeze out the meringue.

4 Squeeze the top of the bag as you would an orange half. It's not really necessary to use your other hand (how many hands do you use to write?), but some people like to guide the bag with the first finger of this hand. DO NOT wrap your hand around the bottom of the bag—you won't be able to see what you are piping, and you will inevitably start squeezing with both hands so your pressure will be uneven.

5 *To pipe a meringue disk,* start in the center of the area you have traced on the parchment paper, usually a circle. Position the bag perpendicular to the pan and touch the tip of the tube to the pan. Squeezing slowly, lift the tube about an inch above the pan and begin to make a

clockwise spiral with the end of the tube, making sure it is always perpendicular to the pan. Don't worry if the lines are a little wavy—it takes a few tries to get used to this. Move from the waist rather than your shoulders—this motion seems to make the flow from the bag more even and less choppy.

6 When you get to the end of the spiral, stop squeezing and lower the tube to the surface again to stop the flow. (If you need to refill the bag during the process, stop the flow in the same way, then just resume at that spot.)

7 *Or, to pipe an oval,* start with a straight line several inches long down the center, then spiral clockwise around that first straight line.

WHIPPING EGG WHITES

Sponge cakes (see Chapter 5) and meringue cakes depend on perfectly whipped egg whites for success. Though it isn't difficult to whip egg whites, here are a few suggestions that will make the process easier.

1 Always separate eggs when they are cold—the whites are more viscous and the white flows out in pretty much one glob.

2 Avoid passing the yolk repeatedly back and forth from one half of the shell to the other—once or twice should do it. Going back and forth too often can break the yolk and mix some yolk into the whites, which would prevent the whites from whipping up well.

3 Always make sure that your mixer bowl and beater are perfectly clean, dry, and free of any grease, which would also prevent the whites from whipping well.

4 Whip egg whites on medium speed—fairly slow whipping builds up a good structure of air cells in the whites and allows them to whip to the highest volume.

5 When adding sugar to whipped egg whites, always wait to add it until the whites can hold a very soft peak. Adding sugar before the egg whites have built up a good volume of air will make it difficult for them to absorb more air.

6 Always use whipped egg whites immediately—if they stand, they will separate and lose the air so carefully whipped into them.

SNOW WHITE

~⚬ ⚬~

I'M NOT ESPECIALLY DRAWN to either fairy tales or cartoon characters, but this is an ideal name for this dessert. It's sort of a lemony version of a Concorde. The whole dessert is white on white—snowy confectioners' sugar over pure white meringue layers. It's perfect for a special occasion when you want to impress everyone. Only two of the meringue layers are used inside the cake—the third one is crushed and used to cover the icing.

1 Set the racks in the upper and lower thirds of the oven and preheat to 250 degrees.

2 To make the meringue, in the bowl of a heavy-duty mixer, whip the egg whites and salt with the whisk attachment on medium speed until very white and frothy. Increase the speed to medium-high, and beat in the sugar about 2 tablespoons at a time, making sure it is well absorbed each time before adding more. Continue to whip the egg whites until they hold a stiff peak. Whip in the vanilla.

3 Use a large rubber spatula to fold in the confectioners' sugar, making sure to get to the bottom of the bowl while folding so that no sugar accumulates there.

4 Pipe a meringue circle onto each pan (see page 141).

MERINGUE LAYERS

1 cup egg whites (from 7 or 8 large eggs)
Pinch of salt
1 cup granulated sugar
1 teaspoon vanilla extract
2 cups confectioners' sugar, sifted after
 measuring

LEMON BUTTERCREAM

4 large egg yolks
½ cup sugar
⅓ cup strained fresh lemon juice
¾ pound (3 sticks) unsalted butter,
 softened

Confectioners' sugar for finishing

Three cookie sheets or jelly-roll pans, lined with parchment; trace a 9-inch circle on each sheet of paper, then turn it over

5 Bake for about an hour, or until the meringue is crisp to the touch but still slightly moist within. Cool the layers on the pans on racks.

6 To prepare the buttercream, whisk together the egg yolks, sugar, and lemon juice in the bowl of a heavy-duty mixer. Place the bowl over a saucepan of simmering water and whisk constantly until the yolks are slightly thickened. Attach the bowl to the mixer and whip with whisk attachment until the mixture has cooled. Switch to the paddle attachment and beat in the butter on medium speed. Continue beating the buttercream until it is smooth.

7 To assemble the dessert, trim each layer to an even 9-inch diameter with a serrated knife. Choose the two best for the cake. Crush the scraps and the least attractive layer.

8 Use a dab of the buttercream to anchor one meringue layer to a cardboard round or platter and spread with about half the buttercream. Top with the second layer and press down gently so it adheres. Spread the remaining buttercream over the top and sides of the cake. Press the meringue crumbs into the buttercream. Chill briefly to set the buttercream, but serve at a cool room temperature so that the buttercream isn't hard.

9 Just before serving, dust the cake with confectioners' sugar.

Serving: Cut this rich cake into small portions with a very sharp serrated knife.

Storage: Wrap and refrigerate. Bring to room temperature before serving.

Makes one 9-inch cake, about 12 servings

Variations

Substitute any flavor of buttercream you like for the lemon buttercream—raspberry and coffee are particularly good.

Sheri Portwood's Brown Sugar Meringue: Replace the granulated sugar with dark brown sugar. Fill and frost the cake with Rich Ganache (page 281).

CHOCOLATE MERINGUE CAKE

⤳ ❡ ❡ ↶

MOST CHOCOLATE MERINGUE CAKES are versions of Gaston LeNotre's famous Concorde cake. The Concorde consists of oval layers of chocolate meringue sandwiched with ganache and covered with broken cylinders of meringue, made by piping straight lines of meringue onto the baking sheet. This version uses the chocolate meringue layers, but fills and frosts them with a light chocolate buttercream and finishes the outside with crushed chocolate meringue—easier to do and just as good.

1 Set the racks to divide the oven in thirds and preheat to 300 degrees.

2 To make the meringue, in the bowl of a heavy-duty mixer, whip the egg whites and salt with the whisk attachment on medium speed until white and opaque, about 3 to 4 minutes. Increase the speed to medium-high, and whip in the granulated sugar in a stream. Continue to whip until the egg whites hold a very stiff peak.

3 Sift the confectioners' sugar and cocoa powder together several times. With a rubber spatula, fold the cocoa mixture into the beaten egg whites.

4 Using a pastry bag filled with a ½-inch plain tube (Ateco 806), pipe four 9-inch disks of meringue on the prepared pans (see page 141 for complete instructions).

CHOCOLATE MERINGUE LAYERS

1¼ cups egg whites (from 9 or 10 large eggs)

Pinch of salt

1¼ cups sugar

2 cups confectioners' sugar

⅓ cup alkalized (Dutch-process) cocoa powder

CHOCOLATE BUTTERCREAM

½ cup egg whites (from about 3 to 4 large eggs)

1 cup sugar

¾ pound (3 sticks) unsalted butter, softened

4 ounces bittersweet chocolate, melted with ¼ cup water

Confectioners' sugar for finishing

Four cookie sheets or jelly-roll pans, lined with parchment

5 Bake for about 30 to 35 minutes, or until the meringues are firm on the outside and almost baked through. Bake in 2 batches, if necessary. Cool the meringue layers on the pans.

6 To make the buttercream, combine the egg whites and sugar in the bowl of a heavy-duty mixer and whisk over a pan of simmering water until the mixture is hot and the sugar is dissolved, about 3 minutes. Attach the bowl to the mixer and whip with the whisk on medium speed until the mixture is cooled. Switch to the paddle attachment and beat in the butter about 3 tablespoons at a time. Continue to beat until the buttercream is smooth and thick. Beat in the cooled chocolate.

7 To assemble, trim the 3 best meringue disks to an even 9-inch diameter. Crush the trimmings and the remaining layer. Place one layer on a platter or cardboard round and spread it with one-third of the buttercream. Repeat with another disk and another third of the buttercream. Place the last layer on top and spread the top and sides of the dessert with the rest of the frosting. Press the crushed meringue onto the top and sides of the dessert. Chill to set the frosting.

8 Just before serving, dust the cake with confectioners' sugar.

SERVING: Cut this rich cake into small portions with a very sharp serrated knife.

STORAGE: Wrap and refrigerate. Bring to room temperature before serving.

MAKES ONE 9-INCH CAKE, ABOUT 12 SERVINGS

VARIATIONS

RASPBERRY MERINGUE CAKE: Make a raspberry buttercream by adding ⅓ cup cooled, strained, and reduced raspberry puree (see page 109) to the buttercream instead of the chocolate.

WHIPPED CREAM MERINGUE CAKE: Substitute 3 cups heavy whipping cream, whipped with ⅓ cup sugar and 2 teaspoons vanilla extract, for the buttercream.

HAZELNUT DACQUOISE

‿◦◦‿

A CRISP AND CHEWY COMBINATION of hazelnut meringue layers and a rich coffee cream, a dacquoise is the ultimate elegant dessert. This recipe is an adaptation of Gino Coffaci's classic incorporating the additions to the original dacquoise we made for the opening of Windows on the World in 1976—making it all hazelnut and leaving the top bare. The top of the dacquoise is not covered with buttercream but lightly dusted with confectioners' sugar.

1 Position the racks in the upper and lower thirds of the oven and preheat to 300 degrees.

2 To make the layers, combine the nuts, 1 cup of the sugar, and cornstarch in a food processor and coarsely grind the nuts.

3 In the bowl of a heavy-duty mixer, whip the egg whites and salt with the whisk on medium speed until white and opaque. Increase the speed to high and gradually whip in the remaining 1 cup sugar. Continue to whip until the whites hold a firm peak.

4 Use a large rubber spatula to fold the extract and the nut mixture into the meringue.

5 Using a pastry bag fitted with a ½-inch plain tube (Ateco 806), pipe three 10-inch disks of meringue onto the prepared pans (see page 141).

HAZELNUT MERINGUE LAYERS

3 cups (about 12 ounces) hazelnuts, toasted and skinned

2 cups sugar

3 tablespoons cornstarch

1¼ cups egg whites (from 9 or 10 large eggs)

Pinch of salt

2 teaspoons vanilla extract

MOCHA BUTTERCREAM

½ cup egg whites (from 3 or 4 large eggs)

1 cup sugar

¾ pound (3 sticks) unsalted butter, softened

3 tablespoons triple-strength brewed coffee or 2 to 3 tablespoons instant espresso mixed with 2 tablespoons hot water, cooled

½ cup (about 2 ounces) chopped, toasted hazelnuts for finishing

Three cookie sheets or jelly-roll pans, lined with parchment; trace a 10-inch circle on each piece of paper, then turn it over

6 Bake for about 30 minutes, until the meringues are firm. Bake in two batches if necessary. Leave on the pans to cool.

7 To make the buttercream, combine the egg whites and sugar in the bowl of a heavy-duty mixer and whisk over a pan of simmering water until the mixture is hot and the sugar is dissolved, about 3 minutes. Attach the bowl to the mixer and whip the whites with the whisk on medium speed until cooled. Switch to the paddle attachment and beat in the butter about 3 tablespoons at a time. Continue to beat until the buttercream is smooth and thick. Beat in the cooled coffee mixture.

8 To assemble, trim each meringue layer to an even 10-inch circle. Place one on a cardboard round or platter and spread with one-third of the buttercream. Top with a second layer and spread with another third of the buttercream. Place the third layer on top and press gently to level. Cover the sides of the dessert with the remaining buttercream. Press the chopped hazelnuts into the buttercream. Chill to set.

SERVING: Cut this rich cake into small portions with a very sharp serrated knife.

STORAGE: Wrap and refrigerate. Bring to room temperature before serving.

MAKES ONE 10-INCH CAKE, ABOUT 12 TO 16 SERVINGS

(see photograph, pages 138–139)

VARIATIONS

DACQUOISE PRALINEE: For an all-hazelnut dacquoise, flavor the buttercream with ⅓ cup praline paste instead of the coffee. (This cake is sometimes called Gâteau Succès.)

ALMOND DACQUOISE: Substitute toasted blanched almonds for the hazelnuts in the meringue layers. Fill and finish with a coffee or lemon buttercream in Chapter 13.

GATEAU PROGRES: Prepare almond meringue layers as for Almond Dacquoise, above. Fill the layers and cover the top and sides of the dessert with Ganache Pralinée (page 282). Press toasted sliced almonds all over the outside of cake.

SANS RIVAL: This is the most popular cake in the Philippines. Substitute lightly toasted cashews for the hazelnuts in the meringue and the garnish. Omit the coffee from the filling and add 2 teaspoons vanilla extract.

ZUGER KIRSCHTORTE
Kirsch Cake from Zug in Switzerland

THE SWEETNESS OF THE ALMOND MERINGUE LAYERS contrasts very successfully with the strong kirsch flavor in the cake and buttercream.

I Position the racks to divide the oven into thirds and preheat to 325 degrees.

2 To make the Japonais, combine the almonds and confectioners' sugar in the bowl of a food processor and process until the almonds are ground very fine.

3 In the bowl of a heavy-duty mixer, whisk the egg whites with the whip at medium speed until white and opaque. Increase the speed and beat in the sugar in a stream. Continue to beat until the egg whites hold a firm peak.

4 Use a rubber spatula to fold in the almond mixture.

5 Spread the meringue to make two thin 9½-inch disks on the paper-lined pans. Bake for about 30 minutes.

6 To make the syrup, bring the sugar and water to a boil. Cool, then add the kirsch.

7 To make the buttercream, combine the egg whites and sugar in the bowl of a heavy-duty mixer, set it over simmering water,

JAPONAIS

¾ cup (about 3 ounces) whole blanched almonds

1 cup confectioners' sugar

½ cup egg whites (from 3 or 4 large eggs)

½ cup sugar

KIRSCH SYRUP

⅓ cup sugar

¼ cup water

¼ cup kirsch

KIRSCH BUTTERCREAM

½ cup egg whites (from 3 or 4 large eggs)

1 cup sugar

¾ pound (3 sticks) unsalted butter, softened

⅓ cup kirsch

Pink food coloring

One 9-inch layer Plain Genoise, page 116
Confectioners' sugar and toasted sliced almonds for finishing

Two cookie sheets or jelly-roll pans, lined with parchment; trace a 9½-inch circle on each sheet, then turn it over

and whisk gently until the mixture is hot and sugar is dissolved. Attach the bowl to the mixer and whip with the whisk on medium speed until completely cooled. Switch to the paddle attachment and gradually beat in the butter. Continue beating until the buttercream is smooth. Beat in the kirsch a little at a time, beating until smooth after each addition. Beat in just enough food coloring to tint the buttercream a pale pink.

8 To assemble, trim the crust from the top and sides of the génoise. Using a 9-inch cardboard cake round as a guide, trim the Japonais layers to even 9-inch circles. Place a dab of the buttercream on the cardboard and place one of the Japonais layers on it. Spread it with one-third of the buttercream. Moisten the génoise layer with half the syrup and invert it onto the buttercream. Moisten with the remaining syrup. Spread the génoise with another third of the buttercream and place the second Japonais layer on top. Spread the remaining buttercream around the sides of the cake.

Press the toasted, sliced almonds into the buttercream and dust the top of the cake with confectioners' sugar. Use a serrated knife to trace a diagonal lattice pattern across the top of the cake.

SERVING: Cut this rich cake into small portions with a very sharp serrated knife.

STORAGE: Wrap and refrigerate. Bring to room temperature before serving.

MAKES ONE 9-INCH CAKE, ABOUT 12 SERVINGS

VARIATION

ZUGER RAHMKIRSCHTORTE: The whipped cream version of this cake is a popular specialty at Confiserie Heini in Lucerne, Switzerland. Whip 2 cups heavy whipping cream with ¼ cup sugar and ¼ cup kirsch until the cream holds a firm peak. Use the whipped cream in place of the buttercream, and cover both the top and outsides of the cake with whipped cream. Press white chocolate shavings into the whipped cream.

RATHAUSTORTE
Town Hall Cake

~ ⚬ ~

THIS IS A SPECIALTY OF CONFISERIE SCHIESSER in Basel, Switzerland. The pastry shop is right next to the famous medieval town hall and the cake is decorated with an outline of the building silhouetted with confectioners' sugar. It's a slightly complicated cake, but the various elements can be prepared over several days.

ALMOND SPONGE LAYER

4 large eggs, separated

Pinch of salt

¾ cup sugar

¾ cup cake flour

1 cup (about 4 ounces) blanched almonds, finely ground

JAPONAIS

¾ cup (about 3 ounces) whole unblanched almonds

1 cup confectioners' sugar

4 large egg whites

½ cup sugar

RUM SYRUP

⅓ cup sugar

¼ cup water

¼ cup dark rum

HAZELNUT-RUM BUTTERCREAM

4 large egg yolks

⅓ cup dark rum

½ cup sugar

¾ pound (3 sticks) unsalted butter

1 cup (about 4 ounces) skinned toasted hazelnuts or ½ cup praline paste (see Sources)

3 tablespoons water

CHOCOLATE GLAZE

½ cup heavy whipping cream

4 ounces bittersweet chocolate, cut into ¼-inch pieces

FOR FINISHING

½ cup chopped toasted hazelnuts

Confectioners' sugar

One 2-inch-deep 9-inch round cake pan, buttered and bottom lined with parchment or wax paper; two cookie sheets or jelly-roll pans, lined with parchment paper–trace a 9-inch circle on each sheet, then turn it over

1 Position the racks to divide the oven into thirds and preheat to 350 degrees.

2 To make the sponge layer, whisk the yolks with 6 tablespoons of the sugar until light and thickened.

3 In the bowl of a heavy-duty mixer, whip the egg whites and salt with the whisk attachment on medium speed until very white and increased in volume. Increase the speed to medium-high and add the remaining 6 tablespoons sugar in a stream. Continue to beat until the whites hold a firm peak. Fold in the yolks, then fold in the flour and ground nuts.

4 Pour the batter into prepared cake pan and bake for about 25 minutes. Remove the cake from the oven and lower the oven temperature to 325 degrees. Immediately unmold the cake layer onto a rack, leave paper on, then invert it onto another rack to cool.

5 To make the Japonais, combine the almonds and confectioners' sugar in the bowl of a food processor and process until the nuts are finely ground.

6 In the bowl of a heavy-duty mixer, whip the egg whites with the whisk attachment on medium speed until white and opaque. Increase the speed to medium-high and beat in the sugar in a stream. Continue to

beat until the whites hold a firm peak. Use a rubber spatula to fold in the almond mixture.

7 Spread the meringue Japonais thinly in layers to make two thin 9½-inch disks on the paper-lined pans. Bake for about 30 minutes.

8 To make the syrup, bring the sugar and water to a boil. Cool, then add the rum.

9 To make the buttercream, whisk the yolks in the bowl of an electric mixer, then whisk in the rum and sugar. Place the bowl over a pan of simmering water and whisk continuously until the mixture thickens. Attach the bowl to the mixer and whip with the whisk attachment on medium speed until cooled. Switch to the paddle attachment and gradually beat in the butter. Continue beating until the buttercream is smooth.

10 Place the hazelnuts in the food processor with the water and process until very smooth. Beat into the buttercream. (If you use praline paste, omit the water.)

11 To assemble, trim the crust from the top of the almond sponge. Using a 9-inch cardboard cake round as a guide, trim the Japonais layers to even 9-inch circles. Place a dab of the buttercream on the cardboard and place one of the Japonais layers on it. Spread it with one-quarter of the buttercream. Slice

the almond cake into two layers and place one over the buttercream. Moisten it with half of the syrup and spread with another quarter of the frosting. Place the other almond layer on top and moisten with the rest of the syrup. Spread the layer with another quarter of the buttercream and place the second Japonais layer over it. Spread the remaining buttercream over the top and sides of the cake. Chill the cake while you prepare the glaze.

12 Bring the cream to a simmer in a small saucepan over low heat. Remove from the heat and add the chocolate. Let stand for 2 minutes, then whisk until smooth. Pour into a small bowl and allow to cool to room temperature.

13 When the glaze has cooled, remove the cake from the refrigerator and pour the glaze onto the center of the top. Use an offset spatula to spread the glaze to the edges—if some drips down the sides, just smooth it away with the spatula. Press the chopped hazelnuts into the buttercream on the sides of the cake.

14 Just before serving dust the top edges of the cake with confectioners' sugar.

SERVING: Cut this rich cake into small portions with a very sharp serrated knife.

STORAGE: Wrap and refrigerate. Bring to room temperature before serving.

MAKES ONE 9-INCH CAKE,
ABOUT 12 SERVINGS

IF ASKED FOR THEIR FAVORITE CAKE, most people will come up with something replete with pecans or coconut, perhaps remembered from childhood, perhaps from a great bakery or restaurant. Such memories are testimony to the richness and flavor nuts impart.

Before you begin to prepare any of these recipes, review the instructions for toasting, blanching, and grinding nuts on pages xviii to xx—the cakes will turn out much better if you do.

NUT CAKE LAYER

THIS EASY RECIPE makes a moist and flavorful layer, which can be served as is with a sprinkling of confectioners' sugar, or used for some of the more elaborate cakes in Chapter 9.

1 Position a rack in the middle of the oven and preheat to 350 degrees.

2 Pulse the nuts repeatedly in a food processor to finely grind them; make sure they do not become pasty. Transfer the nuts to a bowl and stir with a small whisk to aerate. Sift the flour over the nuts, but do not mix them together.

3 In the bowl of a heavy-duty mixer fitted with the whisk, whip the yolks with 6 tablespoons of the sugar on medium speed until light, about 3 to 4 minutes.

4 In a clean, dry mixer bowl, beat the egg whites and salt with the whisk on medium speed until the whites hold a very soft peak. Increase the speed to high and beat in the remaining 6 tablespoons sugar in a stream.

1 cup (about 4 ounces) whole
    unblanched almonds, pistachios,
    or skinned hazelnuts or 1¼ cups
    (about 4 ounces) walnut or
    pecan pieces
¾ cup cake flour
4 large eggs, separated
¾ cup sugar
Pinch of salt

One 2-inch-deep 9- or 10-inch round
cake pan, buttered and bottom lined
with buttered parchment or wax paper

Continue to beat until the whites hold a soft peak.

5 Using a rubber spatula, fold in the yolks, then fold in the ground nuts and cake flour.

6 Scrape the batter into the prepared pan and smooth the top with a metal spatula. Bake the cake for about 30 minutes, until well colored and firm.

7 Unmold the cake onto a rack, then invert onto another rack to cool right side up. Remove the paper when the cake is cool.

SERVING: Serve this cake as a tea cake, or use it in layer cakes.

STORING: Wrap in plastic and keep at room temperature for up to a week, or double-wrap and freeze for longer storage.

MAKES ONE 9- OR 10-INCH CAKE

VARIATION

CHOCOLATE NUT CAKE: Substitute ½ cup cake flour and 3 tablespoons alkalized (Dutch-process) cocoa powder, sifted together, for the ¾ cup cake flour.

BROWN BUTTER–HAZELNUT FINANCIER

❧ ❧

THIS TRADITIONAL FRENCH DESSERT probably got the name *financier* because of its richness. It is made with an unusual batter in which ground hazelnuts, sugar, and flour and a large quantity of melted butter are folded into egg whites that have been beaten with sugar. The egg whites fall and liquefy as the butter is folded in, but the cake rises well nonetheless.

1 Position a rack in the middle of the oven and preheat to 350 degrees.

2 Pulse the hazelnuts and ¾ cup of the sugar in a food processor until the nuts are finely ground. Pour into a bowl and stir in the flour.

3 Melt the butter over low heat and continue to cook for a minute or so, until it turns a light golden color. Remove from the heat and let cool, then add the rum and vanilla.

4 In the clean, dry bowl of a heavy-duty mixer fitted with the whisk, beat the egg whites with the salt until they form a very soft peak. Beat in the remaining ¾ cup sugar in a very slow stream, and continue beating until the egg whites hold a soft peak again.

5 Beginning with the hazelnut mixture, alternately fold in the hazelnut and butter mixtures, one-third at a time. Pour the batter into the prepared pan and smooth the top.

1 cup (about 4 ounces) blanched whole hazelnuts, lightly toasted and skinned

1½ cups sugar

1 cup all-purpose flour (spoon flour into dry-measure cup and level off)

10 tablespoons (1¼ sticks) unsalted butter

2 tablespoons dark rum

2 teaspoons vanilla extract

1 cup egg whites (from 7 or 8 large eggs)

Pinch of salt

Confectioners' sugar for finishing

One 2-inch-deep 10-inch round cake pan, buttered and bottom lined with buttered parchment or wax paper

6 Bake for about 50 minutes, until the cake is well risen and golden. The center should feel firm when pressed with the palm of your hand.

7 Cool the financier briefly on a rack, then unmold and remove the paper. Turn the cake right side up to finish cooling.

8 Just before serving, dust very lightly with confectioners' sugar.

MAKES ONE 10-INCH CAKE, ABOUT 12 SERVINGS

BALOIS

Almond Cake from Basel

❧ ❦

THIS RICH, MOIST ALMOND CAKE is a specialty of Confiserie Schiesser in Basel, Switzerland. I've organized the ingredients list a little differently from the usual form, because I think having each step in the assembly process identified simplifies the preparation. It makes the recipe look more complicated than it is—basically this is just a very rich almond sponge cake.

½ cup (about 2 ounces) sliced blanched almonds

ALMOND PASTE

2 cups (about 8 ounces) sliced blanched almonds

1 cup sugar

2 tablespoons light corn syrup

1 teaspoon vanilla extract

2 large egg whites

EGGS AND YOLKS

3 large eggs

3 large yolks

EGG WHITES

⅓ cup egg whites (from 2 or 3 large eggs)

¼ cup sugar

FLOUR AND BUTTER

1 cup all-purpose flour (spoon flour into dry-measure cup and level off)

8 tablespoons (1 stick) unsalted butter, melted and still hot

Confectioners' sugar for finishing

One 12-cup Bundt or tube pan, generously buttered

1 Set a rack in the lower third of the oven and preheat to 350 degrees. Coat the buttered pan with the ½ cup blanched sliced almonds.

2 To make the almond paste, pulse the almonds and sugar in a food processor until

the nuts are finely ground, then let the machine run until the mixture starts to become somewhat pasty. Add the corn syrup and vanilla and process for 1 minute. Then add the egg whites and let process for another minute. Scrape the almond mixture into a medium bowl.

3 In the bowl of a heavy-duty mixer fitted with the whisk attachment, beat the eggs and yolks on medium speed until very aerated, about 5 minutes. One-third at a time, fold the egg mixture into the almond mixture.

4 In a clean, dry mixer bowl, whip the egg whites with the clean, dry whisk attachment on medium speed until they are very white and opaque and just beginning to hold a shape. Increase the speed to medium-high and add the sugar in a stream. Continue to whip until the whites hold a soft peak.

5 Fold one-third of the egg whites into the batter. Fold in all the flour, then another third of the egg whites. Fold in the butter and, finally, the remaining egg whites.

6 Pour the batter into the prepared pan and bake for about 45 to 50 minutes, or until the cake is well risen and colored and a toothpick inserted midway between the side of the pan and the central tube emerges dry.

7 Cool the cake in the pan on a rack for 5 minutes, then unmold onto a rack to cool.

SERVING: Serve with fruit or a fruit sauce.

STORAGE: Keep wrapped in plastic at room temperature, or double-wrap and freeze for longer storage.

MAKES ONE 10-INCH BUNDT OR TUBE CAKE

FARINA GARGANTAG
Almond and Farina Cake

೧ ೧

THIS RECIPE IS FROM one of my oldest and dearest friends, Sandy Leonard. He recently moved into an Armenian neighborhood and has learned to prepare many wonderful ethnic dishes, among them this excellent cake.

1 Position a rack in the middle of the oven and preheat to 350 degrees.

2 In the bowl of an electric mixer fitted with the whisk, beat the eggs and sugar at medium speed until light. Beat in the melted butter, nuts, lemon zest, vanilla, and cinnamon until smooth. Stir in the farina (or Cream of Wheat) and baking powder.

3 Pour the batter into the prepared pan. Bake for 45 minutes, or until the cake is firm to the touch and a toothpick inserted in the center comes out clean. Transfer to a rack to cool in the pan.

4 To make the syrup, bring the sugar, water, and lemon juice to a boil in a small pan over medium heat. Continue to boil for 5 minutes without stirring, then remove from the heat and let cool to lukewarm.

5 To finish, cut the cooled cake into diamonds or rectangles in the pan, and pour the warm syrup over it. Top each piece with an almond.

CAKE BATTER

5 large eggs

1 cup sugar

½ pound (2 sticks) unsalted butter, melted

1 cup (about 4 ounces) coarsely chopped blanched or unblanched almonds

Grated zest of 1 lemon

1 teaspoon vanilla extract

½ teaspoon ground cinnamon

2 cups farina or Cream of Wheat

1 tablespoon baking powder

LEMON SYRUP

2 cups sugar

1 cup water

1 tablespoon fresh lemon juice

24 blanched whole almonds for finishing

One 9 × 13-inch baking pan, bottom lined with parchment or wax paper

VARIATIONS

This cake can also be baked in a 10-inch round cake pan. Cut it into 24 slim slices, with an almond on each.

Some recipes use semolina instead of farina. Some add ½ teaspoon rose water to the syrup after it has cooled to lukewarm.

NOTE: Grate the zest of the lemon before squeezing the juice—it is much easier than trying to do it the other way around.

CAPRICCIO ALLE NOCCIOLE

Hazelnut Cake from Ticino

༄ ༅

THE RECIPE FOR THIS buttery Swiss hazelnut cake was given to me by Paolo Loraschi, executive pastry chef for the Al Porto pastry shops in Lugano, Locarno, and Ascona.

1 Position a rack in the lower third of the oven and preheat to 350 degrees. Coat the buttered pan with ground unblanched hazelnuts.

2 In the bowl of a heavy-duty mixer fitted with the paddle attachment, beat the butter and 6 tablespoons of the sugar on medium speed for about 5 minutes, or until soft and light. One at a time, beat in the egg yolks, beating until smooth after each addition.

3 Stir the flour, baking powder, ground hazelnuts, and chocolate together. Add half the mixture to the egg yolk mixture and mix on low speed until just incorporated. Beat in the milk, then beat in the rest of the flour mixture.

4 Stir the batter with a large rubber spatula to give it a final mix.

5 In a clean, dry mixer bowl, whip the egg whites with the whisk attachment on medium speed until very white and opaque

½ cup ground unblanched hazelnuts
    for the pan
16 tablespoons (2 sticks) unsalted
    butter, softened
1 cup sugar
3 large eggs, separated
2 cups all-purpose flour (spoon flour
    into dry-measure cup and level off)
2 teaspoons baking powder
1 cup (4 ounces) ground unblanched
    hazelnuts
3 ounces bittersweet chocolate,
    coarsely grated
1 cup milk

One 12-cup Bundt or tube pan,
buttered

and just beginning to hold a shape. Increase the speed to medium-high, and add the remaining 6 tablespoons sugar in a stream. Continue to whip until the egg whites hold a soft peak.

6 Stir one-third of the egg whites into the batter to lighten it, then fold in the remaining whites.

7 Pour the batter into the prepared pan. Bake for about 50 to 60 minutes, or until the cake is well risen and colored and a toothpick inserted midway between the side of the pan and the central tube emerges dry.

8 Cool the cake in the pan on a rack for 5 minutes, then unmold onto the rack to cool.

SERVING: Serve with sweetened whipped cream.

STORAGE: Keep wrapped in plastic at room temperature, or double-wrap and freeze for longer storage.

MAKES ONE 10-INCH BUNDT OR TUBE CAKE, ABOUT 12 SERVINGS

BRAUNE LINZERTORTE

Dark Linzertorte

~᠀᠀~

THIS TRADITIONAL VIENNESE SWEET has a texture more like cake than pastry. It's a perfect make-ahead dessert because it freezes and defrosts perfectly.

1 Position a rack in the middle of the oven and preheat to 350 degrees.

2 To make the dough, mix all the dry ingredients together in a bowl. Rub in the butter until the mixture looks like fine sand. Beat the egg and yolk together and use a fork to stir them into the dough, stirring only until the dough is smooth. It will be very soft.

3 Spread half the dough over the bottom of the springform pan. Cover the dough with the raspberry preserves, leaving a 1-inch border of pastry all around. Using a pastry bag fitted with a ⅜-inch plain tube (Ateco 804), pipe a diagonal lattice of dough over the preserves, then pipe a border of large dots around the outer rim. Gently paint the lattice and border with the beaten egg white and strew with the sliced almonds.

DOUGH

1½ cups all-purpose flour (spoon flour into dry-measure cup and level off)

1 cup (about 5 ounces) ground hazelnuts

¾ cup sugar

1 teaspoon ground cinnamon

¼ teaspoon ground cloves

1 teaspoon baking powder

12 tablespoons (1½ sticks) butter

1 large egg

1 large egg yolk

FOR FINISHING

⅔ cup raspberry preserves

1 large egg white, lightly beaten

¼ cup (about 1 ounce) sliced blanched almonds

Confectioners' sugar

One 9-inch springform pan, buttered

4 Bake the torte for about 40 minutes. Cool in the pan on a rack.

5 Remove the sides of the pan and loosen the bottom of the torte with the point of a small knife. Slide the torte onto a platter and dust with confectioners' sugar.

SERVING: This is good as either a dessert or a tea cake.

STORAGE: Store loosely covered at room temperature for up to 2 days, or wrap tightly and freeze.

MAKES ONE 9-INCH CAKE, ABOUT 12 SERVINGS

(see photograph, pages 156–157)

VARIATION

WEISSE LINZERTORTE (LIGHT LINZERTORTE): Substitute ground blanched almonds for the hazelnuts. Omit the cinnamon and add the grated zest of 1 lemon and 1 teaspoon vanilla to the egg and yolk before stirring them into the dough.

TORTA DI NOCCIOLE ALLA VERONESE

Hazelnut Cake from Verona

~ ෙ ෙ ~

THIS RICH AND VIRTUALLY FLOURLESS CAKE is popular in the hazelnut-growing areas outside Verona. Although the original does not demand it, the torta would be wonderful with a little lightly whipped unsweetened cream.

1   Set a rack in the middle of the oven and preheat to 350 degrees.

2   Put the hazelnuts in a food processor and pulse until finely ground but not oily. Transfer them to a bowl and pour the bread crumbs over them, but don't mix them together.

3   With a heavy-duty mixer fitted with the whip, beat the yolks. Beat in the Marsala, then beat in ⅓ cup of the sugar. Continue beating until the mixture is very light.

4   In a clean, dry bowl (and clean beaters), or in a heavy-duty mixer fitted with the clean, dry whip, beat the egg whites with the salt. Continue beating until the whites hold a very soft peak. Increase the speed to medium-high and beat in the remaining ⅓ cup sugar in a slow stream. Continue to beat until the egg whites hold a soft, shiny peak.

2 cups (about 10 ounces) unblanched hazelnuts

½ cup fine dry bread crumbs

4 large eggs, separated

3 tablespoons sweet Marsala or dark rum

⅔ cup sugar

Pinch of salt

8 tablespoons (1 stick) unsalted butter, melted

Confectioners' sugar for finishing

One 2-inch-deep 10-inch round cake pan, buttered and bottom lined with parchment

5   Fold in the yolk mixture, then fold in the hazelnut and bread crumb mixture just until it is half incorporated. Pour the melted butter down the side of the bowl and continue to fold until the batter is smooth,

making sure that the tip of the spatula reaches the bottom of the bowl on every pass through the batter so that none of the ingredients will remain unmixed at the bottom of the bowl. Be careful not to overmix, or the batter will deflate.

6 Pour the batter into the prepared pan. Bake for about 30 minutes, or until the top is well colored and the center is firm when pressed with a fingertip.

7 Cool the torta in the pan for a minute, then loosen it from the sides of the pan with the point of a small paring knife and invert onto a rack. Invert again onto another rack so the cake cools right side up on the paper.

8 Just before serving, lightly dust the torta with confectioners' sugar.

STORAGE: Keep tightly covered with plastic at room temperature, or refrigerate; bring to room temperature before serving.

MAKES ONE 10-INCH CAKE,
ABOUT 12 SERVINGS

ALTHOUGH THERE ARE CHOCOLATE CAKES throughout this book, the ones here are so specifically and unabashedly chocolate with a capital C they need a section of their own.

Many of these recipes call for melted chocolate. There are two ways to melt chocolate. For either method, begin by cutting the chocolate into ¼-inch pieces.

- Place the chocolate in a heatproof bowl. Bring a small pan of water to a boil, then take it off the heat. Set the bowl of chocolate over the pan of water and stir occasionally until the chocolate melts.

- Or, place the cut-up chocolate in a microwave-safe bowl. Microwave the chocolate for 20 seconds at a time, removing it and stirring between blasts.

Using either method, up to a pound of chocolate will melt in 3 to 4 minutes.

PERFECT CHOCOLATE CAKE

THIS ELEGANT AND EASY CAKE is adapted from a recipe in *Sweet Times* (Morrow, 1991), the first book of many by my friend baker and writer Dorie Greenspan, prizewinning author of *Baking with Julia* (Morrow, 1996).

1 Position a rack in the middle of the oven and preheat to 350 degrees.

2 In a bowl, stir together the flour, cocoa, baking powder, and baking soda. Sift the ingredients onto a piece of parchment or wax paper and set aside.

3 In a large bowl with an electric mixer, beat the butter and sugar together at medium speed. Beat in the eggs one at a time, beating until smooth after each addition. Reduce the mixer speed to low and beat in half the dry ingredients. Scrape down the bowl and beater well. Beat in the sour cream, scrape again, and then beat in the remainder of the dry ingredients.

4 Scrape the batter into the prepared pan. Bake for 40 to 45 minutes, or until well risen and a toothpick inserted into the center of the cake emerges clean.

5 Cool the cake in the pan on a rack for 5 minutes, then invert onto a rack and remove the paper. Invert the cake onto a rack again to finish cooling right side up.

1½ cups all-purpose flour (spoon flour into dry-measure cup and level off)

½ cup alkalized (Dutch-process) cocoa powder

1 teaspoon baking powder

¼ teaspoon baking soda

½ pound (2 sticks) unsalted butter, softened

1⅓ cups sugar

2 large eggs, at room temperature

One 8-ounce container sour cream

Confectioners' sugar for finishing

One 9 × 13 × 2-inch baking pan, buttered and bottom lined with parchment or buttered parchment

6 Just before serving, sift a light dusting of confectioners' sugar over the cake.

SERVING: Cut the cake into 3-inch squares.

STORAGE: Store covered at cool room temperature.

MAKES ONE 9 × 13-INCH CAKE, ABOUT 12 SERVINGS

MILK CHOCOLATE MOUSSE CAKE

THIS RICH CAKE is easy to whip up at the last minute.

1 Position a rack in the middle of the oven and preheat to 325 degrees.

2 In a medium saucepan, bring the water and sugar to a simmer over medium heat, stirring occasionally to dissolve the sugar. Add the butter and cook, stirring occasionally, until the butter is melted. Remove the pan from the heat, add the chocolate, and swirl the pan until chocolate is entirely submerged. Let stand for 2 minutes to melt the chocolate.

3 Meanwhile, in a large mixing bowl, whisk the eggs with the rum and orange zest.

4 Whisk the chocolate mixture until smooth, then whisk it into the egg mixture.

5 Pour the batter into the prepared pan and place the cake pan into the larger one. Pour about 1 inch warm water into that larger pan. Bake for about 1 hour, or until the cake is well risen and firm in the center.

6 Remove the pans from the oven and carefully, using a wide spatula, lift the cake pan out of the larger pan. Cool the cake in the pan on a rack, then wrap the cake, in the pan, and refrigerate.

¾ cup water

¼ cup sugar

8 tablespoons (1 stick) unsalted butter, cut into 8 pieces

18 ounces milk chocolate, cut into ¼-inch pieces

7 large eggs

2 tablespoons dark rum or other liqueur

1 tablespoon grated orange zest

Thinned cream and raspberries for finishing

One 2-inch-deep 8-inch round cake pan, buttered and bottom lined with buttered parchment or wax paper; a larger baking pan or roasting pan to hold the cake pan

7 To unmold the cake, set the pan over low heat for a few seconds to melt the butter between the pan and paper lining. Run a small sharp paring knife around the sides of the pan to loosen the cake. Invert the cake onto a platter and pull off the paper if stuck to cake.

8 Sprinkle the cake lightly with chocolate shavings.

Serving: Cut into thin wedges to serve.

Storage: Store loosely covered at cool room temperature for up to 6 hours; wrap and refrigerate leftovers. For longer storage, leave the cake in the pan, wrap, and refrigerate for up to 1 week or freeze for up to 1 month.

Makes one 8-inch cake, about 12 servings

CHOCOLATE MOUSSE CAKE WITH CINNAMON CREAM

You can substitute a sweet fruit liqueur or even orange juice for the coffee in this recipe.

1 Place a rack in the middle of the oven and preheat to 325 degrees.

2 Bring the water and sugar to a simmer in a medium saucepan over medium heat, stirring occasionally to dissolve the sugar. Stir in the butter and stir occasionally until the butter is melted. Off the heat, add the chocolate and swirl the pan so the chocolate is submerged in the hot liquid. Let stand for 3 minutes.

3 Meanwhile, in a large mixing bowl, whisk the eggs with the coffee, rum, if using, and cinnamon.

4 Whisk the chocolate mixture until smooth, then whisk into egg mixture.

5 Scrape the batter into the prepared pan and place the pan in the larger pan. Pour warm water to come to a depth of 1 inch into the larger pan. Bake for about 45 minutes, until the cake is risen and slightly firm. Remove the pans from the oven, then carefully lift the cake pan onto a rack to cool.

CAKE BATTER

⅓ cup water

⅓ cup sugar

8 tablespoons (1 stick) unsalted butter cut into 12 pieces

12 ounces semisweet or bittersweet chocolate, cut into ¼-inch pieces

6 large eggs

⅓ cup strong brewed coffee

2 tablespoons dark rum, optional

½ teaspoon ground cinnamon

CINNAMON CREAM

1 cup heavy whipping cream

2 tablespoons sugar

1 teaspoon ground cinnamon

One 2-inch-deep 8-inch round cake pan, buttered and bottom lined with parchment or foil; a larger baking pan or roasting pan to hold the cake pan

6 To unmold the cake, run a knife around the sides of the pan, then set the pan on a burner for a few seconds over low heat. Invert onto a serving platter and peel off the paper.

7 To make the cinnamon cream, whip the cream with sugar and cinnamon. Spread the cream over the top of the cake or serve a spoonful next to each slice of cake. (If you are spreading the cake with the cream, don't do so until just before serving.)

SERVING: Cut into thin wedges to serve.

STORAGE: Store at room temperature for up to 6 hours; wrap and refrigerate leftovers. For longer storage, wrap the cake in the pan and refrigerate for up to 1 week or freeze for up to 1 month.

MAKES ONE 8-INCH CAKE,
ABOUT 12 SERVINGS

CHOCOLATE PECAN CARAMEL CAKE

THIS IS A GREAT MAKE-AHEAD CAKE for the holiday season. The smooth chocolate of the cake contrasts beautifully with the crunchy pecan caramel topping.

1   Position a rack in the lower third of the oven and preheat to 325 degrees.

2   Stir together the sugar and ¼ cup water in a small saucepan to mix, then bring to a boil over medium heat and cook, without stirring, until the sugar has melted and turned a deep amber. While the sugar is cooking, bring the remaining ¾ cup water to a simmer.

3   Use the water to dilute the caramel to a syrup, adding it a little at a time; make sure to avert your face and to wrap a towel around the hand holding the water pan so you won't be burned by any splattering boiling syrup. Bring the syrup to a good boil to make sure all the caramel is dissolved, and remove from heat. Add the butter and both chocolates and let stand for 2 minutes to melt. Whisk until smooth, then whisk in the eggs two at a time.

4   Pour the batter into the prepared pan, put it into the larger pan, and pour about an inch of hot water into that pan. Bake for about 45 minutes, or until the cake is firm to the touch. Cool on a rack, then refrigerate.

CAKE BATTER

¾ cup sugar

1 cup water

6 tablespoons (¾ stick) unsalted butter
    cut into 6 pieces

8 ounces milk chocolate, cut into
    ¼-inch pieces

6 ounces bittersweet chocolate,
    cut into ¼-inch pieces

8 large eggs

PECAN CARAMEL

1 cup (about 4 ounces) pecan pieces,
    toasted

½ cup sugar

½ teaspoon fresh lemon juice

WHIPPED CREAM

¾ cup heavy whipping cream

1 tablespoon sugar

One 9-inch round cake pan, buttered and bottom lined with buttered parchment; a larger baking pan or roasting pan to hold the cake pan; a jelly-roll pan, buttered for the caramelized pecans

5 To make the pecan caramel, stir the sugar and lemon juice together in a small heavy pan to mix, refrigerate until chilled, place over medium heat, and cook, stirring occasionally, until the mixture becomes a deep amber caramel. Stir in the pecans, then pour out onto the buttered pan to cool and harden.

6 When the pecan caramel is cool, finely chop or grind it.

7 To finish the cake, whip the cream with the sugar. Pipe or spread it over the cake. Just before serving, sprinkle the cake with the chopped pecan caramel.

SERVING: Cut into thin wedges to serve.

STORAGE: Store at cool room temperature for up to 6 hours, or, for longer storage, wrap well and freeze up to 1 month.

MAKES ONE 9-INCH CAKE,
ABOUT 10 SERVINGS

CHOCOLATE EMINENCE

Milk Chocolate–Filled Cake with Crunchy Caramelized Hazelnuts

∼⁊ ⁊∼

THIS IS A GREAT COMBINATION of flavors and textures. The slightly bitter, crunchy caramelized hazelnuts contrast perfectly with the smooth, rich milk chocolate filling.

1 Position a rack in the middle of the oven and preheat to 350 degrees.

2 Combine the chocolate and water in a heatproof bowl, place the bowl over a pan of hot, but not simmering, water, and stir occasionally until the chocolate is melted and the mixture is smooth. Remove from the heat.

3 In the bowl of a heavy-duty mixer fitted with the whip, beat the yolks with ¼ cup of the sugar until very light.

4 In a clean, dry mixer bowl, with the clean, dry whip, beat the egg whites with the salt until they begin to hold a very soft peak. Raise the speed to medium-high and beat in the remaining ¼ cup sugar in a slow stream.

5 Mix the chocolate mixture into the yolk mixture, then fold in the egg whites.

6 Pour the batter into the prepared pan and smooth the top. Bake for about 15 to 20 minutes, until the top is firm to the touch. Remove the pan from the oven and loosen the sides of the cake with a small sharp knife. Use the paper to help you slide the layer onto a work surface to cool.

CAKE BATTER

6 ounces bittersweet chocolate, cut into ¼-inch pieces

3 tablespoons water

5 large eggs, separated

½ cup sugar

Pinch of salt

MILK CHOCOLATE GANACHE

1½ cups heavy cream

4 tablespoons (½ stick) unsalted butter

12 ounces milk chocolate, cut into ¼-inch pieces

HAZELNUT PRALINE

½ cup sugar

½ teaspoon fresh lemon juice

½ cup (about 3 ounces) skinned toasted hazelnuts

Cocoa powder for finishing

One 12 × 18-inch jelly-roll pan, buttered and lined with buttered parchment paper; another jelly-roll pan, buttered, for the praline

7   To make the ganache, bring the cream and butter to a boil. Remove from the heat and add the chocolate. Let chocolate melt, then stir. Whisk until smooth, and refrigerate until thickened, about 1 hour.

8   Meanwhile, prepare the praline. In a medium saucepan, stir the sugar and lemon juice together to mix well. Place over low heat and stir occasionally until sugar is melted and caramelized. Stir in the hazelnuts and scrape the mixture out onto the buttered pan. Allow to cool and harden.

9   Break up the praline and grind to a coarse powder in the food processor.

10   To assemble the cake, using a cake pan as a guide, cut two 9-inch disks out of the cake layer. Dice the scraps and reserve them.

11   In the bowl of a heavy-duty mixer fitted with the whip attachment, whip the ganache to lighten it. Place one cake layer on a cardboard round and spread with one-third of the ganache. Sprinkle with half the praline, and all of the diced cake scraps. Spread another third of the ganache over the cake scraps and top with the other layer. Cover the top and sides of the cake with the rest of the ganache. Press the remaining praline into the sides of the cake.

12   Just before serving, dust the top of the cake with cocoa powder and mark a lattice pattern in the cocoa with a serrated knife.

SERVING: Serve at cool room temperature.

STORAGE: Cover cake lightly and refrigerate for up to two days. Bring to room temperature before serving.

MAKES ONE 9-INCH CAKE, ABOUT 12 SERVINGS

TUNNEL OF FUDGE CAKE

～⌣～

THIS IS THE RECIPE with which Ella Rita Helfrich of Houston, Texas, won the 1966 Pillsbury Bake-Off. It's still a winner. While baking, the cake develops a creamy, fudgy core, like a tunnel, hence the name.

1 Position a rack in the middle of the oven and preheat to 350 degrees.

2 In a large bowl, with an electric mixer, beat the sugar and butter together on medium speed until light and fluffy. Add the eggs one at a time, beating well after each addition. Gradually beat in the confectioners' sugar. Stir in the flour, cocoa, and nuts until well blended.

3 Spoon the batter into the prepared pan and smooth the top. Bake for 45 to 50 minutes, or until the top is set and the edges are beginning to pull away from the sides of the pan (this cake has a soft center, so the ordinary doneness test of inserting a toothpick does not work).

4 Cool the cake (upright) in the pan on a wire rack for 1½ hours, then invert onto a serving plate and let cool for at least 2 hours.

CAKE BATTER

1¾ cups sugar

28 tablespoons (3½ sticks) unsalted butter, softened

6 large eggs

2 cups confectioners' sugar

2¼ cups all-purpose flour (spoon flour into dry-measure cup and level off)

¾ cup alkalized (Dutch-process) cocoa powder

2 cups (about 8 ounces) chopped walnuts

CHOCOLATE GLAZE

¾ cup confectioners' sugar

¼ cup alkalized (Dutch-process) cocoa powder

6 to 8 teaspoons milk

One 10-inch Bundt or tube pan, buttered

5   To make the glaze, in a small bowl, stir together all the ingredients, adding enough milk to achieve a drizzling consistency. Spoon over top of the cake, allowing some to run down the sides.

SERVING: This is really a dessert cake—it's great with some whipped cream.

STORAGE: Store under a cake dome at room temperature; press plastic wrap against the cut surfaces of the cake to prevent excessive ooze.

MAKES ONE 10-INCH BUNDT OR TUBE CAKE, ABOUT 16 SERVINGS

THESE CLASSIC "GOOEY" CAKES, rich with filling and frosting surrounding moist, flavorful cake layers, are among the most popular of all baked sweets.

To ensure success with layer cakes, keep in mind the following points.

1   Use a long very sharp serrated knife to trim or cut through layers. This is a case of the right tool making all the difference between success and failure.

2   After cutting through or trimming cake layer(s), brush the work surface free of crumbs, which otherwise have a way of getting mixed into the frosting when you put your spatula down.

3   Use an offset spatula to spread on fillings and frostings. The side of the blade is best for making flat, even layers of filling.

4   Don't fuss endlessly over the outside of the cake—if it isn't perfect, you can always use some chocolate shavings or chopped nuts to mask any flaws.

LEMON MERINGUE CAKE

LEMON AND MERINGUE is one of the best dessert combinations, but this can also be varied with lime or tangerine.

1   To make the lemon curd, finely grate the zest from 2 of the lemons. Squeeze and strain the juice from all 3 lemons; there should be about ¾ cup. Combine the zest, juice, sugar, and butter in a saucepan and bring to a boil over medium heat. Strain out the zest and return to a boil.

2   Meanwhile, beat the yolks in a bowl until they are liquid.

3   Beat ¼ of the boiling liquid into the yolks, and return the remaining liquid to a boil.

LEMON CURD

3 large lemons

¾ cup sugar

8 tablespoons (1 stick) unsalted butter

8 large egg yolks

Two 9-inch layers Classic White Cake,
    page 207

MERINGUE

¾ cup egg whites (from about
    6 to 7 large eggs)

1 cup sugar

Beat the yolk mixture into the boiling liquid and continue beating over medium heat until it thickens slightly. Do not allow the lemon curd to boil, or it will scramble. Pour the lemon curd into a clean bowl, press plastic wrap against the surface, and chill it.

4   To assemble, slice each layer horizontally in half, making a total of 4 layers. Stack the layers, spreading one-third of the lemon curd between each layer.

5   Preheat the oven to 400°F.

6   To make the meringue, combine the egg whites and sugar in the bowl of an electric mixer. Place the bowl over a pan of simmering water and whisk gently until the egg whites are hot and the sugar is dissolved. Attach the bowl to the mixer and whip with the whip attachment until the meringue has increased in volume and is cool.

7   Spread the meringue over the top and outsides of the cake, reserving about ¼–½ cup for finishing. Using a pastry bag fitted with a star tube (such as Ateco 824), pipe a decorative design on the top.

8   Place the cake on a cookie sheet and bake for a few minutes to color the meringue.

SERVING: Serve the same day you color the meringue.

STORAGE: Keep at cool room temperature until serving time. Refrigerate leftovers.

MAKES ONE 9-INCH CAKE, ABOUT 12 SERVINGS

RASPBERRY CREAM CAKE

༺∽୨ ୧∽༻

THIS CAKE IS A SORT OF RASPBERRY VERSION of the famous Black Forest cherry cake.

1 To make the whipped cream, combine the cream, sugar, and vanilla in a large bowl and whip until soft peaks form.

2 To assemble, place one of the cake layers on a cardboard cake round and spread with a thin layer of whipped cream. Cover with most of the raspberries, reserving a few for garnish, then cover the berries with more cream. Add the second layer and cover the top and sides of the cake with the remaining whipped cream. Press chocolate shavings into the sides of the cake and decorate the top with the reserved raspberries.

3 Just before serving, dust the cake lightly with confectioners' sugar.

SERVING: This cake is best served as soon as it is assembled. It is delicious with additional fresh raspberries on the side.

WHIPPED CREAM
2 cups heavy whipping cream
¼ cup sugar
1 teaspoon vanilla extract

Two 9-inch layers 1942 Devil's Food Cake, page 212

Two ½-pint baskets raspberries

FOR FINISHING
Chocolate shavings
Confectioners' sugar

STORAGE: Store in the refrigerator, covered, for up to 2 days.

MAKES ONE 9-INCH CAKE, ABOUT 12 SERVINGS

GATEAU DES ILES

~⚬⚬~

THIS "ISLAND CAKE" COMBINES the flavors of the Caribbean in a sweet, delicate tribute.

1   To make the syrup, bring the water and sugar to a boil in a small saucepan. Let cool, and stir in the rum.

2   To make the filling, combine the cream, coconut cream, and vanilla in a bowl and whip to form soft peaks.

3   To assemble the cake, split the génoise horizontally into 3 layers. Place the bottom layer on a cardboard cake round and moisten with some of the syrup. Spread with one-third of the whipped cream and top with half the pineapple. Repeat with the next layer, more syrup, another third of the cream, and most of the remaining pineapple. Top with the last layer and moisten with the remaining syrup.

4   Cover the top and sides of the cake with the remaining whipped cream and press the coconut into it. Decorate with the pineapple wedges.

NOTE: Coconut cream is a sweetened coconut product usually used for making drinks. The most common brand is Coco Lopez.

RUM SYRUP
⅓ cup water
⅓ cup sugar
⅓ cup white rum

COCONUT FILLING
2 cups heavy whipping cream
½ cup coconut cream (see Note)
1 teaspoon vanilla extract
1 cup chopped fresh pineapple

One 9-inch layer Plain Génoise, page 116

2 cups (about 3½ ounces) sweetened shredded coconut for finishing
6 or 8 pineapple wedges

SERVING: This cake is best served as soon as it is assembled.

STORAGE: Store loosely covered in the refrigerator for up to 2 days.

MAKES ONE 9-INCH CAKE, ABOUT 12 SERVINGS

CHOCOLATE-PISTACHIO-RASPBERRY CAKE

~⤳ ৩ ⤶~

THIS STRIKING AND UNUSUAL DESSERT combines three flavors that harmonize beautifully in both taste and appearance.

CAKE BATTER

1 cup (about 4 ounces) blanched
    pistachios

½ cup all-purpose flour (spoon flour
    into dry-measure cup and level off)

4 large eggs, separated

¾ cup sugar

Pinch of salt

GANACHE FILLING

8 ounces bittersweet chocolate, cut into
    ¼-inch pieces

2 ounces milk chocolate, cut into
    ¼-inch pieces

1 cup heavy whipping cream

FRAMBOISE SYRUP

⅓ cup water

⅓ cup sugar

⅓ cup framboise (raspberry eau-de-vie)

WHIPPED CREAM

1½ cups heavy whipping cream

2 tablespoons sugar

2 tablespoons framboise

FOR FINISHING

Two ½-pint baskets raspberries

Milk chocolate shavings

Blanched pistachios

One 2-inch-deep 10-inch round cake pan,
buttered and bottom lined with
parchment or wax paper

1 Position a rack in the middle of the oven and preheat to 350 degrees.

2 Grind the pistachios until fine in the food processor; make sure they don't become pasty. Combine with the flour.

3 In the bowl of a heavy-duty mixer fitted with the whisk, beat the egg yolks with 6 tablespoons of the sugar until light.

4 In a clean, dry mixer bowl, with the clean, dry whisk, beat the egg whites with the salt on medium speed until they become

white and opaque. Increase the speed to medium-high and beat in the remaining 6 tablespoons sugar. Continue to beat until the whites hold a firm peak. Fold in the yolks, then fold in the pistachio mixture.

5 Pour the batter into prepared pan and bake for about 30 minutes. Unmold the layer onto a rack, then invert onto another rack to cool.

6 To make the ganache, combine the chocolates in a bowl. Bring the cream to a boil and pour over the chocolate. Let stand for 2 minutes, then whisk until smooth. Refrigerate the ganache, whisking often, until cool but not set.

7 To make the syrup, combine the water and sugar in a small pan and bring to a boil. Let cool, and stir in the framboise.

8 To make the whipped cream, combine the cream, sugar, and framboise in a large bowl and whip until light but not firm.

9 To assemble the dessert, split the pistachio cake horizontally into 2 layers. Place one on a cardboard cake round. Moisten with half the syrup and spread with most of the ganache, reserving some for decoration. Distribute most of the raspberries over the ganache, again saving some for decorating. Cover with a layer of whipped cream. Place the second layer on the cream and moisten it with the remaining syrup. Cover the top and sides of the cake with the remaining whipped cream and press the chocolate shavings into the sides of the cake.

10 Pipe a border of rosettes around the top edge of the cake with the remaining ganache and decorate the rosettes with the reserved raspberries and some pistachios. Place some chopped pistachios in the center and dust them lightly with confectioners' sugar.

Serving: Serve chilled.

Storage: Store covered in the refrigerator for up to 2 days.

Makes one 10-inch cake, about 12 servings

STRAWBERRY MERINGUE CAKE

THIS IS AN IDEAL CAKE for June and July, when strawberries are at their peak. The fruit filling and the meringue are light, and because the recipe calls for neither whipped cream nor buttercream, there is nothing to melt in hot weather.

1 To make the filling, rinse, hull, and slice the berries. Place one-quarter of the berries in a saucepan with the sugar and bring to a boil.

2 Meanwhile, combine the lemon juice, kirsch, and cornstarch. Off the heat, stir the cornstarch mixture into the strawberry mixture. Return to a boil, stirring, and cook for 2 minutes. Remove from the heat and cool, then stir in the remaining sliced berries.

3 To make the syrup, combine the water and sugar in a small pan and bring to a boil; cool. Stir in the lemon juice and kirsch.

4 Use a sharp serrated knife to slice each of the génoise layers into 2 layers. Only 3 layers will be used to assemble the cake. Place one layer on a cardboard round or platter and brush with one-third of the syrup. Spread with half the filling. Top with the second layer and, brush with syrup, and spread with the remaining filling. Place the last layer on top and moisten with the remaining syrup.

STRAWBERRY FILLING

2 pints strawberries

½ cup sugar

1 tablespoon fresh lemon juice

1 tablespoon kirsch

2 tablespoons cornstarch

LEMON-KIRSCH SYRUP

⅓ cup water

⅓ cup sugar

2 tablespoons fresh lemon juice

2 tablespoons kirsch

COVERING MERINGUE

¾ cup egg whites (from 6 or 7 large eggs)

1 cup sugar

Two 10-inch layers Classic Génoise, page 116

5 Meanwhile, preheat the oven to 400°F.

6 To make the meringue, combine the egg whites and sugar in the bowl of an electric mixer. Whisk over simmering water until

the egg whites are hot and the sugar is dissolved. Attach the bowl to the mixer and beat with the whisk at medium speed until the meringue has increased in volume and is cool.

7 Frost the top and sides of the cake with the meringue.

8 Place the cake on a cookie sheet and put in the oven for just 3 to 4 minutes to color the meringue. Remove the cake from the oven and cool, then decorate with the reserved strawberries and the sliced almonds.

SERVING: Serve the cake as soon as it has cooled.

STORAGE: Refrigerate leftovers.

MAKES ONE 9-INCH CAKE,
ABOUT 12 SERVINGS

APRICOT MARZIPAN CAKE

~ 9 C ~

THIS IS A VARIATION OF A FAMOUS Viennese sponge cake called a Punschtorte, which is soaked with a flavorful rum syrup and covered with marzipan. It is a perfect summer cake because there is no filling or frosting to melt in the heat.

1   To make the syrup, bring the sugar and water to a boil in a small saucepan. Cool, and stir in the rum, orange juice, lemon juice, and vanilla.

2   To make the glaze, bring the preserves and water to a boil in a small saucepan over medium heat, stirring occasionally. Strain into another pan and simmer until the glaze becomes sticky. Set aside.

3   To make the marzipan, in the bowl of a heavy-duty mixer, beat the almond paste and 1 cup of the sugar with the paddle attachment on low speed until the sugar is almost absorbed. Add the remaining 1 cup sugar and beat slowly until the mixture resembles fine crumbs. Add the corn syrup a little at a time, stopping frequently and checking to see if you can knead the marzipan smooth; the marzipan will still appear crumbly, and you may not need all the syrup. Remove to a work surface and knead until smooth. Pull off a small piece of the marzipan and wrap in plastic. Add

PUNCH SYRUP

¼ cup water

⅓ cup sugar

¼ cup dark rum

¼ cup fresh orange juice

2 tablespoons fresh lemon juice

1 teaspoon vanilla extract

APRICOT GLAZE

1½ cups apricot preserves

¼ cup water

MARZIPAN

4 ounces almond paste

2 cups confectioners' sugar

About ⅓ cup light corn syrup

Red food coloring

Cornstarch for rolling out the marzipan

One 9-inch layer Classic Génoise, page 116

DECORATION

1 ounce semisweet chocolate, melted

enough coloring to the remaining marzipan to tint it a pale pink, then wrap it in plastic.

4 Slice the cake horizontally into 3 layers and place one on a platter or cardboard round. Moisten with syrup and brush with glaze. Top with the second layer, moisten it, and brush with glaze. Place the remaining layer on top and brush the top and sides of the cake with the glaze.

5 Dust a work surface with cornstarch. Roll out the pink marzipan to a thin round about 14 inches in diameter. Drape it over the cake and trim away the excess. Gather the scraps together, and roll into a rope under your palms. Use the rope to finish the bottom of the cake. Use a paper cone (see Chapter 14) to pipe a chocolate design on the cake with the melted chocolate. Finally, make a flower or other decoration from the reserved white marzipan for the center of the cake.

SERVING: Cut into thin slices to serve.

STORAGE: Store at a cool room temperature for up to 2 days.

MAKES ONE 9-INCH CAKE, ABOUT 16 SERVINGS

CHOCOLATE TRUFFLE RASPBERRY CAKE

This is one great, elaborate, and celebratory cake—save it for the most important occasions.

1 To make the syrup, bring the sugar and water to a boil in a small saucepan. Let cool, and stir in the liqueur.

2 To make the ganache, bring the raspberries to a boil in a small saucepan and cook for 5 minutes, or until slightly reduced. Puree in processor, and strain. Let cool.

3 Bring the cream to a boil in a medium saucepan. Off the heat, add the chocolate and allow to stand for 2 minutes, then whisk in the butter and whisk until smooth. Whisk in the raspberry puree and liqueur. Let cool until thickened in the refrigerator, about 1 hour.

4 To assemble, slice the cake into 3 layers and place one on a cardboard round or a platter. Moisten with syrup and spread with ¼ cup of the preserves. Cover with a layer of chocolate ganache. Repeat with the second layer. Place the last layer on top and moisten with the remaining syrup. Spread the top and sides of the cake with ganache, reserving ½ cup for decoration. Chill to set the outside of the cake.

RASPBERRY SYRUP

⅓ cup water

⅓ cup sugar

⅓ cup raspberry liqueur

CHOCOLATE-RASPBERRY GANACHE

One 10-ounce package frozen raspberries

1¼ cups heavy whipping cream

1 pound semisweet chocolate, cut into ¼-inch pieces

4 tablespoons (½ stick) unsalted butter, softened

2 tablespoons raspberry liqueur

One 9-inch layer Chocolate Génoise, page 117

½ cup raspberry preserves

GANACHE GLAZE

1 cup heavy whipping cream

8 ounces semisweet chocolate, cut into ¼-inch pieces

5 To make the glaze, bring the cream to a boil in a small saucepan. Remove from the heat, add the chocolate, and allow to stand for 2 minutes. Whisk until smooth, then strain and cool to room temperature.

6 To glaze the cake, place it on a rack on a baking sheet and pour the cooled glaze through a strainer onto the top of the cake. Sweep the excess glaze from the top with a metal spatula. Chill to set the glaze.

7 To decorate, use the reserved ganache to make a circle of rosettes around the top edge of the cake and a 4-inch circle of rosettes in the center of the cake.

SERVING: Serve at cool room temperature.

STORAGE: Refrigerate, loosely covered, for up to 2 days.

ONE 9-INCH CAKE, ABOUT 12 SERVINGS

MILANESE ORANGE CAKE

~⟋⟍~

THIS SPECTACULAR CAKE is a re-creation of one I remember from an elegant Milanese pastry shop. Finishing the outside of the cake with tiny squares of sponge cake is a typical Italian technique.

SPONGE CAKE BATTER

5 large eggs

5 large egg yolks

1 teaspoon orange extract

1 cup sugar

Pinch of salt

¾ cup cake flour (spoon flour into dry-measure cup and level off)

½ cup cornstarch

ORANGE SYRUP

¼ cup water

¼ cup sugar

¼ cup fresh orange juice

¼ cup orange liqueur

ORANGE FILLING

4 large egg yolks

⅓ cup sugar

1 teaspoon finely grated orange zest

¼ cup fresh orange juice

¼ cup orange liqueur

¾ pound (3 sticks) unsalted butter, softened

Confectioners' sugar for finishing

One 9-inch springform pan and one 9 × 13 × 2-inch baking pan, both buttered and bottoms lined with parchment

1   Position the racks to divide the oven into thirds and preheat to 350 degrees.

2   To make the cake layers, whisk together the eggs, yolks, extract, sugar, and salt in the bowl of an electric mixer. Place the bowl over a pan of gently simmering water and whisk until the mixture is lukewarm. Attach to the mixer and beat with the whip attachment until increased in volume and cold.

3   Sift the remaining ingredients together onto wax paper. In three additions, sift the dry ingredients into the egg mixture, folding them in with a rubber spatula. Pour a third of the batter into the rectangular pan and the remainder into the round pan.

4   Bake the layer in the rectangular pan for about 15 to 20 minutes, and the one in the

springform for 30 minutes or more. Unmold onto racks to cool right side up.

5 To make the syrup, bring the water and sugar to a boil in a small saucepan. Then add the juice and liqueur.

6 To make the filling, whisk all the ingredients except the butter together in a mixer bowl. Place over a pan of simmering water and whisk constantly until the mixture is hot and thickened, about 2 minutes. Attach to the mixer and whip with the whisk until cooled and increased in volume. Gradually switch to the paddle attachment and beat in the butter.

7 Using a sharp serrated knife, slice the round cake into 5 layers. Set aside 2 layers. Cut one of the remaining layers into an 8-inch layer, another into a 7-inch layer, and the third into a 6-inch layer. Patch the scraps together to make one 5- and one 4-inch layer. Cut the rectangular layer into ½-inch dice.

8 Place one of the 9-inch layers on a cardboard round or a platter and moisten with the syrup. Spread with a couple of tablespoons of filling. Top with the 8-inch layer, moisten, and spread with filling. Continue layering the successively smaller layers until you reach the smallest layer. Moisten it with syrup, reserving a little, and cover the top and sides of the cake with buttercream, reserving about ⅓ cup. Use the second 9-inch layer to cover the outside of the cake, moisten it, and spread with the last of the buttercream. Press the squares of cake into the buttercream all over the cake and dust with confectioners' sugar.

SERVING: Serve at cool room temperature.

STORAGE: Cover loosely and refrigerate for up to 2 days; bring to cool room temperature before serving.

MAKES ABOUT 12 SERVINGS

TORTA BIANCO E NERO

~⌒⌒~

THIS ELEGANT HARLEQUIN CAKE is filled with alternating layers of vanilla and chocolate buttercream.

1　To make the buttercream, whisk together the yolks and sugar in the bowl of an electric mixer. Beat in the brandy, then place the bowl over a pan of simmering water and whisk constantly until the mixture thickens. Attach the bowl to the mixer and whip with the whisk attachment on medium speed until cold and increased in volume. Beat in the butter in 5 or 6 additions, and continue beating until the buttercream is smooth and light.

2　Bring the water to a boil in a small saucepan. Remove from the heat, add the chocolate, and stir until the chocolate melts. Cool.

3　Transfer half the buttercream to a large bowl. Beat the cooled chocolate mixture into one half and the vanilla into the other.

4　To make the syrup, bring the sugar and water to a boil in a small saucepan. Cool, then stir in the rum.

BUTTERCREAM

4 large egg yolks

½ cup sugar

⅓ cup Italian brandy

1 pound (4 sticks) unsalted butter, softened

3 tablespoons water

4 ounces bittersweet chocolate, finely chopped

2 teaspoons vanilla extract

RUM SYRUP

⅓ cup water

⅓ cup sugar

⅓ cup white rum

One 10-inch layer Pan di Spagna, page 124

2 dozen Italian macaroons (such as Amaretti di Saronno)

Confectioners' sugar for finishing

5 Using a sharp serrated knife, slice the cake into 6 layers. Set 2 layers aside. Trim the remaining 4 layers into a 9-, an 8-, a 7-, and a 6-inch layer. Use the scraps to make a 5- and a 4-inch layer.

6 Place one of the 10-inch layers on a cardboard round or a platter and moisten with syrup. Spread with some of the chocolate buttercream. Place the 9-inch layer on top, moisten with syrup, and spread with a couple of tablespoons vanilla buttercream. Continue stacking the successively smaller layers, moistening each one with syrup and alternating the buttercreams, until you reach the 4-inch layer. Moisten it and spread the top and sides of the cake with the remaining chocolate cream. Place the second 10-inch layer over the cake, moisten it, and spread with the remaining vanilla cream.

7 Coarsely crush the macaroons and press them all over the outside of the cake. Chill to set the buttercream. Dust lightly with confectioners' sugar just before serving.

Serving: Serve at cool room temperature.

Storage: Cover loosely and refrigerate for up to 2 days; bring to cool room temperature before serving.

Makes about 16 servings

BUTTER CAKE LAYERS

MOST OF THE FOLLOWING RECIPES, which are used for the layer cakes in this chapter, are mixed according to traditional methods, but none of them includes whipped egg whites as a component—I think they make the cake layers more complicated to prepare and don't really contribute much to the lightness of the finished cake.

If the sugar weighs the same as the flour or more, you can use the high-ratio method (see page 44) to mix the batter. Mix and match these layers with the recipes in this chapter and with fillings, frostings, and glazes in Chapter 13.

CLASSIC WHITE CAKE LAYERS

THE FINE, MOIST CRUMB of this cake makes it perfect for any type of filling or frosting.

1 Position a rack in the middle of the oven and preheat to 350 degrees.

2 Combine the flour, baking powder, and salt in a bowl, mixing well.

3 Place the butter and sugar in the bowl of a heavy-duty mixer fitted with the paddle attachment and beat on medium speed for about 5 minutes, or until very soft and light. Beat in the vanilla.

4 Whisk together the egg whites and milk by hand in a medium mixing bowl until just combined.

5 Reduce the mixer speed to low and beat in one-quarter of the flour mixture, then one-third of the milk mixture, stopping and scraping down the bowl and beater after each addition. Beat in another quarter of the flour, then another third of the milk mixture. Scrape again. Repeat with another quarter of the flour and the remaining milk mixture; scrape. Finally, beat in the remaining flour mixture.

6 Scrape the bowl well with a large rubber spatula. Pour the batter into the prepared pans and smooth the tops.

2 cups all-purpose flour (spoon flour into dry-measure cup and level off)

2 teaspoons baking powder

¼ teaspoon salt

12 tablespoons (1½ sticks) unsalted butter, softened

1½ cups sugar

2 teaspoons vanilla extract

6 large egg whites

¾ cup milk

Two 9-inch round cake pans, buttered and bottoms lined with buttered parchment or wax paper

7 Bake the layers for about 30 to 35 minutes, until they are well risen and firm and a toothpick inserted in the center emerges clean. Cool the layers in the pans on racks for 5 minutes, then unmold onto racks to finish cooling right side up.

STORAGE: If you are going to use the layers the day you bake them, wrap in plastic and keep them at room temperature. Double-wrap and freeze for longer storage.

MAKES TWO 9-INCH ROUND LAYERS

BUTTERMILK CAKE LAYERS

~ ⦿ ⦿ ~

BUTTERMILK AND EVEN SOUR MILK used to be very popular ingredients because they made moist cake layers with a slight tang. These layers are perfect for either a fruit or chocolate finish.

1 Position a rack in the middle of the oven and preheat to 350 degrees.

2 Stir together the flour, baking soda, and salt in a bowl, mixing well.

3 Place the butter and sugar in the bowl of a heavy-duty mixer fitted with the paddle attachment and beat on medium speed for about 5 minutes, or until very soft and light. Beat in the vanilla, then beat in the eggs one at a time, beating well after each addition.

4 Reduce the speed to low and beat in one-third of the flour mixture, then half the buttermilk, stopping and scraping down the bowl and beater after each addition. Beat in another third of the flour, then the remaining buttermilk, stopping and scraping again. Finally, beat in the remaining flour mixture.

5 Scrape the bowl well with a large rubber spatula. Pour the batter into the prepared pans and smooth the tops.

6 Bake the layers for about 30 to 35 minutes, until they are well risen and firm and a toothpick inserted in the center

2¾ cups all-purpose flour (spoon flour into dry-measure cup and level off)
½ teaspoon salt
½ teaspoon baking soda
½ pound (2 sticks) unsalted butter, softened
2 cups sugar
2 teaspoons vanilla extract
4 large eggs
1 cup buttermilk

Two 9-inch round cake pans, buttered and bottoms lined with buttered parchment or wax paper

emerges clean. Cool the layers in the pans on racks for 5 minutes, then unmold onto racks to finish cooling.

STORAGE: If you are going to use the layers on the day you bake them, wrap in plastic and keep at room temperature. Double-wrap and freeze for longer storage.

MAKES TWO 9-INCH ROUND LAYERS

GOLDEN CAKE LAYERS

꧁꧂

THE WORD *GOLD* OR *GOLDEN* usually signifies a cake made with egg yolks rather than whole eggs. I especially like to use these layers as a shortcake—split and spread with whipped cream and berries.

1 Position a rack in the middle of the oven and preheat to 350 degrees.

2 Stir together the flour, baking powder, and salt in a bowl, mixing well.

3 Place the butter and sugar in the bowl of a heavy-duty mixer and beat with the paddle attachment on medium speed for about 5 minutes, or until very soft and light. Beat in the vanilla and lemon extracts, then beat in the egg yolks one at a time, beating well after each addition.

4 Reduce the speed to low and beat in one-third of the flour mixture, then half the milk, stopping and scraping down the bowl and beater after each addition. Beat in another third of the flour, then the remaining milk, stopping and scraping again. Finally, beat in the remaining flour mixture.

5 Scrape the bowl well with a large rubber spatula, then pour the batter into the prepared pans and smooth the tops.

6 Bake the layers for about 30 to 35 minutes, until they are well risen and firm and a toothpick inserted in the center

2½ cups bleached all-purpose flour
(spoon flour into dry-measure cup
and level off)
2 teaspoons baking powder
½ teaspoon salt
12 tablespoons (1½ sticks) unsalted
butter, softened
1⅓ cups sugar
1 teaspoon vanilla extract
1 teaspoon lemon extract
6 large egg yolks
1 cup milk

Two 9-inch round cake pans, buttered and bottoms lined with buttered parchment or wax paper

emerges clean. Cool the layers in the pans on racks for 5 minutes, then unmold onto racks to finish cooling.

STORAGE: If you are going to use the layers the day you bake them, wrap in plastic and keep at room temperature. Double-wrap and freeze for longer storage.

MAKES TWO 9-INCH ROUND LAYERS

COCONUT CAKE LAYERS

_~୨ ୨ ୯~_

THESE VERSATILE CAKE LAYERS, which are, of course, perfect for an all-coconut cake with coconut filling and frosting, are also great with fruit fillings. The coconut makes for a very moist layer that everyone always loves.

1   Set a rack in the middle of the oven and preheat to 350 degrees.

2   Stir together the flour, baking powder, and salt in a bowl, mixing well.

3   Place the butter and sugar in the bowl of a heavy-duty mixer and beat on medium speed with the paddle for about 5 minutes, or until soft and light. Beat in the vanilla and lemon zest, then beat in the eggs and yolks one at a time, beating well after each addition.

4   Reduce the speed to low and add one-third of the flour mixture, then add half the coconut milk and scrape down the bowl and beater. Repeat with another third of the flour mixture and the remaining coconut milk. Scrape down the bowl and beater again. Finally, beat in the remaining flour mixture.

5   Use a large rubber spatula to scrape the bowl well and give a final mix to the batter. Fold in the chopped coconut. Pour the batter into the prepared pans and smooth the tops.

1¾ cups bleached all-purpose flour (spoon flour into dry-measure cup and level off)

1½ teaspoons baking powder

¼ teaspoon salt

12 tablespoons (1½ sticks) unsalted butter, softened

1⅓ cups sugar

1 teaspoon vanilla extract

1 teaspoon finely grated lemon zest

2 large eggs, at room temperature

2 large egg yolks

½ cup coconut milk (see Note)

1 cup (about half a 7-ounce bag) sweetened shredded coconut, finely chopped

Two 9-inch round cake pans, buttered and bottoms lined with buttered parchment or wax paper

6 Bake the layers for about 30 to 35 minutes, until they are well risen and firm and a toothpick inserted in the center emerges clean. Cool the layers in the pans on racks for 5 minutes, then unmold onto racks to finish cooling.

STORAGE: If you are going to use the layers the day you bake them, wrap in plastic and keep at room temperature. Double-wrap and freeze for longer storage.

MAKES TWO 9-INCH ROUND LAYERS

VARIATION

COCONUT PECAN LAYERS: Add ¾ cup (about 3 ounces) chopped—not ground—pecans along with the coconut.

NOTE: I always use Thai canned coconut milk for this recipe.

1942 DEVIL'S FOOD CAKE LAYERS

THIS RECIPE COMES FROM Virginia Lo Biondo, my aunt Virginia's sister-in-law. Mrs. Lo Biondo told me she got the recipe from a neighbor during World War II and that it was already an old recipe at the time. It's her family's favorite cake. Frost with fluffy white icing, page 285 or whipped ganache, page 284.

1 Position a rack in the middle of the oven and preheat to 350 degrees.

2 Melt the chocolate in a large heatproof bowl set over hot, but not simmering, water. Let cool.

3 Stir together the flour, baking soda, and salt in a bowl, mixing well.

4 Add the butter to the chocolate, then pour in the boiling water and stir well to mix. Whisk in the sugar and sour cream. Stir in the flour mixture. Whisk in the eggs.

5 Pour the batter into the prepared pans and smooth the tops.

6 Bake for about 25 to 30 minutes, or until the layers are well risen and firm to the touch; and a toothpick inserted emerges clean. Cool the layers in the pans on racks for 5 minutes, then unmold onto racks to finish cooling.

3 ounces unsweetened chocolate

1⅓ cups bleached all-purpose flour (spoon flour into dry-measure cup and level off)

¾ teaspoon baking soda

½ teaspoon salt

6 tablespoons (¾ stick) unsalted butter, cut into 6 pieces

¾ cup boiling water

1½ cups sugar

6 tablespoons sour cream or buttermilk

2 large eggs

Two 9-inch round cake pans, buttered and bottoms lined with parchment or wax paper

STORAGE: If you are going to use the layers the day you bake them, wrap in plastic and keep at room temperature. Double-wrap and freeze for longer storage.

MAKES TWO 9-INCH ROUND LAYERS

CHOCOLATE FUDGE CAKE LAYERS

～ ৩ ৫ ～

THESE RICH LAYERS ARE SOMETHING like brownies. I especially like to finish them with a light chocolate or vanilla buttercream (see page 279).

1 Set a rack in the middle of the oven and preheat to 350 degrees.

2 Melt the butter in a 2-quart saucepan over medium heat, swirling the pan occasionally so the butter melts quickly. Let the melted butter bubble for a few seconds, so it is really hot. Off the heat, add the chocolate, swirling the pan to submerge the chocolate. Set the pan aside to allow the chocolate to melt while you prepare the other ingredients.

3 In a medium bowl, whisk the eggs to break them up. Whisk in the sugar in a stream. Whisk in the salt and vanilla, then whisk briefly until the mixture lightens a little.

4 Whisk the chocolate and butter mixture just until smooth. With a rubber spatula, scrape the chocolate into the egg mixture and stir it in. Fold in the flour, then the chopped nuts, if using.

5 Scrape the batter into the prepared pans and smooth the tops.

6 Bake the layers for about 30 to 35 minutes, or until they are firm to the touch but not dry all the way through—a toothpick inserted in the center should emerge with

1 pound (4 sticks) unsalted butter, cut into 12 pieces
8 ounces unsweetened chocolate, cut into 1/4-inch pieces
6 large eggs
2 2/3 cups sugar
1 teaspoon salt
2 teaspoons vanilla extract
2 1/3 cups all-purpose flour (spoon flour into dry-measure cup and level off)
Chopped pecans or walnuts, optional

Two 9-inch round cake pans, buttered and bottoms lined with parchment or wax paper

some batter still clinging to it, but not completely wet. Cool the layers in the pans on racks for 10 minutes, then unmold onto racks to cool completely.

STORAGE: If you are going to use the layers the day you bake them, wrap in plastic and keep at room temperature. Double-wrap and freeze for longer storage.

MAKES TWO 9-INCH ROUND LAYERS

213

10 ROLLED CAKES

ROLLED CAKES FALL INTO THE CATEGORY of baked things that are as much fun and as interesting to make as they are to eat! Most rolled cakes are really easy to prepare. To make sure they turn out perfectly, just bear in mind a few tricks.

1 Be sure not to overbake the cake—a dry cake is impossible to roll.

2 To help conserve moisture after the cake is baked, cool it, on the paper it was baked on, on a countertop rather than a rack.

3 Spread the filling over the top of the cake, so that the surface that was against the bottom of the pan becomes the outside of the roll.

4 Don't be afraid of rolling the cake: once you have positioned the cake on its paper as directed, give a fold and just lift the paper—the paper will push the cake and make it roll itself up.

5 To tighten the cake around the filling, holding the bottom of the paper, press on the top of the roll, through the paper, with the side of a clipboard or cookie sheet.

6 Chill the roll to set the filling in a nice cylindrical shape. Then finish the cake after it has chilled. Bring it back to room temperature to serve unless it is filled and finished with whipped cream, in which case, keep it refrigerated until serving.

7 When serving, two thinner slices of a rolled cake look better to serve than one thick one.

CHOCOLATE SOUFFLE ROLL

~ ⚬ ⚬ ~

LOOSELY BASED ON JAMES BEARD'S chocolate roll, this is a perfect dessert to prepare on short notice.

1 Position a rack in the middle of the oven and preheat to 350 degrees.

2 Combine the chocolate with the liqueur or water and the butter in a heatproof bowl. Place the bowl over a pan of hot, but not simmering, water and stir occasionally with a rubber spatula until the chocolate is melted and the mixture is smooth. Stir in the yolks one at a time, beating well after each addition.

3 In the bowl of a heavy-duty mixer fitted with the whisk, whip the egg whites with the salt at low speed until they are just beginning to hold a very soft peak, then raise the speed and whip in the sugar in a slow stream. Continue whipping until the egg whites hold a firm peak. Stir one-quarter of the egg whites into the chocolate batter to lighten it, then fold the chocolate batter into the remaining egg whites.

4 Pour the batter into the prepared pan and smooth the top. Bake for about 15 minutes, until the layer is firm to the touch.

CAKE BATTER

6 ounces semisweet chocolate, finely chopped

¼ cup orange or raspberry liqueur or water

2 tablespoons unsalted butter

6 large eggs, separated

Pinch of salt

½ cup sugar

FOR FINISHING

1 cup heavy whipping cream

2 tablespoons sugar

1 tablespoon liqueur, optional

One ½-pint basket raspberries

One 10 × 15-inch jelly-roll pan, buttered and lined with parchment or wax paper

5 Remove the pan from the oven and loosen the sides of the cake with a small sharp knife. Using the paper to help, slide the layer onto the work surface to cool, about 20 minutes.

6   To assemble the roll, slide a cookie sheet under the layer. Cover the layer with a clean piece of parchment or wax paper and another pan, and turn the cake over. Lift off the top pan and peel off the paper stuck to the layer. Replace with a clean sheet of paper, replace the pan, and invert again. Remove the top pan and paper.

7   In a medium bowl, whip the cream with the sugar and liqueur, if using, until it holds a firm peak. Use a metal spatula to spread the cream over the layer. To roll the cake, pick up one long edge of the paper and use it to help you ease the layer into a curve, then continue lifting the paper to roll the layer and roll it directly onto a platter, seam side down. Trim the ends of the roll and refrigerate, loosely covered until ready to serve.

8   To serve, decorate each slice with some of the raspberries.

STORAGE: Keep refrigerated until serving time, and refrigerate leftovers.

MAKES ABOUT 12 SERVINGS

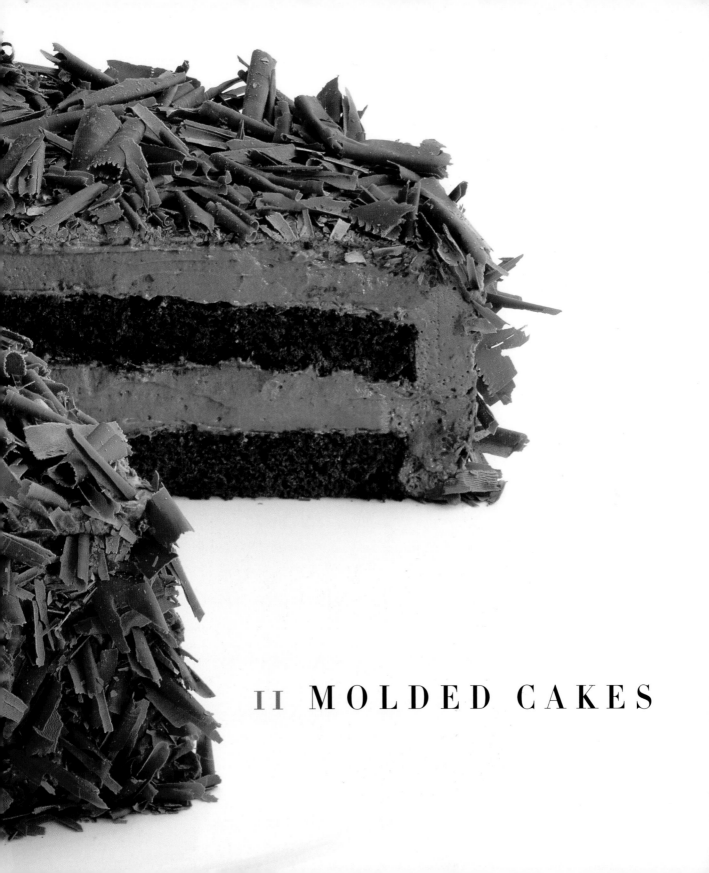

II MOLDED CAKES

MOST OF THESE CAKES have fillings that are soft or liquid until they set. Such cakes are made in molds to contain the filling so it sets neatly within the cake. Although there are many types of molds for making such cakes, I still prefer to use a springform pan for most of them: they're easy to find and relatively inexpensive, and, of course, they can be used for cheesecakes and other types of cakes as well. Some of the molded cakes here are made in a dome shape. I usually like to use Pyrex mixing bowls for these. Although they have a flattish bottom, which gives a slightly flat top to the dessert, you can compensate by doming the frosting slightly.

APRICOT BAVARIAN CAKE

TRY THIS DESSERT WITH PEACHES or nectarines when they are in season.

APRICOT PUREE
2 pounds apricots
1 cup sugar

RUM SYRUP
¼ cup water
¼ cup sugar
¼ cup white rum

APRICOT BAVARIAN CREAM
¼ cup white rum
2 envelopes gelatin

2 cups apricot puree (from above)
2 cups heavy whipping cream

One 9-inch layer Classic White Cake,
    page 207
2 tablespoons apricot jam

FOR FINISHING
1 cup heavy whipping cream
½ cup toasted sliced almonds

One 9-inch springform pan

1 To make the puree, rinse, halve, and pit the apricots. Combine them with the sugar in a nonreactive saucepan and bring to a simmer, stirring occasionally. Bring to a boil, lower the heat, and simmer for about 10 minutes, until the apricots thicken slightly. Cool, then puree in a blender.

2 To make the syrup, bring the water and sugar to a boil in a saucepan. Cool, and stir in the rum.

3 To make the Bavarian, pour the rum into a small bowl and sprinkle the gelatin over the surface. Allow the gelatin to soften for several minutes, then place the bowl over a pan of simmering water and heat, stirring, until the mixture is clear. Remove the bowl from the water and whip in ½ cup of the apricot puree. Whip the gelatin mixture into the remaining puree.

4 Whip the cream until it holds a soft shape, then fold it into the apricot mixture.

5 To assemble, using a serrated knife, split the cake layer into 2 layers. Place one layer in the bottom of the springform pan and brush it with half the syrup. Spread with a tablespoon of the jam. Pour in half the Bavarian. Repeat with the second layer and the remaining syrup, jam, and Bavarian. Cover and chill overnight to set.

6 To unmold, run a knife around the inside of the pan, open the buckle and remove the sides of the pan.

7 To finish, whip the cream. Spread the cream around the sides of the dessert only. Press the almonds into the cream. Use a pastry bag fitted with a star tube to pipe rosettes on the top of the cake.

SERVING: Serve chilled.

STORAGE: Store loosely covered in the refrigerator for up to 2 days.

MAKES ONE 9-INCH CAKE,
ABOUT 12 SERVINGS

VELOUTE AU CITRON

❧ ❧

The name of this dessert is, literally, "lemon velvet." The lemon mousse has a suave velvety texture that makes it worthy of the name and the sweetness of the meringue covering contrasts perfectly with the lemons.

1 To make the mousse, whisk together the yolks, zest, lemon juice, and sugar in the bowl of an electric mixer. Place the bowl over a pan of simmering water and whisk constantly until the mixture thickens. Attach to the mixer and beat with the whip attachment on medium speed until the mixture has cooled, about 5 minutes.

2 Meanwhile, pour the rum into a small bowl and sprinkle the gelatin over the surface. Allow the gelatin to soften, then place the bowl over the pan of simmering water and heat, stirring, until clear. Remove from the water.

3 Whisk ½ cup of the cooled lemon mixture into the gelatin. Beat the gelatin into the remaining lemon mixture.

4 Whip the cream until it holds a shape and fold it into the lemon mixture. Set aside at room temperature.

5 To make the syrup, bring the sugar and water to a boil in a small saucepan. Cool, then stir in the rum.

LEMON MOUSSE
6 large egg yolks
3 tablespoons grated lemon zest
¾ cup strained fresh lemon juice
¾ cup sugar
½ cup white rum
2 envelopes gelatin
2½ cups heavy whipping cream

RUM SYRUP
¼ cup water
¼ cup sugar
¼ cup white rum

2 Biscuit Batter Layers, page 118

MERINGUE
4 large egg whites
¾ cup sugar
½ cup (about 2 ounces) toasted, sliced almonds, crushed, for finishing

One 10-inch springform pan

6   To assemble, trim each layer to an even 9-inch circle. Place one of the layers in the bottom of the springform pan. Moisten with half the syrup. Pour half the mousse over the layer, making sure that it fills the space between the sides of the layer and the pan. Moisten the other layer with the remaining syrup and slide it on top of the mousse. Cover with the remaining mousse and smooth the top. Chill until set, at least 6 hours.

7   When ready to finish the dessert, make the meringue. Whisk the egg whites and sugar together in the bowl of an electric mixer. Place the bowl over a pan of simmering water and whisk constantly until the egg whites are hot and the sugar is dissolved. Attach to the mixer and beat with the whip attachment on medium speed until firm and cooled.

8   To unmold the dessert, warm the sides of the mold with a blowtorch or a cloth wrung out in hot water. Run a small sharp knife around the inside of the mold and remove the sides. Spread or pipe the meringue over the top and sides of the dessert and press the almonds around the sides.

9   Use a blowtorch to color the meringue, or place in a preheated 400-degree oven for 1 to 2 minutes, turning often to color the meringue evenly.

SERVING: Use a thin knife dipped in hot water and wiped clean after each slice to cut the cake.

STORAGE: Store loosely covered in the refrigerator for up to 8 hours before serving. If you prepare this in advance, you can keep the mousse covered in the refrigerator, but don't finish with meringue until the day it is to be served.

MAKES ONE 10-INCH CAKE, ABOUT 12 SERVINGS

ERDBEEROBERSTORTE
Strawberry Whipped Cream Cake

ALTHOUGH VIENNA HISTORICALLY has been famous for desserts with mountains of whipped cream, this dessert is a little less rich. Try it with raspberries or cherries when they are in season.

CAKE BATTER

5 large eggs

1 teaspoon grated lemon zest

½ cup sugar

1 cup cake flour (spoon flour into dry-measure cup and level off)

ORANGE SYRUP

¼ cup water

¼ cup sugar

¼ cup orange liqueur

STRAWBERRY FILLING

2 pints strawberries

¾ cup sugar

2 envelopes gelatin

⅓ cup water

2 cups heavy whipping cream

FOR FINISHING

1½ cups heavy whipping cream

¼ cup sugar

2 teaspoons vanilla extract

1 pint strawberries, rinsed, halved, and patted dry

Chocolate shavings

Confectioners' sugar

One 10-inch springform pan, buttered and bottom lined with parchment or wax paper

1 Position a rack in the middle of the oven and preheat to 350 degrees.

2 Whisk the eggs, lemon zest, and sugar together in the bowl of an electric mixer. Set over simmering water and whisk until lukewarm. Attach the bowl to the mixer and beat with the whisk on medium speed until increased in volume, and cold.

3 Sift the cake flour over the egg mixture in three or four additions, folding it in with a rubber spatula.

4 Pour the batter into the prepared pan and bake for about 30 minutes. Unmold the cake onto a rack, then invert onto a rack to cool right side up.

5 To make the syrup, bring the sugar and water to a boil in a saucepan. Cool, and stir in the orange liqueur.

6 To make the filling, rinse, hull, and halve the strawberries. Puree half of them in the food processor (you should have 1 cup puree). Whisk the sugar into the puree and set it aside. Reserve the remaining strawberries.

7 Sprinkle the gelatin over the water in a small bowl and let stand until softened. Set the bowl over simmering water and stir to melt the gelatin. Stir a little of the puree into the melted gelatin, then whisk the gelatin into the remaining puree.

8 Whip the cream until it holds a shape and fold it into the puree.

9 Slice the cooled cake horizontally into 2 equal layers. Slice one of the layers horizontally in half. Place the thicker layer in the bottom of the springform pan and moisten it with one-third of the syrup. Pour in half the strawberry filling and distribute the reserved strawberries over the filling. Cover with one of the thin layers and moisten it. Pour in the remaining filling and top with the last layer. Moisten it with the remaining syrup. Refrigerate to set the filling, 4 to 6 hours.

10 To finish, whip the cream with the sugar and vanilla until it holds a shape. Run a knife between the side of the springform and the cake, then unbuckle the side of the pan. Unmold the cake. Cover it completely with the whipped cream, reserving some for decoration. Using a pastry bag fitted with a star tip, decorate the top of the cake with rosettes of whipped cream. Decorate the top of the cake with the strawberries. Press chocolate shavings into the sides of the cake and sprinkle some onto the very center of the top. Dust the chocolate shavings on the top very lightly with confectioners' sugar.

SERVING: Serve the cake shortly after finishing.

STORAGE: Store the filled cake in the refrigerator for up to 2 days. Don't finish with whipped cream and shavings until just prior to serving.

MAKES ONE 10-INCH CAKE, ABOUT 12 SERVINGS

NOTE: You may substitute a 9-inch génoise layer, page 116, for the cake layer here.

PASSION-FRUIT BAVARIAN CREAM CAKE

⌒ ⌒ ⌒

THE TART FLAVOR OF FRESH PASSION FRUIT may come as a surprise. This dessert has a tailored appearance and exquisite, subtle flavor. (To purchase passion fruit puree, see Sources.)

1 To make the puree, bring the juice, sugar, and water to a boil in a large saucepan over medium heat. Lower the heat and simmer for about 5 to 10 minutes, until slightly reduced. Puree in a blender, strain, and chill.

2 To make the syrup, bring the sugar and water to a boil. Cool, and stir in the rum.

3 To make the Bavarian, place the 1½ cups puree in a large bowl. Place the rum in a small bowl and sprinkle the gelatin over the surface. Let soak for 5 minutes, then place the bowl over a pan of simmering water and stir to melt the gelatin.

4 Whip the cream until it holds a shape. Beat 1 cup of the puree into the gelatin mixture, then beat the gelatin mixture into the remaining puree. Fold in the whipped cream.

5 To assemble the dessert, trim the biscuit layer to an even 9-inch round and place it in the bottom of the springform pan. Moisten it well with the rum syrup. Pour the Bavarian over and smooth the top. Chill to set the Bavarian.

PASSION FRUIT PUREE

1½ cups fresh passion fruit juice
    or frozen puree

1 cup sugar

⅓ cup water

RUM SYRUP

¼ cup sugar

¼ cup water

¼ cup white rum

PASSION FRUIT BAVARIAN CREAM

1½ cups passion fruit puree (from
    above)

⅓ cup white rum

1½ envelopes gelatin

1½ cups heavy whipping cream

PASSION FRUIT GLAZE

1 envelope gelatin

2 tablespoons water

⅓ cup passion fruit puree (from above)

½ cup apple jelly

One 10-inch springform pan

Biscuit batter layers, page 118

6   To make the glaze, sprinkle the gelatin over the water in a small bowl and let soften for 5 minutes. Bring the ⅓ cup puree and the jelly to a boil in a small saucepan. Add the soaked gelatin and return to a boil. Pass through a very fine strainer. Cool to room temperature.

7   To finish, pour the cooled glaze over the set Bavarian and tilt to cover the surface evenly. Chill again to set the glaze.

8   To unmold, run a thin knife dipped into hot water around the inside of the pan. Release the spring and lift off the sides. Smooth the sides of the dessert with a wet spatula if necessary.

SERVING: Use a thin knife dipped in hot water and wiped clean after each slice to cut the cake.

STORAGE: Store loosely covered in the refrigerator for up to 8 hours before serving. To prepare in advance, keep the unglazed cake, covered, in the refrigerator for a day or two. Glaze on the day it is to be served.

MAKES ONE 10-INCH CAKE, ABOUT 12 SERVINGS

SHOGGITORTE

~◦❂◦~

THIS IS A TYPICAL SWISS CHOCOLATE CAKE—Swiss bakers like to combine a rich sponge cake with a light chocolate mousse.

1   To make the mousse, whip the cream in a large bowl until it holds a soft peak. Refrigerate while you prepare the other ingredients.

2   Sprinkle the gelatin over the water in a small bowl and allow to soften for 5 minutes.

3   Whisk the egg whites and sugar together in the bowl of an electric mixer. Set the bowl over a saucepan of simmering water and whisk constantly until the egg whites are hot and the sugar is dissolved, about 3 minutes: test a little between your thumb and forefinger—if the mixture is gritty, continue to heat until all the sugar is dissolved. Whisk the softened gelatin into the egg whites. Attach the bowl to the mixer, fitted with the whisk attachment, and beat the whites until increased in volume, somewhat cooled, and soft and creamy. Do not overbeat, or the meringue will become dry or grainy. Allow the meringue to cool to room temperature, stirring occasionally.

CHOCOLATE MOUSSE FILLING

2 cups heavy whipping cream

1 envelope gelatin

¼ cup cold water

1 cup egg whites (from 7 or 8 large eggs)

1 cup sugar

8 ounces bittersweet chocolate, melted

One 9-inch layer Chocolate Génoise, page 117

Chocolate shavings for finishing

One 10-inch springform pan

4   When the meringue is cool, whisk about one-third of it into the chocolate, then quickly fold the chocolate mixture back into the remaining meringue. Quickly rewhip the cream if it has separated, and fold the cream into the chocolate mixture.

5 To assemble, using a sharp serrated knife, slice the génoise into 2 layers. Place one of the cake layers in the springform pan and top with half the mousse. Repeat with the remaining layer and remaining mousse. Refrigerate for at least 8 hours, or overnight.

6 To unmold the cake, run a small knife around the inside of the pan. Release the spring and lift off the sides of the pan. Top with chocolate shavings and press more against the side of the cake.

SERVING: Use a thin knife dipped in hot water and wiped clean after each slice to cut the cake.

STORAGE: Store loosely covered in the refrigerator for at least 8 hours before serving.

MAKES ONE 9-INCH CAKE, ABOUT 12 SERVINGS

(see photograph, pages 226-227)

STRAWBERRY STREUSEL CAKE

~⊙ ⊙ ⌒~

THIS IS A GREAT MAKE-AHEAD CAKE—it keeps well for a full day in the refrigerator. Just make sure to bring it to room temperature for about an hour before serving. This cake is loosely based on a cake originated by the great Parisian pastry chef Pierre Hermé.

1 Preheat the oven to 350 degrees.

2 To make the streusel, stir together all the ingredients except the butter in a medium bowl, mixing well. Stir in the butter and continue stirring until the mixture forms large crumbs. Place the crumbs on second prepared pan and bake for about 20 minutes, until golden and firm. Cool on the pan.

3 For the mousse, in the bowl of a heavy-duty mixer, beat the cream cheese and confectioners' sugar with the paddle on medium speed until very light, about 5 minutes. Beat in the kirsch and vanilla.

4 Whip the cream to a soft peak, and fold it into the cream cheese mixture.

5 To assemble, trim the biscuit layer to an even 9-inch round and place it in the springform pan. Spread half the mousse over the layer, making sure the mousse goes to the edges of the pan. Cover with the

STREUSEL

1¼ cups all-purpose flour (spoon flour into dry-measure cup and level off)

½ cup sugar

1 teaspoon baking powder

Pinch of ground cinnamon

8 tablespoons (1 stick) unsalted butter, melted

One 10-inch biscuit layer, page 118

CREAM CHEESE FILLING

1 pound cream cheese, softened

1 cup confectioners' sugar, sifted

1 tablespoon kirsch

1 teaspoon vanilla extract

½ cup heavy whipping cream

1 pint strawberries, rinsed, hulled, and quartered

Confectioners' sugar for finishing

One 10-inch springform pan plus one jelly-roll pan

berries, then the remaining mousse. Press the streusel into the top of the filling. Refrigerate for at least 8 hours, or overnight, to set the filling.

6 To unmold, run a knife around the inside of the pan and remove the side.

7 Just before serving, dust the dessert lightly with confectioners' sugar.

SERVING: Use a thin knife dipped in hot water and wiped clean after each slice to cut the cake.

STORAGE: Store loosely covered in the refrigerator.

MAKES ONE 10-INCH CAKE, ABOUT 12 SERVINGS

BLANC-MANGER AUX FRAMBOISES

Almond Mousse Cake with Raspberries

~⊙~⊙~

BLANC-MANGER, A TYPE OF ALMOND CREAM that dates from the eighteenth century, is making a major comeback in pastry shops in Paris. Essentially simple, the dessert is light and satisfying.

1 Trim the sponge disk to an even 9-inch diameter and place in the springform pan; set aside.

2 To make the blancmange, whip the cream; refrigerate.

3 Sprinkle the gelatin over the surface of the water in a small cup and allow to soften for 5 minutes. Whisk the egg whites and sugar together in a mixer bowl, then whisk over simmering water until the egg whites are hot and the sugar is dissolved. Scrape in the gelatin and stir well to mix. Attach the bowl to the mixer and whip with the whisk on medium speed until cooled and increased in volume.

4 Remove the whipped cream from the refrigerator and fold in the almonds and extract. Fold the cream into the meringue.

One 10-inch Sponge Base, page 95

BLANC-MANGER

2 cups heavy whipping cream

1½ envelopes gelatin

¼ cup water

4 large egg whites

¾ cup sugar

1 cup (about 4 ounces) ground toasted almonds

1 teaspoon almond extract

One ½-pint basket fresh raspberries

FOR FINISHING

1 cup heavy whipping cream

1½ cups toasted sliced almonds

Confectioners' sugar

One 10-inch springform pan

5   Spread half the blancmange over the cake base in the pan. Scatter with the raspberries, then top with the remaining blancmange. Smooth the top and chill to set, 8 hours or overnight.

6   To finish, unmold the dessert by running a knife around the inside of the pan. Release the pan sides and remove. Spread the top and sides evenly with the whipped cream, then press the almonds into the cream to cover the entire dessert. Refrigerate.

7   Just before serving, sprinkle the cake lightly with confectioners' sugar.

SERVING: Use a thin knife dipped in hot water and wiped clean after each slice to cut the cake.

STORAGE: Store loosely covered in the refrigerator.

MAKES ONE 10-INCH CAKE, ABOUT 12 SERVINGS

DEVIL'S FOOD BOMBE

୬୬ ౭

THIS IS A DELICIOUS AND AMUSING WAY to present a chocolate cake filled with whipped cream. You probably won't use all of both layers to assemble the bombe, but you can save the scraps for a trifle.

1   For the filling, whip the cream with the sugar and vanilla to a soft peak.

2   Cut the cake into thin strips no more than 3/16-inch thick. Line the bowl with strips of cake, trimming to fit as necessary. Sprinkle with rum. Spread a layer of whipped cream over the bottom, then cover with strips of cake. Sprinkle the cake with rum and spread with more cream. Continue layering in this manner until the bowl is full, ending with a layer of cake. Wrap the bowl and chill for at least several hours, or overnight.

3   Unmold the cake onto a cardboard round or platter. Whip the cream with the sugar and vanilla to a soft peak, and spread all over the outside of the cake.

SERVING: Use a thin knife dipped in hot water and wiped clean after each slice to cut the cake.

FILLING

3 cups heavy whipping cream

½ cup sugar

2 teaspoons vanilla extract

One 9-inch layer 1942 Devil's Food
    Cake, page 212

⅓ cup dark rum

FOR FINISHING

1 cup heavy whipping cream

2 tablespoons sugar

½ teaspoon vanilla extract

One 2½-quart bowl, buttered and lined
with plastic wrap

STORAGE: Store loosely covered in the refrigerator for up to 8 hours before serving.

MAKES ABOUT 12 SERVINGS

CASINO

୬ ୭ ୧

WHEN THIS CAKE IS UNMOLDED, it is covered with whimsical-looking swirls of cake and jam.

I Trim the edges of the rectangular cake layer, then cut it into two 9 × 12-inch rectangles. Spread each with a very thin layer of the preserves, lay on parchment paper, roll them up tightly, and chill.

2 To assemble, slice the rolls into thin slices and use them to line the bowl.

3 To make the mousse, sprinkle the gelatin over water and allow to soften for 5 minutes. Whisk the yolks, vanilla seeds, sugar, and rum in the bowl of an electric mixer. Place over a saucepan of simmering water and whisk until thickened. Attach the bowl to the mixer, fitted with the whisk attachment, and whip until cool.

4 Place the gelatin mixture over the simmering water and stir to melt. Whip the cream until soft peaks form. Whisk the gelatin mixture into the yolk mixture, then fold in the whipped cream. Pour into the lined mold. Cover the mousse with the cake disk. Trim the sides to even them. Chill to set.

Biscuit base and layer, page 118
½ cup seedless raspberry preserves

VANILLA BEAN MOUSSE
1½ envelopes gelatin
¼ cup water
4 large egg yolks
2 Tahitian vanilla beans, split and seedy pulp scraped out (see page xiv)
½ cup sugar
3 tablespoons white rum
1½ cups heavy whipping cream

One 1½-quart bowl, buttered and lined with plastic wrap

5 To unmold, invert the bowl onto a platter. Lift off the bowl and plastic wrap.

SERVING: Use a thin knife dipped in hot water and wiped clean after each slice to cut the cake.

STORAGE: Store loosely covered in the refrigerator.

MAKES ABOUT 12 SERVINGS

ZUCCOTTO ALLA RICOTTA

~୨ ୧~

THIS ELEGANT FLORENTINE DESSERT uses a layer of pan di Spagna to line a bowl which is then filled with a rich ricotta mousse. The chocolate and pistachios add a bit of crunch to the rich filling.

1 Cut out a disk the size of the top of your bowl from the pan di Spagna and cut the rest of it into 2 large wedges. Cut the wedges into thin slices and line the bowl with them. Sprinkle with the rum. Reserve the disk to cover the filling.

2 To make the filling, combine the ricotta and confectioners' sugar in the food processor and process until smooth, about 2 minutes. Transfer to a large bowl.

3 Combine the rum and anisette in a small bowl and sprinkle the gelatin over the surface. Allow it to soak until softened, about 5 minutes, then place over a saucepan of simmering water and stir to melt. Whisk the dissolved gelatin into the ricotta mixture, then stir in the chocolate and pistachios. Whip the cream to soft peaks, and fold it in.

4 Pour the filling into the prepared mold and cover with the reserved disk of pan di Spagna. Cover with plastic wrap and chill until set, about 6 hours.

One 9-inch layer Pan di Spagna, page 124
¼ cup white rum for sprinkling

FILLING

One 15-ounce container ricotta
1 cup confectioners' sugar
3 tablespoons white rum
1 tablespoon anisette
1 envelope gelatin
3 tablespoons (about 1 ounce) chopped bittersweet chocolate
3 tablespoons (about 1 ounce) chopped pistachios
1 cup heavy whipping cream

FOR FINISHING

1 cup heavy whipping cream
2 tablespoons sugar
½ cup chopped pistachios

One 1½-quart bowl, buttered and lined with plastic wrap

5 Remove the plastic wrap and invert the bowl onto a platter. Remove the bowl and plastic wrap. Whip the cream with the sugar to soft peaks. Cover the Zuccotto with the cream. Sprinkle with the chopped pistachios.

SERVING: Serve the cake shortly after finishing.

STORAGE: Store the cake without the whipped cream, covered, in the refrigerator for up to 2 days. Finish the cake just prior to serving.

MAKES ONE 8- TO 9-INCH CAKE, ABOUT 16 SERVINGS

STRAWBERRY CHARLOTTE
WITH STRAWBERRIES

A CHARLOTTE IS ALWAYS ELEGANT in appearance and it's easy to prepare ahead of time. For the best flavor, use ripe local strawberries for the filling. That makes this a seasonal dessert, but it's worth waiting for.

1 Trim the ladyfingers to height of the sides of the springform pan. Line the bottom of the pan with the scraps. Line the sides of the pan with the trimmed ladyfingers, rounded sides out. Refrigerate until the filling is ready.

2 To make the Bavarian, rinse, hull, and slice the berries. Place in a saucepan with the sugar, bring to a boil over low heat, and simmer gently for about 10 minutes, until slightly thickened. Cool, then puree in a blender or processor. Transfer to a bowl and stir in the kirsch and lemon juice.

3 Place the water in a small heatproof bowl and sprinkle the gelatin over the surface. Allow to stand for 5 minutes, then place over a pan of simmering water and stir to melt. Cool the gelatin slightly.

Ladyfingers, page 118 in sponge cake
  chapter

STRAWBERRY BAVARIAN

2 pints strawberries

¾ cup sugar

2 tablespoons kirsch

1 tablespoon fresh lemon juice

1½ envelopes gelatin

¼ cup cold water

2 cups heavy whipping cream

FINISHING

1 pint strawberries, rinsed and halved

One 10-inch springform pan

4 Whip the cream until it holds a shape but is not too stiff. Whisk the dissolved gelatin into the puree, then fold in the cream. Pour the filling into the lined mold and chill for at least 8 hours, or overnight.

5 To unmold the charlotte, run a knife around the inside of the pan, release the sides of the pan, and remove. Decorate with strawberries.

SERVING: Use a thin knife dipped in hot water and wiped clean after each slice to cut the cake.

STORAGE: Store loosely covered in the refrigerator for up to 8 hours before serving. To prepare in advance, keep the cake covered in the refrigerator, but only glaze strawberries on the day you plan to serve the dessert.

MAKES ONE 10-INCH CAKE, ABOUT 12 SERVINGS

CLASSIC CHOCOLATE CHARLOTTE

_9 9 C_

IN A CLASSIC CHARLOTTE SHAPE, this dessert is as elegant in appearance as in flavor.

1 To line the mold, trim the ends of 6 or 8 of the sponge fingers to a V shape and fit them together in the bottom of the mold. Line the sides of the mold with sponge fingers, saving some to cover the top of the mousse after the mold is filled.

2 To make the mousse, put the chocolate in a heatproof bowl and melt it over a saucepan of hot, but not simmering, water. Remove from the water and beat in the butter.

3 Whisk the yolks, liqueur, and sugar together in the bowl of an electric mixer. Place the bowl over a pan of simmering water and whisk until slightly thickened. Attach the bowl to the mixer and beat with the whisk attachment until cool. Fold in the chocolate mixture.

4 Whip the cream into soft peaks. Fold it into the chocolate mixture and pour into the lined mold. Cover with the reserved sponge fingers. Chill to set the mousse, at least 8 hours, or overnight.

Ladyfingers, page 118 in sponge cake chapter

CHOCOLATE MOUSSE FILLING
1 pound semisweet chocolate, finely chopped
8 tablespoons (1 stick) unsalted butter cut into 8 pieces
4 large egg yolks
⅓ cup orange liqueur
⅓ cup sugar
1 cup heavy whipping cream

One 2½-quart charlotte mold, buttered and lined with plastic wrap

5 Unmold the charlotte onto a platter.

SERVING: Use a thin knife dipped in hot water and wiped clean after each slice to cut the cake.

STORAGE: Store loosely covered in the refrigerator for up to 8 hours before serving.

MAKES ABOUT 12 SERVINGS

NATILLA DE SANTA CLARA

~๑ ໑~

THIS CUBAN DESSERT, somewhat like a combination of zuppa Inglese, the Italian version of trifle, and crème Brûlée, because it is topped with caramelized sugar, is one that I first encountered at the Versailles, Miami's best-known Cuban restaurant. There, the natilla is served as an "individual" portion in a shallow 6-inch gratin dish—actually enough for several people. The dessert is named for a suburb of Havana.

CAKE BATTER

4 large eggs, separated

¾ cup sugar

Pinch of salt

1 cup cake flour (spoon flour into dry-
  measure cup and level off)

ANISE SYRUP

1 cup water

½ cup sugar

3 tablespoons Anis Gorila or other
  Spanish anisette

NATILLA (CUSTARD)

4 cups milk

1½ cups sugar

¼ teaspoon salt

A 3-inch strip lemon zest

½ cup water

½ cup cornstarch

8 large egg yolks

2 teaspoons vanilla extract

¼ cup sugar for caramelizing the top

One 9 × 13 × 2-inch baking pan, buttered and bottom lined with parchment or wax paper; a 2-quart oval gratin dish or one 9 × 13 × 2-inch Pyrex baking dish, buttered

1 Position a rack in the middle of the oven and preheat to 350 degrees.

2 To make the cake layer, in the bowl of a heavy-duty mixer fitted with the whisk, whip the yolks with 6 tablespoons of the sugar until light and increased in volume.

3 In a clean, dry mixer bowl, with the clean, dry whisk attachment, whip the whites with the salt on medium speed until they are opaque and beginning to hold a shape. Gradually whip in the remaining 6 tablespoons remaining sugar, and continue to whip until the whites hold a soft peak.

Fold in the yolk mixture, then sift the cake flour over the bowl in three or four additions and fold it in.

4 Scrape the batter into the prepared pan and smooth top. Bake for about 20 to 25 minutes, or until the cake is well colored and firm. Unmold onto a rack then turn right side up to cool.

5 To make the syrup, combine the water and sugar in a small saucepan and bring to a boil over medium heat, stirring occasionally to dissolve the sugar. Cool, and stir in the liqueur.

6 Slice the cake into 2 layers and place one in the baking dish. Brush with half the syrup. Cover the other layer and reserve it, along with the rest of the syrup, until the natilla is ready.

7 For the natilla, bring the milk, sugar, salt, and lemon zest to a boil in a large nonreactive saucepan over low heat. Meanwhile, in a medium bowl, whisk together the cornstarch and water until smooth. Whisk in the yolks. When the milk mixture has come to a boil, whisk half into the yolk mixture. Return the remaining milk to a boil and whisk in the yolk mixture

in a stream, then continue to whisk constantly until the natilla thickens and returns to a boil. Remove the pan from the heat, remove the lemon zest, and whisk in the vanilla.

8 Pour half the natilla over the moistened cake layer in the baking dish. Top with the other layer, moisten that layer with the remaining syrup, and pour on the remaining natilla. Smooth the top. Cover loosely with plastic wrap and refrigerate until cold.

9 To caramelize the top, blot any condensation that has formed on the surface. Sprinkle the top evenly with the sugar and run under a hot broiler, or caramelize using a small propane torch.

SERVING: Serve within an hour of caramelizing the top so that the sugar crust does not melt.

STORAGE: Store at cool room temperature for 1 hour. To prepare this dessert in advance, assemble the dessert, cover loosely with plastic wrap, and chill for up to 2 days, but do not caramelize the top until right before serving.

MAKES 8 TO 10 SERVINGS

TIRAMISU

❧ ❧

I HAVE SERVED THIS WITH GREAT RESULTS for more than 20 years.

1   To make the syrup, combine the water and sugar in a saucepan and bring to a boil. Cool, and stir in the coffee and brandy.

2   To make the filling, whisk the yolks in the bowl of an electric mixer, then whisk in the sugar and Marsala. Set over a pan of simmering water and whisk until thickened. Attach the bowl to the mixer and beat with the whisk attachment until cooled. (This is the zabaione.)

3   Mash the mascarpone in a bowl with a rubber spatula until smooth. Fold in the zabaione. Whip the cream, and fold it in.

4   Cut the pan di Spagna crosswise into thin slices. Place a layer of slices in the bottom of the gratin dish and brush with syrup. Spread with half the filling. Repeat with another layer of syrup and cake filling, ending with a layer of pan di Spagna and the remaining syrup.

5   Whip the cream with the sugar. Spread the whipped cream over the surface of the dessert. Sprinkle with cinnamon and coffee grounds. Refrigerate for several hours.

SERVING: Use a large spoon to serve.

ESPRESSO SYRUP
½ cup water
½ cup sugar
½ cup very strong brewed espresso
¼ cup Italian brandy, such as Stock (*not* grappa)

FILLING
3 large egg yolks
⅓ cup sugar
⅓ cup sweet Marsala
1 cup mascarpone, at room temperature
1 cup heavy whipping cream

One 9- or 10-inch layer Pan di Spagna, page 124

FOR FINISHING
1 cup heavy whipping cream
2 tablespoons sugar
Ground cinnamon
Coffee grounds

One 2-quart gratin dish or glass bowl

STORAGE: Store covered in the refrigerator for up to 2 days.

MAKES ABOUT 12 SERVINGS

CHOCOLATE-RASPBERRY TRIFLE

〜♋〜

LOOSELY BASED ON THE ITALIAN SWEET zuppa inglese, this trifle is easy to make in advance for holiday entertaining.

1   To make the custard creams, in a heavy nonreactive pan, combine the milk and ¾ cup of the sugar and bring to a boil. Meanwhile, whisk the yolks with the remaining ¾ cup sugar in a large bowl. Sift the flour over the yolks and whisk it in. When the milk boils, whisk one-third of it into the yolk mixture. Return the remaining milk to a boil and whisk in the yolk mixture, then continue to whisk until the mixture thickens and comes back to a boil. Whisk constantly for 30 seconds, remove from the heat, and whisk in the vanilla.

2   Scrape half the cream into a bowl and cover with plastic wrap; refrigerate to cool. Whisk the chocolate into remaining cream until melted, scrape into a bowl, cover, and cool.

3   To make the syrup, bring the water and sugar to a boil in a saucepan. Cool, and stir in the rum.

4   For the whipped cream, combine all the ingredients and whip to a soft peak.

CUSTARD CREAMS

4 cups milk

1½ cups sugar

12 large egg yolks

⅔ cup all-purpose flour (spoon flour into dry-measure cup and level off)

2 teaspoons vanilla extract

6 ounces semisweet chocolate, finely chopped

RUM SYRUP

¾ cup water

¾ cup sugar

½ cup dark rum

WHIPPED CREAM

2 cups heavy whipping cream

¼ cup sugar

2 teaspoons vanilla extract

One 9-inch plain or chocolate génoise, page 116

FOR FINISHING

Two ½-pint baskets raspberries

Chocolate shavings

One 2-quart glass serving bowl

5 To assemble, cut cake crosswise into thin slices. Place a layer of slices in the bottom of the glass serving bowl and moisten with syrup. Spread with half the vanilla cream and scatter with about half the raspberries. Top with half the chocolate cream, then half the whipped cream. Repeat the layering with the remaining ingredients, reserving a few raspberries for garnish. Sprinkle lightly with chocolate shavings and the reserved raspberries.

SERVING: Use a large spoon to serve.

STORAGE: Store loosely covered in the refrigerator.

MAKES 12 TO 16 SERVINGS

STRAWBERRY-LEMON TRIFLE

TRADITIONALLY, TRIFLE WAS OFTEN MADE from odds and ends, so think of making this when you have some extra lemon curd or sponge cake on hand.

LEMON FILLING

¾ cup fresh lemon juice

1 cup sugar

8 tablespoons (1 stick) unsalted butter

6 large egg yolks

1¼ cups heavy whipping cream

STRAWBERRY SYRUP

1 pint strawberries

½ cup water

½ cup sugar

2 tablespoons kirsch

One 9-inch layer Plain Génoise, page 116

FOR FINISHING

2 pints strawberries

½ cup (about 2 ounces) toasted sliced almonds

1 cup strawberry jam

1 cup heavy whipping cream

One 2-quart glass serving bowl

1   To make the lemon filling, bring the lemon juice, sugar, and butter to a boil in a nonreactive saucepan over low heat. Meanwhile, whisk the yolks in a medium bowl. Whisk one-third of the lemon mixture into the yolks. Return the remaining lemon mixture to a boil over low heat and whisk in the yolk mixture. Continue whisking constantly until the mixture is thickened and just at a boil. Pour into a bowl, press plastic wrap against the surface, and chill.

2   To make the syrup, rinse and hull the strawberries; puree in a blender. Bring the water and sugar to a boil in a medium saucepan. Off the heat, add the puree and kirsch. Strain and chill.

3   Immediately before assembling the dessert, finish the filling: Whip the cream and fold it into the lemon curd.

4   To assemble, cut the génoise crosswise into thin vertical slices. Rinse the berries and reserve 6 to use for decoration. Hull and slice the remaining berries. Place a layer of cake in the bottom of the glass serving bowl. Moisten the cake with syrup and strew with one-quarter of the sliced berries and one-quarter of the almonds. Dot with one-quarter of the jam. Spread with one-quarter of the lemon filling. Repeat the pattern, ending with a final layer of cake slices and syrup.

5   Whip the cream, and spread half over the top of the trifle. Pipe a decorative border with the remaining cream, using a pastry bag fitted with a star tube, and garnish with the reserved strawberries.

SERVING: Use a large spoon to serve.

STORAGE: Store in the refrigerator.

MAKES 16 SERVINGS

12 INDIVIDUAL CAKES

THE MAIN ATTRACTION OF INDIVIDUAL CAKES lies in the fact that you get your very own whole cake. Seriously, though, these are elegant, and, for the most part, easy, ways to make a great impression when you want to keep things fairly simple. The madeleines and financiers are also perfect accompaniments to a simple dessert like ice cream, or with coffee after dessert.

PETITS FINANCIERS

THESE SMALL SQUARE OR RECTANGULAR buttery cakes are found in almost all Parisian pastry shops. Allowing the butter to color slightly as it cooks adds a nutty flavor to the baked cakes. Deflating the batter prevents the molds from overflowing during baking.

1 Mix the ground nuts, flour, and ¾ cup of the sugar together, and set aside.

2 Melt the butter in a small saucepan and continue to heat until it foams and colors slightly. Pour into a bowl to cool; add the rum and vanilla.

3 In the bowl of a heavy-duty mixer, beat the egg whites with the salt with the whisk attachment on medium speed until white and opaque. Increase the speed and add the remaining ¾ cup sugar in a stream. Continue to beat until the whites hold a firm peak. Fold in the almond mixture and the butter mixture.

½ cup (about 2 ounces) ground
    almonds

½ cup (about 2 ounces) ground
    hazelnuts

1 cup all-purpose flour (spoon flour
    into dry-measure cup and level off)

1½ cups sugar

10 tablespoons (1¼ sticks) unsalted
    butter

2 tablespoons dark rum

1 teaspoon vanilla extract

8 large egg whites (about 1 cup)

Pinch of salt

Chopped almonds and hazelnuts for
    finishing

Small square or rectangular molds,
buttered and floured

4 If possible, refrigerate the batter overnight, then bring to room temperature before using. If you haven't the time, stir the batter over a bowl of cold water for 5 minutes, or until it deflates.

5 Meanwhile, position a rack in the middle of the oven and preheat to 350 degrees.

6 Pipe each mold half-full with batter. Sprinkle the tops with a mixture of chopped almonds and hazelnuts.

7 Bake for about 20 minutes. Cool for several minutes in the pans, then carefully invert onto a work surface. Cool the financiers on a rack.

SERVING: Serve with dessert or alone with a favorite beverage.

STORAGE: Store well wrapped in the refrigerator for a few days, or freeze for longer storage.

MAKES ABOUT 24 INDIVIDUAL CAKES, DEPENDING ON THE SIZE OF THE MOLDS

PISTACHIO FINANCIERS

～◌ ◌～

THESE LITTLE CAKES with a delicate green color are as rich as they are light and delicate.

1 Position a rack in the middle of the oven and preheat to 350 degrees.

2 Place the pistachios and ¾ cup of the sugar in a food processor and pulse until finely ground. Pour into a bowl and stir in the flour.

3 Melt the butter. Remove from the heat and add the kirsch and vanilla extract. Set aside to cool slightly.

4 In the clean, dry bowl of a heavy-duty mixer, beat the egg whites with the salt with the whip until they hold a very soft peak. Beat in the remaining ¾ cup sugar in a very slow stream, and continue beating until the egg whites hold a soft peak again.

5 Beginning with the nuts and ending with the butter, alternately fold the pistachio and butter mixtures into the egg whites, one-third at a time.

6 Use a spoon or a pastry bag fitted with a ½-inch plain tube (Ateco 806) to fill the little pans ¾ full.

7 Bake the financiers for about 20 minutes, until well risen and golden. The center of a cake should feel firm when pressed with the

1 cup pistachios (about 4 ounces), blanched whole
1½ cups sugar
1 cup unbleached all-purpose flour (spoon flour into dry-measure cup and level off)
10 tablespoons (1¼ sticks) unsalted butter
2 tablespoons kirsch or maraschino liqueur
2 teaspoons vanilla extract
8 large egg whites (about 1 cup)
Pinch of salt
Confectioners' sugar for finishing

Four 12-cavity mini-muffin pans, buttered and floured

palm of your hand. Cool the financiers briefly in the pan on a rack, then unmold.

8 Just before serving, dust very lightly with confectioners' sugar.

SERVING: Serve with or as dessert.

STORAGE: Store well wrapped in the refrigerator, or freeze for longer storage.

MAKES ABOUT 48 INDIVIDUAL CAKES, DEPENDING ON THE SIZE OF THE MOLDS

CHOCOLATE-GLAZED FINANCIERS

❧ ❧

THESE RICH ALMOND CAKES can be served alone, with just a light dusting of confectioners' sugar, or with raspberries or other fruit.

1   Position the racks to divide the oven into thirds and preheat to 350 degrees.

2   To make the batter, place the almonds and ¾ cup of the sugar in a food processor and pulse until finely ground. Pour into a bowl and stir in the flour.

3   Melt the butter. Remove from the heat and add the kirsch and vanilla extract. Set aside to cool slightly.

4   In the clean, dry bowl of a heavy-duty mixer fitted with the whisk attachment, beat the egg whites with the salt until they form a very soft peak. Beat in the remaining ¾ cup sugar in a very slow stream, and continue beating until the egg whites hold a soft peak again.

5   Beginning with the almonds and ending with the butter, alternately fold the almond and butter mixtures into the egg whites, one-third at a time.

6   Use a pastry bag or a measuring spoon to fill the molds about three-quarters full.

FINANCIER BATTER

1 cup (about 4 ounces) blanched whole almonds

1½ cups sugar

1 cup all-purpose flour (spoon flour into dry-measure cup and level off)

10 tablespoons (1¼ sticks) unsalted butter

2 tablespoons kirsch

2 teaspoons vanilla extract

8 large egg whites (about 1 cup)

Pinch of salt

CHOCOLATE GLAZE

⅓ cup water

⅓ cup light corn syrup

1 cup sugar

8 ounces semisweet chocolate, finely chopped

Toasted sliced almonds for finishing

Four 12-cavity mini-muffin pans, buttered and floured

7 Bake the cakes for about 20 minutes, until well risen and firm. Unmold onto racks to cool.

8 To make the glaze, combine the water, corn syrup, and sugar in a small saucepan, stir well to mix, and bring to a boil over low heat, stirring occasionally. Off the heat, add the chocolate and allow to stand for 2 minutes. Whisk until smooth.

9 Dip the bottom of each little cake into the glaze and place glaze side up on a rack over paper, allowing any extra glaze to drip down the sides. Decorate the top of each cake with a sliced almond.

SERVING: Serve these delightful cakes anytime.

STORAGE: Store loosely wrapped at cool room temperature.

MAKES ABOUT 48 SMALL CAKES

FRUIT FINANCIERS

THIS FRUIT-FILLED VERSION OF A FINANCIER is made with softened, as opposed to melted, butter for a moist texture that holds the fruit in suspension (rather than having it all fall to the bottom).

¾ cup (about 3 ounces) ground almonds

¾ cup all-purpose flour (spoon flour into dry-measure cup and level off)

¾ cup sugar

Grated zest of 1 lemon

6 tablespoons (¾ stick) unsalted butter, softened

1 tablespoon rum

1 teaspoon vanilla extract

3 large egg whites

1 pint blueberries or raspberries

½ cup sliced almonds for finishing

Nine 3¾-inch tart pans, buttered and floured

1 Position the racks to divide the oven into thirds and preheat to 350 degrees.

2 In the bowl of a heavy-duty mixer, mix the ground almonds, flour, sugar, and lemon zest with paddle until combined. Add the butter and continue beating for 2 minutes.

3 Beat the rum and vanilla into the egg whites, then beat into the butter mixture in two additions, beating for 2 minutes after each addition and scraping down the bowl and beater as necessary.

4 Fill each pan with ¼ cup of batter. Sprinkle with the berries and sliced almonds.

5 Bake for about 35 minutes. Unmold and serve.

SERVING: Serve the cakes alone or with whipped cream and/or a fruit sauce or compote.

STORAGE: Store covered at room temperature, or wrap well and freeze for longer storage.

MAKES ABOUT 9 INDIVIDUAL CAKES, DEPENDING ON THE SIZE OF THE MOLDS

NICOLE KAPLAN'S MADELEINES

~⑤ ⓒ~

THIS RECIPE COMES FROM the talented pastry chef of New York's Eleven Madison Park restaurant.

1 In a small pan, melt the butter over medium heat and then continue to cook until it begins to smell nutty and turns brown. Remove from the heat and strain through a fine sieve into a bowl.

2 In the bowl of a heavy-duty mixer fitted with the whisk, beat the eggs and sugar until fluffy. Sift the flour, baking powder, and salt over the eggs and fold in with a rubber spatula. Fold in the butter and lemon zest. Spoon the batter into a pastry bag fitted with a ¼-inch plain tip. Refrigerate for at least 2 hours, or overnight.

3 When you are ready to bake, set the racks to divide the oven into thirds and preheat to 375 degrees.

4 Pipe the batter into the prepared molds, filling them three-quarters full. Bake until the madeleines form humps and are nut brown around the edges, about 12 minutes.

5 Remove the pans from the oven and bang them on a countertop to release the

7 tablespoons unsalted butter

5 large eggs

½ cup plus 3 tablespoons sugar

1¼ cups unbleached all-purpose flour (spoon flour into dry-measure cup and level off)

1 teaspoon baking powder

Large pinch of fine sea salt

Grated zest of 1 lemon

Madeleine molds, buttered and floured

madeleines. Carefully lift out any that stick, using the point of a knife to help you. Wrap in a napkin to keep warm. Repeat with the remaining batter.

SERVING: These are great for dessert, exquisite with tea.

STORAGE: Store in an airtight container at room temperature.

MAKES 24 MADELEINES, DEPENDING ON THE SIZE OF THE MOLDS USED

OTHELLOS

~⎯⎯⎯⎯⎯⎯⎯~

THIS CLASSIC SMALL VIENNESE PASTRY is made from two spherical sponge bases sandwiched with pastry cream and covered with a chocolate glaze—an indulgent morsel.

1 Position the racks to divide the oven into thirds and preheat to 350 degrees.

2 To make the sponge bases, in the bowl of a heavy-duty mixer fitted with the whisk, whip the yolks with the vanilla and 6 tablespoons of the sugar until very light.

3 In the clean, dry mixer bowl, with the whisk attachment, whip the whites with the salt until white and opaque. Increase the speed and whip in the remaining 6 tablespoons sugar in a stream. Continue whipping until the whites hold a firm peak. Fold in the yolks, then sift the cake flour over the mixture and fold in gently with a rubber spatula.

4 Scrape the batter into a pastry bag fitted with a ½-inch plain tube (Ateco 806) and pipe the batter into 2-inch-wide domes on the prepared pans. Bake for about 10 to 15 minutes. Slide the papers off the pans onto racks to cool.

5 To make the pastry cream, combine 1½ cups of the milk with the sugar in a saucepan and bring to a boil over low heat.

SPONGE BASES

6 large eggs, separated

¾ cup sugar

1 teaspoon vanilla extract

Pinch of salt

1½ cups cake flour (spoon flour into dry-measure cup and level off)

PASTRY CREAM FILLING

2 cups milk

½ cup sugar

⅓ cup cornstarch

4 large egg yolks

¾ cup heavy whipping cream

2 teaspoons vanilla extract

APRICOT GLAZE

1½ cups apricot preserves

⅓ cup water

CHOCOLATE GLAZE

½ cup water

½ cup light corn syrup

1½ cups sugar

9 ounces semisweet chocolate, finely chopped

Two 12 × 18-inch jelly-roll pans, lined with parchment paper

Meanwhile, in a bowl, whisk the remaining ½ cup milk with the cornstarch to mix. Whisk in the yolks. When the milk boils, whisk one-third of it into the yolk mixture. Return the remaining milk to a boil and whisk in the yolk mixture, then continue whisking until the cream thickens and comes to a boil. Boil, whisking constantly, for about 30 seconds. Remove from the heat, scrape into a reactive bowl, and press plastic wrap against the surface. Refrigerate until cold.

6 To make the apricot glaze, bring the preserves and water to a boil in a saucepan over low heat, stirring occasionally. Strain into another small pan and reduce until slightly sticky.

7 Detach the bases from the paper and hollow out the center of each one slightly with a melon ball scoop. Arrange the bases on racks set over parchment or wax paper and paint with the hot apricot glaze. Allow the glaze to set and dry.

8 To make the chocolate glaze, bring the water, corn syrup, and sugar to a boil in a saucepan over low heat, stirring often.

Remove from the heat, add the chocolate, and allow to stand for 3 minutes. Whisk until smooth. Pour the glaze over the bases on racks. Allow the glaze to dry.

9 Immediately before assembling the cakes, finish the pastry cream filling. Whip the cream with the vanilla, and fold into the cooled cream.

10 To assemble, place half the bases upside down on a parchment- or wax paper–lined pan or in paper cases. Pipe a large rosette of the pastry cream onto each. Top each with another base right side up and press together gently just once with a finger on the center of the top, to avoid marring the glaze. Reheat the leftover glaze in a bowl over a pan of gently simmering water and pipe a spiral with a paper cone on each Othello, making sure to cover the mark you made pressing the bases together.

SERVING: Serve the cakes shortly after they have been assembled.

STORAGE: Store leftovers well wrapped in the refrigerator for up to 2 days.

MAKES ABOUT 30 INDIVIDUAL CAKES

CHOCOLATE-RASPBERRY CUBES

〜 ❧ 〜

TRY FOLDING A BASKET OF FRESH RASPBERRIES into the raspberry filling before spreading it over the cake layer.

1 To make the syrup, bring the water and sugar to a boil in a small saucepan. Cool, and add the raspberry eau-de-vie.

2 To make the filling, bring the raspberries to a boil in a nonreactive saucepan and reduce slightly. Puree in a food processor or blender and strain to remove the seeds. Set aside to cool.

3 Whisk the egg whites and sugar together in the bowl of an electric mixer. Set over a pan of simmering water and whisk until the egg whites are hot and the sugar has dissolved. Attach the bowl to the mixer and beat with the whisk attachment until the mixture has cooled. Switch to the paddle attachment and beat in the butter gradually. Continue to beat until smooth, then beat in the raspberry puree and eau-de-vie.

4 To make the glaze, bring the cream to a boil in a small saucepan. Remove from the heat, add the chocolate, and allow to stand for five minutes. Whisk until smooth, then strain and cool.

RASPBERRY SYRUP

¼ cup water

⅓ cup sugar

2 tablespoons raspberry Framboise

RASPBERRY FILLING

One 10- or 12-ounce package frozen
    raspberries

4 large egg whites

¾ cup sugar

½ pound (2 sticks) unsalted butter,
    softened

2 tablespoons raspberry eau-de-vie

CHOCOLATE GLAZE

1 cup heavy whipping cream

8 ounces semisweet chocolate, cut into
    ¼-inch pieces

1 Chocolate Génoise Sheet, page 117

FOR FINISHING

20 raspberries

Gold leaf

5 Cut the génoise in half to make two 9 × 12-inch layers. Place one on a cardboard rectangle and moisten with half the syrup. Spread with three-quarters of the raspberry filling. Top with the remaining layer and moisten with the remaining syrup. Spread the top with the remaining filling, and chill to set.

6 Spread the cooled glaze over the top of cake, and chill to set.

7 Using a sharp knife dipped into hot water and wiped clean between each cut, cut the cake into 2-inch cubes. Decorate with the raspberries and gold leaf.

SERVING: Serve these delicate but rich cakes as dessert.

STORAGE: Store at cool room temperature for up to 6 hours. For longer storage, cover loosely and refrigerate or freeze.

MAKES ABOUT 20 INDIVIDUAL CAKES

ORANGE-HAZELNUT MERINGUES

Delicate meringue fingers are sandwiched together with a rich orange cream and sprinkled with toasted hazelnuts.

1 Position the racks to divide the oven into thirds and preheat to 300 degrees.

2 To make the meringues, in the bowl of a heavy-duty mixer, beat the egg whites and salt with the whisk attachment on medium speed until white and opaque. Increase the speed to medium-high and beat in ½ cup of the sugar in a stream. Continue to beat until the egg whites are very firm, but not dry.

3 Combine the remaining ½ cup sugar, the ground nuts, cinnamon, and cornstarch and fold into the egg whites. Spoon the batter into a pastry bag fitted with a ½-inch plain tube (Ateco 806) and pipe 3-inch fingers onto the prepared pans.

4 Bake the meringues for about 25 minutes, until golden and fairly dry. Watch them carefully, as they burn easily.

5 To make the buttercream, whisk the yolks in the bowl of an electric mixer. Whisk in the liqueur and then the sugar, then place over a pan of simmering water and whisk until thickened. Attach to the mixer and beat with the whisk on medium

HAZELNUT MERINGUES
4 large egg whites, at room temperature
Pinch of salt
1 cup sugar
¾ cup (about 3 ounces) ground hazelnuts
¼ teaspoon ground cinnamon
2 tablespoons cornstarch

ORANGE BUTTERCREAM FILLING
4 large egg yolks
½ cup sugar
⅓ cup orange liqueur
½ pound (2 sticks) unsalted butter, softened

FOR FINISHING
Chopped toasted hazelnuts
Confectioners' sugar

Three 12 × 18-inch jelly-roll pans, lined with parchment paper

speed until cold. In 5 or 6 additions, beat in the butter.

6 Line up half the fingers on a parchment- or wax paper–lined pan, rounded side

down. Pipe a line of the buttercream down each finger, then top with the remaining fingers, flat side facing the filling. Sprinkle with chopped nuts and dust very lightly with confectioners' sugar.

SERVING: Serve at cool room temperature.

STORAGE: Store the filled meringues at cool room temperature until serving time.

MAKES ABOUT 24 INDIVIDUAL CAKES

COFFEE-PECAN MERINGUES

THE SWEETNESS OF PECANS contrasts perfectly with the slight bitterness of the coffee filling.

PECAN MERINGUES
4 large egg whites
Pinch of salt
1 cup sugar
¾ cup (about 3 ounces) ground pecans
¼ teaspoon ground cinnamon
2 tablespoons cornstarch

COFFEE BUTTERCREAM FILLING
4 large egg yolks
½ cup sugar

⅓ cup very strong brewed coffee
½ pound (2 sticks) unsalted butter, softened
2 tablespoons dark rum

FOR FINISHING
Chopped toasted pecans
Confectioners' sugar

Two 12 × 18-inch jelly-roll pans, lined with parchment paper

1 Position the racks to divide the oven into thirds and preheat to 300 degrees.

2 To make the meringues, in the bowl of a heavy-duty mixer, beat the egg whites and salt with the whisk attachment on medium speed until white and opaque. Increase the speed to medium-high and beat in ½ cup of the sugar in a stream. Continue to beat until the egg whites are very firm, but not dry.

3 Combine the remaining ½ cup sugar with the ground pecans, cinnamon, and cornstarch and fold into the egg whites. Spoon the batter into a pastry bag fitted with a ½-inch plain tube (Ateco 806) and pipe 3-inch fingers onto the prepared pans.

4 Bake the meringues for about 25 minutes, until golden and fairly dry. Watch them carefully, as they burn easily.

5 To make the buttercream, whisk the yolks together in the bowl of an electric mixer. Whisk in the coffee, then the sugar. Place the bowl over a pan of simmering water and whisk until the mixture is thickened. Attach to the mixer and beat with the whisk on medium speed until cold. In 5 or 6 additions, beat in the butter, then beat in the rum.

6 Line up half the fingers, rounded side down, on a parchment- or wax paper–lined pan. Pipe a line of the buttercream down each finger, then top with the remaining fingers, flat side facing the filling. Pipe a rosette of buttercream onto the center of each. Sprinkle the rosettes with chopped pecans and dust very lightly with confectioners' sugar.

SERVING: Serve at cool room temperature.

STORAGE: Store the unfilled meringues in the freezer, well wrapped, until 6 hours before serving. Defrost before finishing.

MAKES ABOUT 24 INDIVIDUAL CAKES

CHOCOLATE-RASPBERRY MERINGUES

～⌐◌ ⌐～

CHOCOLATE AND RASPBERRIES are one of my favorite flavor pairings—here the creamy chocolate filling is garnished with fresh raspberries.

1   Position the racks to divide the oven into thirds and preheat to 300 degrees.

2   To make the meringues, in the bowl of a heavy-duty mixer, beat the egg whites and salt with the whisk attachment on medium speed until white and opaque. Increase the speed to high and beat in ½ cup of the sugar in a stream. Continue to beat until the whites are very firm, but not dry.

3   Combine the remaining ½ cup sugar, the ground almonds, and cornstarch and fold into the egg whites. Spoon the batter into a pastry bag fitted with a ½-inch plain tube (Ateco 806) and pipe 2-inch fingers onto the prepared pans.

4   Bake the meringues for about 25 minutes, until golden and fairly dry. Watch them carefully, as they burn easily. Cool on a rack.

ALMOND MERINGUES

4 large egg whites

1 cup sugar

Pinch of salt

¾ cup (about 3 ounces) ground almonds

2 tablespoons cornstarch

CHOCOLATE FILLING

1 cup heavy whipping cream

2 tablespoons unsalted butter

1 tablespoon light corn syrup

12 ounces semisweet chocolate, finely chopped

One ½-pint basket raspberries for finishing

Three 12 × 18-inch jelly-roll pans, lined with parchment paper

5   To make the filling, bring the cream, butter, and corn syrup to a boil in a medium saucepan. Remove from the heat and add the chocolate. Allow to stand for 2 to 3 minutes, then whisk until smooth. Cool to room temperature until thickened.

6   Line up half the fingers on a parchment- or wax paper–lined pan, rounded sides down. Pipe a line of the chocolate filling down each finger, then top with the remaining fingers, flat sides facing the filling. Pipe a rosette of buttercream onto the center of each finger. Top the rosettes with the raspberries.

SERVING: Serve these fingers as is, or with extra raspberries if you like.

STORAGE: Store at cool room temperature on the day the cakes are prepared, or wrap well and refrigerate for longer storage.

MAKES ABOUT 24 INDIVIDUAL CAKES

13 FROSTINGS, FILLINGS, AND GLAZES

SOME OF MY FAVORITE CAKES require no more finishing than putting them on a platter and serving them—or maybe dusting them with a sprinkling of confectioners' sugar. Many cakes, however, need a filling or frosting to finish them off properly. Once you know the ins and outs of cake fillings, icings, and glazes, you can confidently turn an ordinary cake into a master confection. Silky buttercreams, shiny glazes, and smooth frostings are not difficult—they just require a good recipe and a meticulous hand, both for preparation and for presentation.

At the end of this chapter, there are recipes for a few sauces and other accompaniments to finished cakes as well as some necessary components for cake finishing.

WHIPPED CREAM

NOTHING COULD BE SIMPLER than whipped cream, but many people have trouble getting that perfect billowy texture. There are two main reasons for failure with whipped cream: warmth and overbeating. If the cream, the room, or the utensils are warm, the cream will just stay liquid and eventually separate. For successful whipped cream, always chill—in warm weather, put the cream in the mixer bowl, then put the bowl and the whisk in the freezer for 10 minutes before you whip. And, don't overwhip the cream. The cream has to be fairly firm to spread it over the outside of a cake or to use for piping, but if the cream is whipped too much, it will separate, as water weeps from the curds.

1 Place the chilled cream, sugar, and vanilla in the chilled bowl of a heavy-duty mixer. Whip on medium speed with the chilled whisk attachment until the cream begins to hold a shape. Stop the mixer occasionally and check the texture of the cream with a rubber spatula. Stop whipping when the spatula leaves a wide trail in the cream.

2 Increase the speed to medium-high and whip until the cream holds a firm peak. Be careful not to whip the cream until it starts to separate.

2 cups heavy whipping cream, chilled
¼ cup sugar
1 teaspoon vanilla extract

3 Use the cream immediately, or cover the bowl with plastic wrap and refrigerate until you need it. If you leave the cream for more than a few minutes, it will separate and soften somewhat. Use a hand whisk to rewhip the cream immediately before you use it.

MAKES ABOUT 4 CUPS

BUTTERCREAM

❦

THIS BUTTERCREAM RECIPE is based on Swiss meringue, an easy technique that ensures success every time. The simmering water will heat the meringue ingredients enough so they will whip nicely, but not enough to cook them. If you're concerned about egg-borne illnesses, use pasteurized egg whites for this recipe.

1 Half-fill a 1½-quart saucepan with water, just a ½-inch or so, and bring to a boil over medium heat. Lower the heat so the water simmers.

2 Use a hand whisk to mix together the egg whites, sugar, and salt in the bowl of a heavy-duty mixer. Place the bowl over the pan of simmering water and gently whisk until the ingredients are hot (about 130 degrees) and the sugar is dissolved.

3 Attach the bowl to the mixer and whip with the whisk attachment on medium speed until the mixture is cooled, about 5 minutes: touch the outside of the bowl—it should feel cool.

4 Stop the mixer, remove the whisk, and attach the paddle. Beating at low speed, add the butter in 8 to 10 additions. The buttercream will look very soft and fluffy.

¾ cup egg whites (from about 5 large eggs)
1½ cups sugar
Pinch of salt
1 pound (4 sticks) unsalted butter, softened
Flavoring (see Box, page 280)

5 After all the butter has been added, increase the mixer speed to medium and continue to beat until the buttercream is thick and smooth—up to 5 minutes longer. At one point, the buttercream may appear to be separating—this is a normal stoppage on the way to smoothness, just keep beating.

6 Once the buttercream is firm and smooth, add the flavoring a little at a time and continue to beat until smooth.

7 Use the buttercream immediately, or refrigerate or freeze.

STORAGE: Buttercream keeps well in the refrigerator or the freezer. If you plan to store the buttercream, don't add the flavoring until right before using it. Store it in a plastic container with a tight-fitting cover. When you are ready to use the refrigerated or frozen buttercream, let it come to room temperature. Beat with the paddle on medium speed until smooth, then add the flavoring as above.

MAKES ABOUT 2 POUNDS, ENOUGH TO EASILY FILL AND FROST A 9-INCH CAKE

FLAVORING BUTTERCREAM

Use the following amounts to flavor the above batch of buttercream.

CHOCOLATE: 6 ounces bittersweet chocolate, chopped, melted with ¼ cup water, and cooled

COFFEE: ¼ cup triple-strength coffee (see page 252)

LEMON: ⅓ cup strained fresh lemon juice

LIQUOR OR EAU-DE-VIE: 3 tablespoons

SWEET LIQUEUR: ¼ cup

PRALINE: ⅓ cup praline paste

RASPBERRY: ½ cup thick seedless raspberry puree (see page 109)

VANILLA: 1½ tablespoons vanilla extract or the scraped-out pulp of a whole vanilla bean

This pull-out-all-the-stops rich filling is one of the best things that could ever happen to a cake layer. Basically a mixture of chocolate and cream, ganache may vary in texture and use, depending on the proportions. The strongest, sometimes called truffle ganache, has twice as much chocolate as cream; it is usually only used to make truffles or other chocolate candy centers. With a little less chocolate—1½ parts chocolate to 1 part cream—you'll get rich ganache, the type that's used as an icing for cakes. This type of ganache can be whipped by machine to lighten it before it is used. Finally, equal parts of chocolate and cream yield ordinary ganache, which makes a glaze to be poured over cakes. But if ordinary ganache is very cold, you can also whip it and spread it on a cake. I frequently add some butter and corn syrup to ganache to give it extra smoothness and depth of flavor.

RICH GANACHE

USE THIS TO SPREAD BETWEEN THE LAYERS of a cake or to cover the outside of a cake, or both. Sometimes I spread just a little on a cake layer before I add another filling, to add a hint of chocolate richness.

1   Bring the cream to a simmer in a 2-quart nonreactive saucepan over medium heat. Add the corn syrup and butter and remove the pan from the heat. Immediately add the chocolate and swirl the pan to make sure the chocolate is submerged in the hot liquid. Let stand for 3 minutes.

1¼ cups heavy whipping cream

2 tablespoons light corn syrup

4 tablespoons (½ stick) unsalted butter, cut into 6 pieces

1 pound bittersweet or semisweet chocolate, cut into ¼-inch pieces

2 Using a medium wire whisk, start in the center of the pan and begin whisking slowly in a small circle. As soon as the ingredients in the center of the pan are smooth, begin to whisk slowly outward in an ever-widening arc until the ganache is smooth. If a lump or two of unmelted chocolate remains, place the pan over very low heat and whisk gently until all the chocolate is melted.

3 Scrape the ganache into a bowl and cover loosely with plastic wrap. Cool the ganache to spreading consistency, either at room temperature or in the refrigerator. If you refrigerate the ganache, stir and scrape the bowl with a rubber spatula occasionally so the ganache cools evenly.

4 Use the ganache immediately, or refrigerate or freeze.

5 To lighten the ganache, if desired, use the paddle attachment on a heavy-duty mixer and beat the ganache at medium speed for about 30 seconds, or until the color lightens. Don't whip longer or at a higher speed, or the ganache will get too aerated and have a dry, crumbly consistency when spread on the finished cake.

STORAGE: Cover the unwhipped ganache tightly and refrigerate or freeze. Bring back to room temperature and use, or beat to lighten as above.

MAKES ABOUT 1¾ POUNDS, ENOUGH FOR FILLING AND FROSTING A 9- OR 10-INCH CAKE

VARIATIONS

SPIKED GANACHE: Whisk 2 tablespoons of liquor or eau-de-vie, or 3 tablespoons sweet liqueur, into the freshly made ganache.

GANACHE PRALINEE: Using the paddle attachment, beat together 4 tablespoons (½ stick) unsalted butter, softened, with ½ cup pralinée until smooth. Add the ganache and beat on low speed for a few seconds to mix together, then stop, scrape down the bowl and beater, and beat on medium speed for about 30 seconds to lighten. Sublime!

MILK CHOCOLATE GANACHE

~⟋⟍~

I COULD FILL (AND EAT) a cake with this ganache about twice a week. It has that perfect combination of lightness and richness that, as far as I'm concerned, is what a perfect cake filling is all about.

1 In a 2-quart nonreactive saucepan, bring the cream to a simmer over medium heat. Add the butter and remove the pan from the heat. Immediately add the chocolate and swirl the pan to make sure the chocolate is submerged in the hot liquid. Let stand for 3 minutes.

2 Using a medium wire whisk, start in the center of the pan and begin whisking slowly in a small circle. As soon as the ingredients in the center of the pan are smooth, begin to whisk slowly outward in an ever-widening arc until the ganache is smooth. If a lump or two of unmelted chocolate remains, place the pan over very low heat and whisk gently until all the chocolate is melted.

3 Scrape the ganache into a bowl and cover loosely with plastic wrap. Refrigerate the ganache, stirring and scraping down the bowl occasionally with a rubber spatula, until it is quite cold—about 70 degrees. The ganache will still be quite liquid.

4 This ganache is always whipped before it is used: Whip the ganache with the whisk

> 1½ cups heavy whipping cream
> 4 tablespoons (½ stick) unsalted butter, cut into 8 pieces
> 12 ounces best-quality milk chocolate, cut into ¼-inch pieces

on medium speed for about a minute, or until smooth, aerated, and of spreading consistency. Don't whip too long, or the ganache will solidify in the bowl and become unspreadable (see Note).

5 Use immediately to fill and cover a cake.

STORAGE: The unwhipped ganache can be refrigerated overnight in a plastic container with a tight-fitting cover.

MAKES ABOUT 1½ POUNDS

NOTE: Sometimes I divide the ganache into 3 parts—two for between the layers and a third, slightly larger portion to cover the outside of the cake. In that case, I whip each separately to avoid the problem of having any of the ganache solidify before it can be used.

ORDINARY GANACHE

~ ⚬ ~

THERE'S NOTHING ORDINARY about this shiny, elegant glaze, one of the best possible ways to finish off a cake. There aren't a lot of secrets to getting a good ganache glaze—in fact, the less you do to it, the better. If you decide to branch out and use this glaze on cakes other than those recommended for it in this book, remember that the cake must already be finished with whipped ganache, buttercream, a coat of strained reduced fruit preserves, or a sheet of marzipan—ganache glaze needs a smooth surface underneath it to make a smooth, shiny covering. Never pour it over the bare surface of a cake, or it will soak in instead of forming a smooth surface.

1 In a medium saucepan, bring the cream to a simmer. Remove from the heat, add the chocolate, and swirl the pan to make sure all the chocolate is submerged in the hot cream. Allow to stand for 3 minutes.

2 Whisk until smooth, but don't overmix, or the glaze will be riddled with bubbles. Strain the ganache through a fine wire-mesh strainer into a medium bowl. Cool to room temperature, then use immediately.

3 To glaze a cake, place it on a rack set in a jelly-roll pan. If the cake is round, start at the top center and pour the glaze in an ever-widening spiral to the edge of the cake. Quickly, using the side of the blade of a large metal spatula, sweep the excess off the top

1 cup heavy whipping cream
8 ounces bittersweet or semisweet
    chocolate, cut into ¼-inch pieces

of the cake, pressing very gently. Then use the tip of the spatula to touch up the sides if necessary with the glaze that has dripped onto the pan. Leave the cake on the rack until the glaze sets, then move it to a platter.

STORAGE: I prefer to use only freshly made ganache glaze. Leftovers should be refrigerated and may be used to flavor buttercream frosting or whipped cream.

MAKES ABOUT 1 POUND, ENOUGH TO
GLAZE A 9-INCH CAKE

FLUFFY WHITE ICING

꩜

THIS ICING IS ONE OF THE BEST VARIATIONS on meringue. It's really a version of what used to be called seven-minute frosting, because the mixture was beaten with a hand-rotary egg beater in a double boiler for that length of time. Nowadays, with our heavy-duty electric mixers, the ingredients only need to be warmed and then whipped up with the mixer.

1 Half-fill a 1½-quart saucepan with water and bring to a boil over medium heat. Lower the heat so the water simmers.

2 Use a hand whisk to combine the egg whites, sugar, salt, and corn syrup in the bowl of a heavy-duty mixer. Place the bowl over the pan of simmering water and gently whisk until the ingredients are hot (about 130 degrees) and the sugar has dissolved.

3 Attach the bowl to the mixer and whip the icing with the whisk attachment on medium speed until cooled, about 5

3 large egg whites (scant ½ cup)
1 cup sugar
Pinch of salt
⅓ cup light corn syrup

minutes: touch the outside of the bowl—it should feel cool.

4 Use immediately to fill and cover a cake.

MAKES ENOUGH FOR FILLING AND COVERING A 9-INCH TWO-LAYER CAKE

MERINGUE FROSTING

~∾९ ৎ∾~

THIS IS A LITTLE DIFFERENT from the Fluffy White Icing (page 285) because it gets colored in the oven after it is on the cake, the way meringue is on the top of a pie or tart. Also, unlike icing, it is only used on the outside of a cake.

1 Set a rack in the middle level of the oven and preheat to 400 degrees.

2 Half-fill a 1½-quart saucepan with water and bring to a boil over medium heat. Lower the heat so the water simmers.

3 Use a hand whisk to combine the egg whites, sugar, and salt in the bowl of a heavy-duty mixer. Place the bowl over the pan of simmering water and gently whisk until the ingredients are hot (about 130 degrees) and the sugar has dissolved.

4 Attach the bowl to the mixer and whip the icing with the whisk attachment on medium speed until cooled, about 5 minutes: touch the outside of the bowl— it should feel cool.

⅔ cup egg whites (from 4 to 5 large eggs)
Pinch of salt
1 cup sugar

5 Use immediately to cover a cake.

6 To color the meringue, set the cake on a cookie sheet or the back of a jelly-roll pan and bake for about 2 minutes, or until the meringue is lightly colored. Cool the cake before serving.

MAKES ENOUGH TO COVER AND DECORATE A 9- OR 10-INCH CAKE

CHOCOLATE GLAZE
MADE WITH SUGAR SYRUP

~⤬~

THIS IS AN APPROXIMATION of the famous Viennese preserving glaze—an airtight coat of chocolate used on cakes that need to be shipped great distances. Hotels and pastry shops in Vienna still have their "shipping cakes," many of them still enrobed in a glaze like this one.

This glaze can also be poured over a bare cake or one just brushed with the type of glaze made with reduced jam. It's great drizzled over a sponge cake or angel food cake baked in a tube pan. It should never be poured over a ganache or buttercream, because it must be applied hot and would melt the ganache or buttercream.

1 The cake to be glazed should be completely cooled before you start to prepare the glaze. Place the cake on a cardboard round on a rack set over a jelly-roll pan.

2 Bring the water, corn syrup, and sugar to a simmer in a 2-quart saucepan over medium heat, stirring often to dissolve the sugar completely. When the syrup begins to simmer, stop stirring, and let it come to a full rolling boil. Boil the syrup for a few seconds, until it loses its surface foam and becomes clear.

3 Off the heat, add the chocolate and swirl the pan to submerge the chocolate in the hot syrup. Let stand.

⅓ cup water
⅓ cup light corn syrup
1 cup sugar
8 ounces semisweet or bittersweet
    chocolate, cut into ¼-inch pieces

4 Whisk the glaze until smooth, but be careful not to whisk too much, or the glaze will be full of bubbles. Immediately pour the glaze over the prepared cake.

5 Leave the cake on the rack for an hour, then use the point of a small knife to separate the glaze at the bottom of the cake from the rack. Use a wide spatula to transfer the cake to a platter.

MAKES ENOUGH TO COVER A 9- OR 10-INCH CAKE

GLAZE MADE FROM PRESERVES OR JAM

‿༼ ༽‿

SOMETIMES THE OUTSIDE OF A CAKE needs to be sealed with a simple coat of strained, reduced jam before the surface is covered with a chocolate glaze or water icing. The fruit glaze not only seals, it also provides a smooth surface for the application of the next glaze. When you make this type of a glaze, be sure to reduce it enough—if the preserves are not sufficiently reduced, they will just be absorbed by the cake. If you use jelly instead of jam, melt it without the water—and it doesn't need to be strained.

1 If the preserves or jam has very large pieces of fruit in it, puree it in a blender or food processor. Add the water to the machine so that the thick preserves don't stick to the blade and bowl.

2 In a medium saucepan, bring the preserves and water to a simmer over low heat, stirring often. Strain the glaze into another pan and return to low heat. Allow the glaze to simmer for 3 to 4 minutes, or until it is reduced and slightly sticky. Use a scrap of cake to test: if the glaze stays on the surface when it is brushed on the scrap of cake, it is reduced enough.

> 1 cup fruit preserves or jam
> ¼ cup water

3 Use the glaze immediately, or reheat it gently right before you intend to use it, so that it doesn't further reduce.

STORAGE: Keep leftover glaze in a covered jar in the refrigerator. Stir a tablespoon or two of water into the glaze before you put it into the jar so it will be liquid and easy to pour out when you use it again.

MAKES ABOUT 1 CUP, ENOUGH TO GLAZE ONE 9- OR 10-INCH CAKE

WATER ICING

⟿ ❧ ⟾

THIS GLAZE IS REALLY a sort of fake fondant icing, the fine, white cooked-sugar icing. It's so easy to stir together and warm confectioners' sugar with liquid that very few people make fondant icing any more, and those who do use it usually purchase it ready made.

1 Put the cake on a cardboard and set on a rack over a jelly-roll pan to collect drips.

2 With a wooden spoon, stir together all the ingredients in a medium saucepan to make a heavy paste. Place over low heat and stir continuously until the glaze is very warm, about 110 degrees.

3 Immediately brush, pour, or drizzle the glaze over the cake.

4 Leave the cake on the rack for an hour before attempting to move it. Then use a wide spatula to transfer the cake to a platter. Discard any leftover glaze.

3 cups confectioners' sugar
3 tablespoons water
2 tablespoons strained fresh lemon juice or other liquid (see Note)
1 teaspoon vanilla extract

MAKES ABOUT 2 CUPS, ENOUGH TO COVER A 9- OR 10-INCH CAKE

NOTE: Any liquid, including only water, works in this. My favorites are strained lemon or orange juice, white or dark rum, and strong coffee.

PASTRY CREAM

~⚬⚬~

THIS ALL-PURPOSE STARCH-THICKENED custard cream is used as a filling in many different cakes and pastries. I like to use it on its own or add butter to make a crème mousseline, as in the variation below. Good, freshly made pastry cream is hard to beat—it's a perfect filling for a delicate cake. Because pastry cream is made with eggs and milk, it is fairly perishable, so remember: Prepare the pastry cream on the day you are going to use it. Make sure all your utensils, pans, and bowls are scrupulously clean. Cool and refrigerate the pastry cream immediately after it is made.

1 In a medium nonreactive saucepan, combine 1½ cups of the milk, the sugar, and vanilla bean, if using, and bring to a simmer over medium heat.

2 Meanwhile, whisk the remaining ½ cup milk and the cornstarch together in a small bowl until smooth. Whisk in the egg yolks until smooth again.

3 When the milk simmers, remove the vanilla bean, if you used it, and bring the milk to a full rolling boil. Remove the milk from the heat and whisk one-third of it into the yolk mixture.

4 Return the remaining milk to a boil. As it comes to the boil, start to whisk the milk in the pan, then pour in the yolk mixture in a stream. As you pour, whisk continuously across the bottom and into the corners of the pan. Cook the pastry cream, whisking continuously, for about 30 seconds.

2 cups milk

¾ cup sugar

1 vanilla bean, split, or 2 teaspoons vanilla extract

¼ cup cornstarch

6 large egg yolks

2 tablespoons (¼ stick) unsalted butter

5 Remove from the heat and add the vanilla extract, if using, and the butter. Whisk until smooth and pour into a stainless steel or glass bowl. Press plastic wrap against the surface of the pastry cream and refrigerate immediately.

STORAGE: Always keep pastry cream or anything you fill with it in the refrigerator. Use the pastry cream on the day it is made, and use all leftovers within 36 hours of making the pastry cream.

VARIATIONS

Use the vanilla bean or extract in all the following variations.

CHOCOLATE PASTRY CREAM: Add 4 ounces semi-sweet chocolate, melted with ¼ cup water or milk to the pastry cream with the butter.

COFFEE PASTRY CREAM: Replace ½ cup of the milk with triple-strength espresso (see page xiv).

PRALINE PASTRY CREAM: Add ⅓ cup praline paste to the milk and sugar before heating. Reduce the sugar to ½ cup.

MOUSSELINE PASTRY CREAM: Beat ½ pound (2 sticks) unsalted butter, softened, in the bowl of a heavy-duty mixer with the paddle on medium speed until very soft and light. Stop the mixer and add an entire batch of any of the chilled pastry creams. Continue to beat until smooth and light, about 5 to 10 minutes. Use immediately as a filling.

CRÈME ANGLAISE

୬ ୭ ୬

THIS CUSTARD CREAM, one of the great foundation preparations of pastry making, can be used as a sauce, a base for a Bavarian cream, or even, with an equal volume of butter beaten in, as a base for a very delicate buttercream. Crème anglaise is not difficult to make, but you have to be careful with the cooking once the egg yolks have been added—if the temperature exceeds 190 degrees, there is the risk that the yolks will curdle into little shreds, just like the ones in egg-drop soup. But don't worry, my quick method of cooking crème anglaise always yields good results.

1 Set a fine wire-mesh strainer over a bowl and set the bowl in a larger bowl containing ice water.

2 In a 2-quart nonreactive saucepan, bring the milk, cream, sugar, and vanilla bean, if using, to a simmer over medium heat.

3 Meanwhile, whisk the yolks in a 1½-quart bowl.

4 When the milk mixture begins to simmer, remove the vanilla bean, if you used it, and bring to a full rolling boil.

5 Whisk one-third of the milk and cream mixture into the yolks. Return the remaining milk and cream mixture to low heat and bring it back to a simmer. Whisk in the yolks and continue whisking for about 20 seconds until the crème anglaise thickens. The thickening will not be very dramatic (it will not become anywhere near as thick as pastry cream), but it will thicken

> 1 cup milk
> 1 cup heavy whipping cream (or use 2 cups half-and-half to replace the milk and cream)
> ½ cup sugar
> 1 vanilla bean, split, or 2 teaspoons vanilla extract
> 6 large egg yolks

slightly. To test if the cream has thickened enough, remove it from the heat and, still whisking constantly, submerge a metal kitchen spoon in the cream. Lift out the spoon—and if you can easily draw a distinct line through the cream on the back of the spoon with the tip of your finger, the cream has thickened enough. If not, cook, whisking, for a few seconds longer.

6 Immediately strain the cream into the bowl set over ice water. Remove the strainer and whisk the cream occasionally as it

cools. If using the vanilla extract, whisk it in now. After the cream has cooled, cover the bowl with plastic wrap and refrigerate the crème anglaise until it is time to use it.

STORAGE: Use the crème anglaise within 24 hours.

MAKES ABOUT 3 CUPS, ENOUGH TO MAKE A BAVARIAN CREAM OR TO USE AS A SAUCE WITH MOST CAKES

VARIATIONS

CHOCOLATE CREME ANGLAISE: Melt 6 ounces bittersweet chocolate, chopped, with ½ cup milk. Whisk into the crème anglaise before straining it.

CINNAMON CREME ANGLAISE: Crush 2 cinnamon sticks and add to the milk and cream. Bring to a simmer and let stand for 5 minutes, then return the liquid to a simmer and continue with the recipe.

COFFEE CREME ANGLAISE: Add ½ cup triple-strength coffee (see page 252).

LEMON CREME ANGLAISE: Add the coarsely grated zest of 2 lemons to the liquid before heating it (the zest will be strained out later).

ORANGE CREME ANGLAISE: Add the coarsely grated zest of 2 oranges to the liquid before heating it.

LIQUEUR CREME ANGLAISE: Whisk 2 tablespoons or more, according to taste, sweet liqueur or other spirits into the cooled crème anglaise.

14 DECORATING

WHEN THE SUBJECT OF CAKE DECORATING is mentioned, it causes a variety of responses, not all of them pleasant. I think it's enough to say that all decoration, especially decorating done by nonprofessionals, should be simple and understated. Although I have been making and decorating desserts and cakes as a pastry chef, then as a teacher, for a total of thirty-odd years, I still keep decorations to a minimum—nothing is more unappealing or unappetizing than an overdecorated cake.

The decorations in this chapter include the following:

DECORATIONS MADE BY PIPING: Simple borders and flowers that anyone can make; thin piped decorations made with chocolate or royal icing; and linear designs made with a paper cone, or easier-to-make alternatives.

MARZIPAN: Ribbons and simple flowers and leaves made from this versatile (and tasty) medium. (These same decorations can be made from chocolate plastic.)

CHOCOLATE PLASTIC: Ribbons, ruffles, and scrolls made from an easy chocolate dough.

PIPING BUTTERCREAM, GANACHE, AND MERINGUE

It's easy and fun to pipe borders and simple decorations on the top of a cake. The equipment you'll need is a pastry bag fitted with a plain (Ateco 804) or star (Ateco 822 or 824) tip. Any border in any recipe in this book can be executed with either tip. Remember, piping is a manual skill that, like any other, improves with frequent practice. These simple rules will help you develop good piping skills.

1 Insert the tube through the wide end of the bag and make sure it is firmly gripped in the narrow end of the bag. You can seal off the bag with a bull clip or a large paper clip, clipped right behind the tube, or just twist the fabric right behind the tube then insert it into the top (wide) end of the tube. (See illustration #1.)

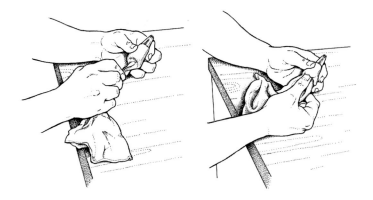

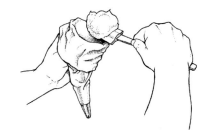

2 Fold over the top third of the pastry bag to make a cuff and grip the bag under the cuff with your nonwriting hand, as if you were holding a glass. (See illustration #2.) Use your writing hand to fill the bag, no more than half-full. Or stand the bag in a large jar or measuring cup and fold the top of the bag down over the container—that way, you can use both hands to fill.

3 When the bag is half-filled (or less), twist the top just above the filling, so the buttercream or other material will only come out the end with the tube.

4 Right before you start piping, remove the clip or undo the twist, closing the bottom of the bag.

5 To pipe, always hold the bag in the hand you use to write. With that hand, grip the top of the bag as though it were an orange half you are about to press over a hand juicer. (See illustration #3.) To steady the bag, use only the index finger of your other hand against the side. DO NOT GRIP THE BAG WITH BOTH HANDS.

6 As soon as you finish piping, remove the tube from the bag, wash it in hot soapy water, and dry it thoroughly. Wash the bag in hot soapy water and rinse it thoroughly. Sometimes I run a pastry bag through a dishwasher cycle, stretched around several of the prongs on the upper rack, wide end down. And occasionally I wash pastry bags in the washing machine with detergent and bleach, when I am doing other kitchen laundry.

Decorating

1 **DOTS:** Hold the bag perpendicular to the cake top and about ⅜ inch above it. Squeeze once, then release the pressure before pulling the bag away to the side, rather than straight upward, to avoid leaving a point. If using a star tube, pull away straight up. If you are using a star tube, this will make little star shapes. Position the tube about ½ inch away from the last dot or star and pipe another one. Continue all around the top rim of the cake.

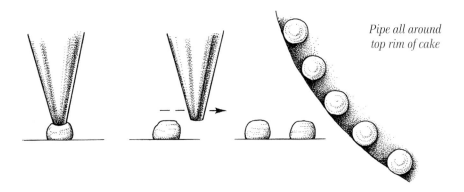

*Pipe all around
top rim of cake*

2 **TEARDROPS:** Use the same position as to make dots, but pull the bag away to a tapering point, gradually releasing the pressure. With a star tube, this movement makes shells. Start the next teardrop or shell right against the side of the previous one.

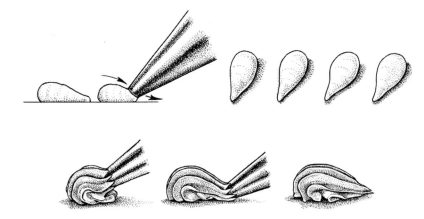

3 **INTERLOCKING TEARDROPS OR SHELLS:** Proceed as for teardrop above, but taper each squirt to a curve, alternating one curve toward the center of the cake and the next toward the outside edge.

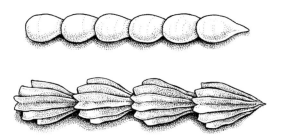

4 **ROSETTES:** Using a star tube, position the bag perpendicular to the cake top and almost touching the surface. Squeeze gently and lift slightly, then move the tube around in a clockwise arc, coming back to where you started. To avoid leaving a stand-up point in the center of the rosette, when you release the pressure, pull away to the side instead of lifting straight up. Piping rosettes next to each other around the rim of the cake makes a decorative border. Rosettes that are piped a distance apart can be used to mark each portion of the cake.

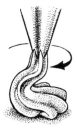

ROYAL ICING

❧ ❧

DELICATE WHITE ROYAL ICING can turn an ordinary cake into a very tailored and elegant presentation. Royal icing decorations are perfect for wedding cakes and other special-occasion cakes, covered with marzipan or rolled fondant. The dramatic contrast between the pure white icing and the off-white marzipan is as beautiful as the extreme subtlety of the white icing against the white rolled fondant. Royal icing is usually piped with a paper cone (it's also possible to use very small decorating tubes). Decorations can be piped onto parchment paper and lifted off onto a cake top, but be careful–this is extremely meticulous work, and you might feel more comfortable piping directly onto the cake after getting your hand in with a few practice rounds on a cake cardboard or an empty cake pan. If you are hesitant to use raw egg whites, use 2 tablespoons pasteurized egg white. To use meringue powder, follow the manufacturer's directions for reconstituting 1 egg white.

1 large egg white

1¼ cups confectioners' sugar, sifted
  after measuring

¼ teaspoon strained fresh lemon juice
  or distilled white vinegar

1 Before you begin to prepare royal icing, wash your mixer bowl and paddle in hot soapy water, then rinse and dry them well with paper towels or a clean dish towel. Any fat on the bowl or paddle will keep the icing from becoming properly aerated.

2 Use the paddle to mix the egg white and sugar together by hand in the mixer bowl. Place on the mixer and beat on low speed until smooth.

3 Add the lemon juice or vinegar, increase the speed to medium, and beat the icing for 4 to 5 minutes, or until it is very light and fluffy.

4 Scrape the icing into a clean bowl. Press plastic wrap against the surface, then cover the plastic wrap with a damp paper towel, and cover the paper towel with more plastic wrap–this will prevent the surface of the icing from crusting. If the icing is going to have to wait more than a couple of hours before you use it, pack it into a plastic container with a tight-fitting cover; cover the surface of the icing with the plastic wrap and paper towel before you put the lid on the container.

MAKES ENOUGH FOR DECORATING A LARGE CAKE

An easy way to pipe royal icing or chocolate is with a cornet, or paper cone, made from parchment paper. Small cones are used for most delicate piping. I usually cut an 18 × 24-inch sheet of parchment paper in half, then into quarters, then into eighths, and finally into triangles. This gives me cones that are about 6 × 9 × 11 inches, small enough to handle easily but large enough to hold a few tablespoons of the icing or chocolate. Use the following instructions and diagrams to make the cones.

1 Start with the right triangle pictured in the first illustration. The area opposite the right angle will be the point of the cone.

2 Curl the larger side angle around to start the cone, as in the second illustration. Make sure the point of the cone is sharp and tightly closed. If the end of the cone you make has even the slightest opening at this point, it will get larger as you use the cone.

3 To finish, wind the other angle around the cone, as in the third illustration.

4 Fold the upper edge over to prevent the cone from unraveling, as in the fourth illustration.

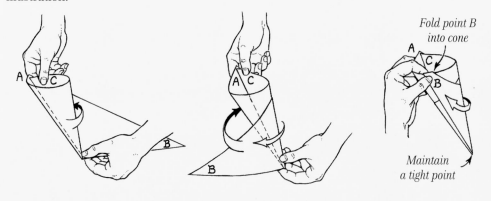

301

MARZIPAN

～೨ ೧～

THIS ELEGANT AND TASTY CAKE COVERING is made of almond paste mixed with confectioners' sugar and a little corn syrup to bind the mixture. It's easy to do in a food processor or a heavy-duty mixer. Then it always has to be kneaded smooth by hand to give it the best consistency. This recipe yields a little over a pound of marzipan. You may need less if you only want to make a few flowers or cover a cake, but marzipan keeps well in the freezer or wrapped well in multiple layers of plastic wrap. You'll notice that the amount of corn syrup used is not exact—that's because both the almond paste and the confectioners' sugar, particularly the almond paste, may be holding more or less liquid.

1   In the bowl of a heavy-duty mixer, beat the almond paste and half the sugar with the paddle on low speed just until the almond paste and the sugar are reduced to fine particles.

2   Keep the mixer running as you add gradually, the remaining sugar, a couple of tablespoons at a time. This is so that the mixture remains a fine, crumbly mass.

3   Add half the corn syrup and mix briefly. Stop and scrape the bowl and beater with a rubber spatula—the corn syrup has a tendency to accumulate on both.

4   Continue mixing until the marzipan is again the consistency of fine crumbs. Stop the mixer, pick up a handful, and try to knead and squeeze it together. If it is too dry

> One 8-ounce can almond paste, cut into ½-inch pieces
> 2 cups confectioners' sugar, sifted after measuring
> About ¼ cup light corn syrup

to stick together after you have gently kneaded it, start the mixer again and add a little more corn syrup, then repeat the test. If the marzipan is still too dry after ¼ cup corn syrup has been added, add more by teaspoons. It's easy to add liquid if the marzipan is too dry, but if it becomes too wet, it's difficult to handle, and if you need to compensate for the extra corn syrup by adding more confectioners' the mixture becomes almost all sugar.

5 Once the marzipan kneads smoothly and easily, turn it out onto a clean work surface and knead it into a smooth, coherent dough.

STORAGE: Double-wrap the marzipan in plastic wrap and keep it at cool room temperature, or freeze for longer storage.

MAKES ABOUT 17 OUNCES

VARIATIONS

COLORING THE MARZIPAN: Paste colors work best, but they are very strong and may easily give too bright a shade. To avoid this problem, break off a 2-tablespoon–sized piece of marzipan. Knead in some of the paste color. Then knead small amounts at a time of the piece of colored marzipan into the larger one, and stop when the big piece is the right shade. Marzipan that has had coloring added always loses some of its brilliance once it is rolled out and dries, so you can make the color slightly more vivid than you want it to be—but you are still aiming for a pastel shade.

CHOCOLATE-FLAVORED MARZIPAN: Knead ¼ cup alkalized (Dutch-process) cocoa powder into this batch of marzipan. If the marzipan gets dry, add a little water, about ½ teaspoon at a time. If you are coloring less than a pound of marzipan, use less cocoa proportionately. This is an excellent and easy medium with which to make chocolate flowers.

NOTE: To mix the marzipan in a food processor, use the metal blade to pulse the ingredients together, then follow the same procedure as above when adding the corn syrup.

COVERING A CAKE WITH MARZIPAN

One pound of marzipan will easily cover a 10-inch cake. Spread the surface of the cake with buttercream, ganache, or another smooth frosting for the marzipan to adhere to. Whipped cream is not suitable, as it would soak into the marzipan and cause it to disintegrate. A reduced apricot or raspberry glaze is fine if brushed onto the cake when hot and allowed to cool and set.

Unwrap the marzipan, plain or colored, and knead until smooth. Shape into a disk about 1 inch thick. Lightly dust a smooth work surface and the marzipan with confectioners' sugar. Start to roll out the marzipan with a rolling pin, making sure not to roll over the edges of the disk. Rotate the disk about 45 degrees and roll again. Move the marzipan every time you roll it to prevent it from sticking to the surface and the rolling pin. Dust very lightly with cornstarch when necessary. Avoid using too much cornstarch, or its taste will become apparent and the marzipan's surface will be dry and cracked.

To make a disk to cover a 9- or 10-inch cake, roll the marzipan out into a round approximately 14 to 16 inches in diameter. Position the rolling pin at the edge of the disk closest to you and gently roll the marzipan up over the rolling pin. Don't press, or the marzipan will stick to itself. Position the rolling pin over the edge of the cake farthest from you, with about ½ inch of the marzipan resting on the work surface behind the cake, then quickly unroll the marzipan over the cake. Smooth the top by pressing gently with the palms of your hand, then gently press the marzipan against the sides of the cake so that there are no creases. Trim away the excess at the bottom and reserve it for finishing the edges. Knead the scraps together and roll between the palms of your hands into a rope the length of the circumference of the cake. Place the cake on a platter, then carefully lift the rope of marzipan and position it around the bottom edge of the cake. Overlap the ends where they meet and trim the rope on the diagonal of a small knife. Remove the excess and press the ends together. Using the back of a small knife, press a pattern of diagonal lines into the rope.

Marzipan Leaves

Knead a drop of green color into 2 ounces of marzipan. Roll the marzipan into a rope about 12 inches long. Flatten the rope with the palm of your hand, then smooth it with the bowl of a spoon: Run the curve of the bowl back and forth along the length of the marzipan, pressing gently, until the marzipan is about ³⁄₁₆-inch thick and about 1 inch wide. Run the blade of a knife or a spatula under the ribbon of marzipan to detach it from the surface.

Cut the ribbon diagonally at 1¼-inch intervals, to make even-sided diamonds. Pick up one leaf at a time and use a fingertip to press one side in slightly along the width to soften the angle into a curve. Vein the leaves with the back of a knife, or leave them plain. Prop the leaves at different angles against the sides of a jelly-roll pan so they dry in different positions. Let some of the leaves dry flat.

SIMPLE MARZIPAN FLOWERS

⁓ ◝ ◜ ⁓

THESE ARE THE EASIEST marzipan flowers to make, and they can be very effective when massed on a cake. They require very little skill, just a little patience.

1   Roll the pink marzipan into a rope about a foot long, then divide it in half and roll each half to a foot in length.

2   With a small sharp paring knife, cut each rope into ¼-inch pieces. Each piece will become a petal, and 5 petals will make a flower. Cover the cut marzipan with plastic wrap and a damp paper towel so that it does not dry out while you are working.

3   To form each petal, roll a piece of marzipan into a little ball, then flatten it between your thumb and first finger.

4 ounces pink marzipan
½ ounce yellow marzipan

One jelly-roll pan, lined with parchment or foil

4   After forming 5 petals, arrange them in a flower shape so they overlap slightly. Insert the last petal over the previous one and behind the first one, as shown in the illustration. Place the flowers on the lined pan as they are formed.

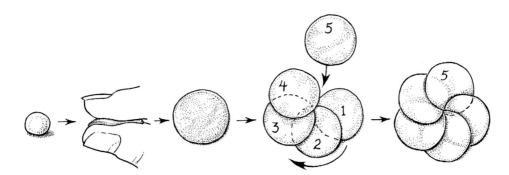

Decorating

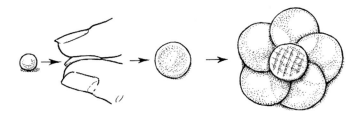

5 Divide the yellow marzipan into as many pieces as you have flowers.

6 Form each piece of yellow marzipan into a ball, then flatten it slightly (not as flat as a petal). Moisten the bottom with a tiny drop of water and place it in the center of a flower, pressing it firmly into place. If you wish, you can mark the yellow center with a little lattice design, as in the illustration.

MAKES ABOUT 20 SMALL
(1-INCH) FLOWERS

MARZIPAN CARNATIONS

Knead a drop of red or yellow color into 2 ounces of marzipan. Roll into a rope about 12 inches long. Flatten the rope with the palm of your hand, then smooth it with the back of the bowl of a spoon: Run the bowl of the spoon back and forth along the length of the marzipan, pressing gently, until the marzipan is about ³/₁₆-inch thick and about 1 inch wide. Continue to rub the side closest to you so the edge is thinner than the rest of the ribbon. Run the blade of a knife or spatula under the ribbon to loosen it from the work surface.

To make a fringe, use the point of a small knife to cut a series of ½-inch slashes ¼ inch apart along the thinner edge of the ribbon. Roll up the fringe, keeping it straight at the slashed edge so it makes a broom-like form. Pick up the flower by the unslashed edge and, holding it slashes upward, pinch below the slashes: Pinch gently at first, rotate the flower, and keep pinching to make the petals unfurl. Finally, pinch away the excess unslashed rolled marzipan at the base. Trim the base of the carnation straight and even with a small knife. Stand the carnation on a pan to dry. If desired, for a dappled effect, dip the edge of a pastry brush in a drop or two of food coloring, position the brush bristles upward close to the carnation, and use your fingertip to flick back the bristles and spray droplets of the coloring onto the petals.

VARIEGATED CARNATIONS Start with three pieces of marzipan, leaving two white and adding coloring to the third. Roll each into a 12-inch rope, as above, then twist the three ropes together. Roll the rope. Cut into four pieces, roll each piece into a thin rope, and twist together again. Roll into another smooth rope and cut into three pieces. Roll each third into a 12-inch rope and make carnations as above. Use the scraps to make more carnations—in these, the marbling will be more subtle, and you will end up with flowers in a range of shades.

MARZIPAN ROSES

For each rose, use 1 ounce of marzipan. Knead until smooth, and roll into a rope about 4 inches long. Cut the rope into 7 equal pieces. To make the base for the flower, fashion one piece into a cone about 1¼ inches high, and set it aside. Roll each remaining piece into a ball, then flatten it against the work surface with the palm of your hand to make a disk. Work with a couple of pieces at a time, keeping the rest under a towel to prevent them from drying.

Using the back of the bowl of a spoon, flatten each disk: Use light pressure with the spoon, beginning in the center of the disk and moving the spoon in an ever-widening circle, increasing the pressure as the spoon reaches the edge of the disk. Form petals that are 2 to 2½ inches in diameter and about ³⁄₁₆-inch thick at the center. Make them paper-thin at the edges, thicker in the center. The edges should be very thin and smooth.

Make 3 petals in this way to be the center bud of the rose. Place these petals on the work surface and make a ½-inch slash in the least attractive edge of each, perpendicular to the edge. Pick up and pleat each petal at the slash: Slide one cut edge under and the other over the petal. Press so that the petal is now concave. Repeat with the other two petals.

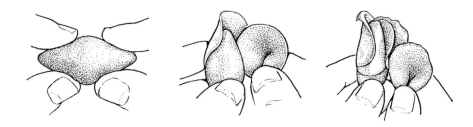

Decorating

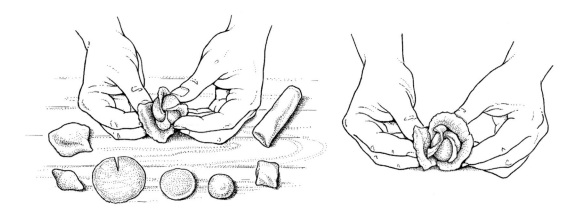

To form the center bud, keep the slashed edges of the petals at the bottom so the slashes will not be visible in the finished rose. Place the cone-shaped base slightly to the left of the center of one of the petals and about ⅛ inch below the edge. Curve the left edge of the petal around the base. Insert the left side of the second petal to the right of the base, between the base and the first petal. Curve the second petal to the left around the base, then insert the third petal between the base and the second petal. At this point, the three petals around the base should appear as a Y from above. Pinch the base of the bud gently so the petals stick together at the bottom, then curve the upper edges of the petals back slightly to give the bud a natural shape.

To make a larger rose, prepare 3 more petals the way you did the first three. Holding one at the slash between your thumb and first finger, use the other hand to curve the edge back, pinching the edge of the petal in two or three places. Press the outside petals one at a time against the very bottom of the bud, attaching them equidistantly around the bud. To make a very full open rose, make 5 more petals from another ounce of marzipan and attach them around the rose.

CHOCOLATE PLASTIC

~◦ ◦~

THIS DECORATING PASTE—used in some of the same ways as marzipan—makes lovely, dramatic cake decorations. Use it as you would marzipan to wrap an entire layer or roll cake, or fashion ruffles and ribbons of it for delicate decorations.

1 Use a rubber spatula to stir the corn syrup thoroughly into the melted chocolate. Be sure to scrape the sides of the bowl to incorporate any unmixed chocolate.

2 Scrape the chocolate plastic out onto the prepared pan and spread it so that it is no more than ⅓ inch thick.

3 Draw the sides of the plastic wrap up around the chocolate to cover it completely. Allow the chocolate plastic to set at a cool room temperature or in the refrigerator. In any case, wait for several hours before you use it.

⅔ cup light corn syrup
1 pound semisweet chocolate, melted

A cookie sheet or jelly-roll pan, lined with a long overhang of plastic wrap

MAKES ABOUT 20 OUNCES, ENOUGH TO DECORATE 2 OR 3 DESSERTS, DEPENDING ON THEIR SIZE

VARIATIONS

Substitute white chocolate or milk chocolate for the semisweet chocolate. Reduce the corn syrup to ½ cup.

WORKING WITH CHOCOLATE PLASTIC

Follow these general instructions for rolling out ribbons from chocolate plastic.

1 Lightly dust the work surface and chocolate plastic with sifted cocoa powder.

2 Divide the batch into 4 pieces and pound each piece with a rolling pin to soften it and make it pliable.

3 Shape each piece into a cylinder about 4 inches long, then flatten with the rolling pin or heel of your hand into an approximately 4-inch square. Lightly dust again with the sifted cocoa powder and roll each square out into a thin ribbon.

   Or use a pasta machine to roll the thin ribbons. Pass each of the 4 pieces through every other setting, from the widest down to the next to last. (If it is extremely cool in the room, you might be able to pass the ribbons through the last setting. If you can, the result will be a wonderfully thin, almost transparent ribbon.)

4 Use the ribbons to encircle a cake. Pleat some into ruffles for a beautiful effect, and cover the entire top of a cake with concentric circles of them.

5 Or, don't divide the chocolate plastic, roll it out thin, and use it to cover a cake or roll. Dust it and the surface of the cake lightly with sifted cocoa powder.

MAKING LEAVES AND FLOWERS FROM CHOCOLATE PLASTIC

1 *To make leaves from the chocolate plastic,* roll the plastic out with a rolling pin or pasta machine, and cut it into 1¼-inch-wide ribbons. Cut the ribbons diagonally to make diamonds, then press the side points of the diamonds in so the sides curve into leaf shapes.

2 *To make carnations,* roll out the chocolate plastic with rolling pin or pasta machine, then cut it into ribbons 1 inch wide and 12 inches long. Use the point of a paring knife to make ½-inch-long cuts ¼ inch apart down one of the long sides of the ribbon, so the ribbon looks like a fringe. Begin at one of the short ends and roll up along the uncut edge. When the whole fringe has been rolled up, hold the carnation with the uncut end between the thumbs and forefingers of both hands and press right under where the slashes end, to make the carnation

open. Pinch or cut away the excess chocolate plastic at the bottom. Carnations are very effective when made in a variety of chocolate colors and massed together.

3 *To make roses,* proceed as above, rolling the chocolate plastic into 4 × 12-inch ribbons. Then use a round cutter about 2 to 2½ inches in diameter to cut out petals. Make conical rose bases by pressing the scraps together, then wrap the petals around the base, as in the illustrations. As in nature, make a closed bud first, then assemble several open petals around it.

4 *To make bell-shaped flowers,* such as morning glories or petunias, roll ½ tablespoon of chocolate plastic into a ball. Point one end to make a cone, then round the end opposite the point. Use a pencil or an awl to drill into the center of the shape from the rounded end, rotate the pencil or awl around to enlarge the opening, then withdraw it and use your fingertips to pinch the edges thinner. Pinch the pointed end to make it thinner too. To make a morning glory, spread out the open end of the flower so that the sides are almost perpendicular to the pointed stem. Pinch the thin edge in four places equidistant around the flower. To make petunias, form a similar shape but leave it more tightly closed and pinch and frill the edge of the petals with your fingertips.

5 *To make 4- and 5-petaled flowers,* divide a tablespoon-sized piece of chocolate plastic into 4 or 5 pieces. Roll each into a ball, then make a point at one end of the ball so you get a cone with a rounded end and a pointed one. Press between your fingertips to flatten into a teardrop shape. Repeat with the other pieces to make other petals. Press the petals together at the pointed bases and squeeze the bases to keep the flower intact. Make a small ball from another piece then flatten it and place it in the center of the petals. Open the petals out and curve them slightly to give the flower a natural look. See the illustration on page 307.

SOURCES

THE BAKER'S CATALOGUE

P.O. Box 876

Norwich, VT 05055-0876

Telephone: (800) 827-6836

General baking ingredients and equipment, candied fruit.

BONNIE SLOTNICK COOKBOOKS

163 West Tenth Street

New York, NY 10014

Telephone: (212) 989-8962

E-mail: bonnieslotnickbook@earthlink.net

My source for the antiquarian and out-of-print cookbooks I collect and use for research on my own books.

BRIDGE KITCHENWARE

214 East 52nd Street

New York, NY 10022

Telephone (212) 688-4220; (800) 274-3435

Web site: bridgekitchenware.com

Catalog available ($3.00, refundable with first order).

Baking pans and baking and decorating equipment of all kinds, including pastry bags and tubes, offset spatulas, and serrated knives of many lengths.

CALPHALON CORPORATION

P.O. Box 583

Toledo, OH 43697-0583

Telephone: (800) 809-7267

Web site: www.calphalon.com

E-mail: consumerrelations@calphalon.com

THE CULTURED CUP

5346 Belt Line Road

Dallas, TX 75254

Telephone: (972) 960-1521; (888) 847-8327

E-mail: info@theculturedcup.com

Green tea.

KAISER BAKEWARE

1200-G Westinghouse Boulevard

Charlotte, NC 28273

Telephone: (704) 588-8090; (800) 966-3009

Web site: kaiserbakeware.com

NEW YORK CAKE AND BAKING DISTRIBUTORS

56 West 22nd Street

New York, NY 10010

Telephone: (212) 675-2253; (800) 942-2539

Web site: nycakesupplies.com

Baking pans, decorating equipment, spatulas, knives, as well as many brands of domestic and imported chocolate. Cardboards, boxes, and other paper goods, Gold leaf.

Nielsen-Massey Vanilla

1550 Shields Drive

Waukegan, IL 60085

Telephone: (800) 525-7873

Web site: nielsenmassey.com

Vanilla products.

Nordicware

Highway 7 at Highway 100

Minneapolis, MN 55416

Telephone: (952) 920-2888; (800) 328-4310

Web site: nordicware.com

Bundt pans.

Penzey's Spices

P.O. Box 933

Muskego, WI 53150

Telephone: (262) 679-7207; (800) 741-7787

Catalog available. Herbs, spices, extracts.

Sur la Table

Pike Place Farmers Market

84 Pine Street

Seattle, WA 98101

Telephone: (206) 448-2245; (800) 243-0852

Web site: surlatable.com

Catalog available. Baking pans and decorating equipment. Cardboards, general cookware, and bakeware.

Sweet Celebrations (formerly Maid of Scandinavia)

7009 Washington Avenue South

Edina, MN 55439

Telephone: (952) 943-1661; (800) 328-6722

Web site: sweetc.com

Catalog available. Decorating supplies of all kinds.

Williams-Sonoma

100 North Point Street

San Francisco, CA 94133

Telephone: (800) 541-2233

Web site: williams-sonoma.com

Catalog available. Cookware and bakeware. Decorating equipment.

BIBLIOGRAPHY

A Treatise on Cake Baking. New York: Standard Brands, 1935.

All About Home Baking. New York: General Foods Corporation, 1937.

Bakers Weekly Revised Recipes. New York: American Trade Publishing Company, 1924.

Blake, Arlyn. *The I Love to Cook Book.* New York: Essandess Special Editions, 1971.

Book of American Baking. New York: American Trade Publishing Company, 1910.

Brooks, William H. *Modern Practical Cake Baking.* Palo Alto: Times Publishing Company, 1915.

Floris, Christopher. *The Floris Book of Cakes.* London: Andre Deutsch, 1981.

Glasse, Hannah. *The Art of Cookery Made Plain and Easy.* Alexandria, Virginia: Cottom and Stewart, 1812.

Greenspan, Dorie. *Sweet Times.* New York: William Morrow, 1991.

Harbaugh, Rose Oller and Mary Adams. *Favorite Torte and Cake Recipes.* New York: Simon and Schuster, 1951.

Harland, Marion. *Breakfast, Luncheon and Tea.* New York: Charles Scribner's Sons, 1875.

Lambeth, Joseph A. *Lambeth Method of Cake Decoration and Practical Pastries.* Detroit: Allied Bakery Products, Inc., 1934.

Lewis, T. Percy. *The Trade's Cake Book.* London: Maclaren and Sons, Ltd., n.d.

Mayer, Eduard. *Wiener Suss-speisen.* Linz, Austria: Trauner Verlag, 1968.

Parloa, Maria. *The Appledore Cook Book.* Boston: Graves, Locke & Co., 1878.

Richards, Paul. *Cakes for Bakers.* Chicago: Bakers' Helper Company, 1932.

Richemont Craft School. *Swiss Confectionery.* Lucerne: Bakers and Confectioners Craft School, Richemont, 1985.

Rorer, Mrs. Sarah Tyson. *Mrs. Rorer's Cakes, Icings and Fillings.* Philadelphia: Arnold and Company, 1905.

Rushing, Lilith and Ruth Voss. *The Cake Cook Book.* Philadelphia: Chilton Company, 1965.

The Art of Home Baking. Toronto: Maple Leaf Mills, Ltd., 1964.

Witzelberger, Richard. *Das Oesterreichische Mehlspeisen Kochbuch.* Vienna: Kremayr & Scheriau, 1979.

Zelf Bakken. Weert. The Netherlands: Omslagdia Jules Dierick, 1987.

Zenker, Hazel G. *Cake Bakery.* Philadelphia: M. Evans and Company, Inc. 1973.

ACKNOWLEDGMENTS

Thanks are due to many people who have been a part of the production of this book. My agent, Phyllis Wender and her associate Sonia Pabley have provided invaluable support. Nancy Nicholas, who edited the manuscript, always lent suggestions, advice, and her great sense of humor. Special thanks to copy editor Judith Sutton for her astute eye.

At HarperCollins, my editor Susan Friedland and her assistants Vanessa Stich and Monica Meline were always on the other end of the phone when I needed them. Thanks to publicists Carrie Weinberg, Gypsy Lovett, and James Hagerty and to production editor Lydia Weaver.

Joel Avirom and his associates Jason and Meghan again provided an outstanding design. Many thanks are due to Tom Eckerle and Ceci Gallini for beautiful photographs and props. Laura Hartman Maestro lent her unerring pencil to some perfect line drawings.

More than anyone else, my friend and associate Andrea Tutunjian worked on this project from outline to photographs. Thanks, Andrea. Barbara Bria Pugliese did all the studio food styling and Barbara, Faith Drobbin, Rebecca Millican, and Cara Tannenbaum prepared cakes for photography and also tested most of the recipes. A big thank you to my friend Bonnie Slotnick who was always ready to help with last-minute emergencies.

Rick Smilow, president of the Institute of Culinary Education (formerly Peter Kump's) generously provided kitchen space for baking and testing. ICE director of purchasing Frank Garofolo and his associate Jami Bovone tracked down specialty food items and also helped with staple items for baking.

Many friends and colleagues contributed recipes. Thanks are due to Ellen Baumwoll, Marilynn Brass, Sheila Brass, Tim Brennan, Sidney Carlisle, Alan Cohen, Pat Coston, Marion Cunningham, Kyra Effren, Dorie Greenspan, Bruno Heini, Hans Heini, Pierre Herme, Chris Hubbuch, Nicole Kaplan, Paul Kinberg, Sandy Leonard, Shari Lepore, Virginia LoBiondo, Paolo Loraschi, Karen Ludwig, Virginia Malgieri, Maureen McKeon, Ann Nurse, Fredi Nussbaum, Gary Peese, Sheri Portwood, Stephen Pyles, Ana Rambaldi, Rosa Ross, Stephan Schiesser, Bonnie Slotnick, Zona Spray, Jayne Sutton, Leslie Sutton, Andrea Tutunjian, Phyllis Vacarelli, and Stephanie Weaver.

And a last special thank you to my friends Maida Heatter, Dorie Greenspan, and Arthur Boehm.

INDEX